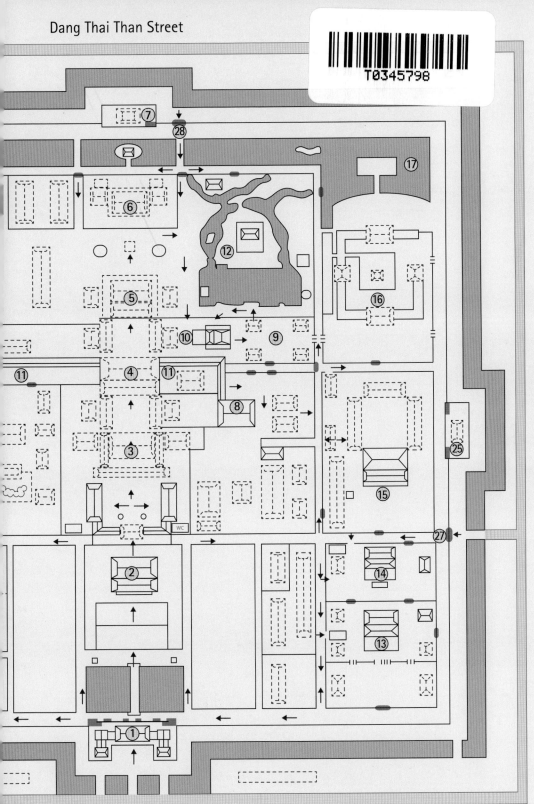

Foan Thi Doun Street

Source: Hue Monuments Conservation Center

ROYAL HUE
Heritage of the Nguyen Dynasty of Vietnam

ROYAL HUE

Heritage of the Nguyen Dynasty of Vietnam

Vu Hong Lien

Photography Paisarn Piemmettawat

First published in Thailand in 2015 by
River Books Co., Ltd
396 Maharaj Road, Tatien,
Bangkok 10200, Thailand
Tel: (66) 2 225-4963, 2 225-0139, 2 622-1900
Fax: (66) 2 225-3861
Email: order@riverbooksbk.com
Website: www.riverbooksbk.com

Editor Narisa Chakrabongse
Photography Paisarn Piemmettawat
Design Ruetairat Nanta
Production Paisarn Piemmettawat

ISBN 978 974 9863 95 4

Printed and bound in Thailand by Bangkok Printing Co., Ltd.

CONTENTS

Acknowledgements

I am indebted to a special group of people who have helped this book come into being and to be as informative as possible. First of all, a heartfelt 'thank you' to my editor Narisa Chakrabongse whose enthusiastic response to the subject was a great encouragement for both my research and my writing. Next, my sincere gratitude to the Hue Monuments Conservation Center for their generous assistance and kind permission for us to photograph many exclusive locations. Another 'thank you' to the Director of the Museum of Royal Antiquities, Nguyen Phuoc Hai Trung, for his insight into the labyrinth of classical poetry and the Nguyen royal games. Last but not least, my deepest gratitude to my dear friends, Dr. Peter Sharrock and Dr. Daniele Moyal-Sharrock, for pushing me forward into the world of publishing.

For my parents who introduced me to Hue
and my son Oliver Daniel Vu-Warder

Upper reaches of the Perfume River.

Foreword

This book is the result of my long association with Hue, from the age of 7 to this day. Although it has been a somewhat intermittent relationship which arose when my professional and emotional paths collided with Hue, each encounter never failed to leave a lingering sense of appreciation that, over time, deepened into affection for this brave city, a phoenix that is beginning to soar from its ashes.

The book is also a response to the positive reaction from my audience at the School of Oriental and African Studies, London University, when I lecture on the Nguyen. They are often astonished to learn that Vietnam has such a rich heritage from an imperial past as recent as the first half of the twentieth century, in spite of the French occupation and the ravages of war, and that a great deal can still be viewed and appreciated. I realised that a book in English could foster a learned understanding of Vietnam under the Nguyen, and of the considerable cultural legacy that the 13 emperors left behind, before the dynasty ended abruptly in August 1945.

To write this book I have dissected a wealth of information gleaned from the French National Archives, Vietnamese historical accounts and documents, the Royal Nguyen's family history, both published and unpublished, the last Emperor Bao Dai's Memoir and the recollections of people who have served, or been opposed to, the Nguyen Court. Many of the technical details of Nguyen arts and architecture came from documents published by the Hue Monuments Conservation Center, conversations with its officials, architects and engineers working on the restoration of Hue, UNESCO's publications, and my own research. To avoid overwhelming the book with footnotes, I do not give footnotes on the pages but, instead, list the sources in the bibliography.

The photographs illustrating this book are by Paisarn Piemmettawat of River Books with whom I worked most enjoyably during a previous project. This time, we again pooled our resources to capture many evocative images of Hue and had a great time in the process. We spent days traipsing around the city and the Nguyen tombs, or waiting by the Perfume River for the clouds to pass and the elusive sun to come out.

Side road along the Imperial Citadel.

Outside Hoa Binh gate – Imperial Citadel.

We travelled up and down the river to capture the beauty of Hue in different moods, or rushed out of our hotel before dawn, laden with photographic equipment, half-written chapters, sunscreen and tripods, at the slightest hint of promising light. We shared our journey with many people of Hue, all of whom were gracious and willing. The days were long and tiring but we were happy knowing that we had managed to preserve moments of Hue in their best light.

Motif of phoenix on Ngu Phung Terrace.

I first came to Hue as an young child living by the south end of Trang Tien Bridge, a corner of the city once the exclusive preserve of the French Governor General, but by then a residential area. From here, I walked down the road to a French school to receive my education while, at home, my parents taught me the basic principles of Confucian and Buddhist teachings, the meaning of the scholarly 'four books', the shining examples of Vietnamese heroes and the beauty of Vietnamese classical poetry. Our favourite outings at the time were to the Thien Mu pagoda and the Nguyen tombs, where I played hide-and-seek with my brothers among the stone mandarins. It was an impressionable time made even more memorable by a grand flood when the Perfume River broke its banks, inundated many streets on the south bank and reached the second of the three steps leading up to my courtyard. Not being able to go to school, I lingered for hours by the window sill, watching in fascination as the swirling brown water rushed down the street, its level slowly but surely rising. At the front of the house, the floor of the Trang Tien Bridge disappeared under a sea of water. Little did I know that this flood had damaged beyond repair many historical sites on both banks of the river, the ghosts of which I desribe in this book. Somehow, after the flood, Hue recovered and life resumed.

Many years later, from Saigon – today's Ho Chi Minh City – I watched the Tet offensive of 1968 unfolding its horror on the streets of Hue and unleashing its merciless destruction on the Imperial Citadel. Again, Hue recovered. Several years went by before I again witnessed the damaging of Hue in 1975, this time, from 6,500 miles away, in London, where I had lived for many years. Evidence of the many bouts of destruction were still visible when I finally returned in 1993, months before the city was included in the UNESCO list of World Heritage Sites. Hue then was a battered but unbowed city, with the former royal domain still mostly in ruins. However, in the centre, Thai Hoa Palace stood shining like a newly-polished gem, having been recently restored. That was the first step on a long and difficult journey to recovery but Hue has managed to keep evolving, its people have never lost their faith in the resilience of this royal city.

Bat motif – Imperial Citadel.

I have returned to Hue several times since and each time the city has emerged a little further from its tragic past, with more parts having been newly restored. Today, the road to recovery is still long but Hue has become a beautiful city once more, a place where the harmony between heaven and earth has been rekindled. Spanning the Perfume River, the Eiffel-built Trang Tien Bridge stretches fully repaired and the banks of the river are again lined with freshly painted monuments. On the north bank, the Imperial Citadel proudly displays the remains of its exquisite structures. On the south bank, some of the Nguyen tombs can once again celebrate their largerly under-rated landscape architecture, now that they have been returned to their former function as palaces for the afterlife of the Nguyen Emperors.

From being a piece of Cham territory annexed by ancient Vietnam in 1307, not only has Hue proven to be a city remarkable in its striving for greatness and beauty, it has now become a city of festivals, when, every two years since 2000, the entire city immerses itself in a grand celebration of Nguyen lifestyle. Alternating with the festivals, Hue traditional handicrafts are showcased every other year, when the finest Nguyen arts are put on display and their techniques of production explained.

According to official statistics, over seven million foreign visitors have come to Hue since 1993. Most were in awe at the lavish architecture and the richness of Nguyen arts, a few perhaps confused by the close relationship between Nguyen and Chinese art. In fact, although classical arts under the Nguyen, may have a Chinese appearance at first glance, on closer inspection their distinctive Vietnamese features emerge, some as a result of the inventiveness of local artists, others as a result of artefacts imported from Europe and elsewhere. What inspired the different Nguyen emperors to make Hue and its arts so uniquely Vietnamese? Before trying to answer this question, let us take a journey back in time, starting with the last event of the Nguyen Dynasty, and then we travel forth to discover a modern Hue, a royal heritage restored and re-invented.

Court of Stone at Minh Mang's tomb.   Thien Mu Pagoda.

Introduction: Bao Dai's abdication

Emperor Bao Dai. (Photo courtesy of Phan Thuan An)

Corner of Ngu Phung Terrace.

On 30th August 1945, standing on the Ngu Phung terrace of Ngo Mon, the royal gateway into the Imperial Citadel of Hue, the last emperor of Vietnam, Bao Dai, formally announced his decision to abdicate to a bemused crowd of thousands who had been waiting impatiently under the glaring afternoon sun.

> *'With sad reminiscence of the four hundred-year-struggle that our glorious ancestors went through to expand our nation from Thuan Hoa to Ha Tien, with some regrets for the twenty years of our reign, during which, we faced the impossibility of providing an appreciable service to our country, we have decided to abdicate…'.*

The surprisingly short statement, dated 25th August 1945, was issued at the request of the newly formed Democratic Republic Government of Ho Chi Minh's Anti-French Alliance, the Viet-Minh. It was a dramatic and ultimate act of the last Nguyen Emperor, after days of confusion at court, when Bao Dai suddenly found himself abandoned by all. 'On the morning of the 21st of August, emptiness was all around me, no prime-minister Tran Trong Kim, no minister at all appearing at the Palace', Bao Dai recalled in his Memoir, published in 1980.

Being alone was a bewildering experience for Bao Dai who had been protected from unpleasantness all his life and reign by his

Emperor Bao Dai at his coronation.

family, his mandarins, the French protectorate authority and the
Japanese occupying force. Those days in August 1945 were a
shocking reality and he recalled them as a time when 'the citizens of
Hue seemed to be seized by a high fever', with demonstrations
occurring daily. His earlier attempt to proclaim independence and
appeal for national unity had been ignored both in Vietnam and
elsewhere. His letters to President Truman, King George VI,
General Chiang Kai-shek and General De Gaulle went unanswered.

With his abdication, Bao Dai closed the last chapter in the
history of the Nguyen Dynasty, a turbulent era of 143 years that, at
times, saw Vietnam engaging in intense diplomatic discourse with
successive French authorities, allied with and then fighting against
the Thai and the French, only to succumb to French domination in
the later half of the 19th century. In his Memoir, Bao Dai recalled:
'the announcement of my abdication met with a profound silence',
'a look of naked astonishment passed through the faces of those
lining up on the first rows'. 'Men and women seemed to have gone
deaf'. 'My announcement appeared as a thunderbolt rendering
everybody petrified'. His private secretary, Pham Khac Hoe, present

Image of the Nguyen Emperor's seal.

at the ceremony, on the other hand, remembered that everybody
clapped and cheered and that Bao Dai had read his statement in an
emotional voice that wavered at times.

In an atmosphere of general confusion on that fateful day, Bao
Dai quickly performed the ceremony of handing over his symbols of
royal authority – his Gold Seal (Kim An) and his Sword of
Mandate   to representatives of Ho Chi Minh: Tran Huy Lieu,

Blue and White ceramic steam bowl.

Nguyen Luong Bang and Cu Huy Can. The form of the ceremony had been discussed and agreed between the court and representatives of the new government only the day before when the delegation from Hanoi arrived. According to Pham Khac Hoe, Bao Dai 'dressed for the last time in his royal golden robes, a golden cloth headdress in place of a crown, and embroidered shoes on his feet'. In negotiating the order of the ceremony, one of Bao Dai's requests was that his royal flag would be raised once more. Thus, during the ceremony, the royal yellow flag was raised and then lowered following his statement of abdication, to be replaced by the Red and Yellow flag of the new revolutionary government. The ceremony ended with a ceremonial 21-gun salute announcing that the exchange of power was complete.

The abdication ceremony over, Bao Dai left quickly and quietly, some said with tears in his eyes, to assume his new role of plain Citizen Nguyen Phuc Vinh Thuy. His mother and the royal family moved out of the Imperial Palace the next day, to be housed in Emperor Khai Dinh's An Dinh palace on the south bank of the Perfume River. Bao Dai alone remained in the Citadel for a few more days and then departed for Hanoi in September, at the invitation of the new government to become their special envoy.

With the departure of Bao Dai, the lifestyle enjoyed by Hue as the nation's royal seat came to an end. It was a lifestyle unrivalled in its excesses, its refinement and its ingenuity, faint echoes of which still resonate in the Imperial Citadel and the royal tombs. It is reflected in the collection of Royal Blue and White ceramics – now housed in the Hue Museum of Royal Antiquities (formerly the Museum of Royal Fine Arts) and in the myths of the Royal Treasure, today lost and unlikely to be reassembled. The Nguyen's lifestyle has been criticised by many historians and sections of the general public, but it is undeniable that the dynasty left an exquisite cultural legacy that in 1993 earned Hue UNESCO World Heritage status.

The city of Hue and the Imperial Citadel were severely damaged during the anti-French struggle which resumed when the French tried to re-establish their rule after the Second World War. Further damage came during the Tet Offensive of 1968, and, again in 1975; several of the original buildings were destroyed by bombing and ground fighting as opposing forces fought for control of the city. The three main palaces of the Forbidden Purple City, where the Emperor lived, were destroyed and only traces of their foundations are visible marked by simple plaques. Some of the remaining palaces and the Imperial Citadel gates have now been lovingly restored. Today, the royal motifs of dragon and phoenix again occupy honourable places on the palace roofs, the brick-paved paths have been scrubbed clean of moss, and the Courtyard of Salutation at Thai Hoa Palace once again welcomes those who have come to pay homage, not to the Emperor, but to the heritage that the Nguyen left for Vietnam and for the world.

Emperor Bao Dai's shoes.

Ngo Mon – view from inside the Citadel.

Thai Hoa Palace seen through a Ceremonial Gate.

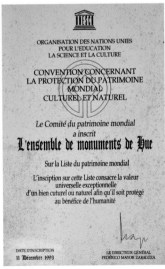

UNESCO Certificate.

History of Hue

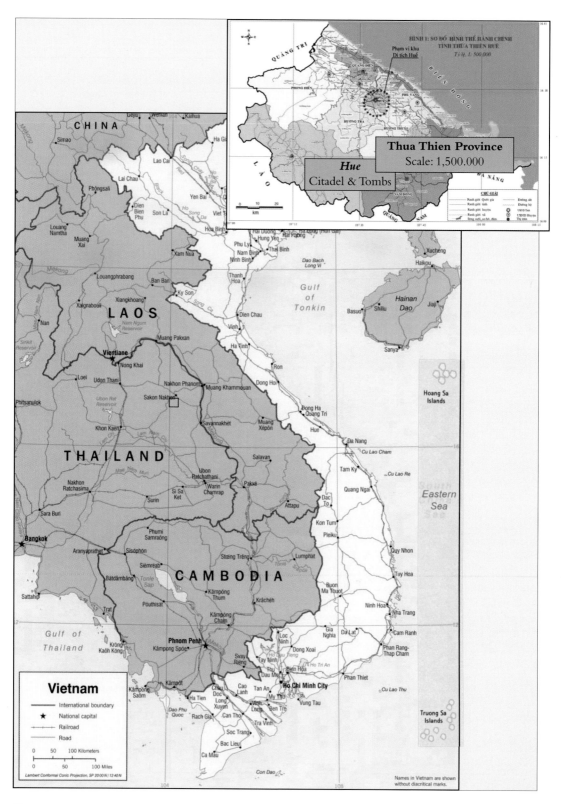

Thua Thien Province
Scale: 1,500.000

Hue
Citadel & Tombs

HÌNH 1: SƠ ĐỒ HÌNH THẾ HÀNH CHÍNH
TỈNH THỪA THIÊN HUẾ
Tỷ lệ: 1: 500.000

Phạm vi khu
Di tích Huế

Vietnam
— International boundary
★ National capital
+++ Railroad
— Road

| 0 | 50 | 100 Kilometers |
| 0 | 50 | 100 Miles |

Lambert Conformal Conic Projection, SP 20.00 N / 12.40 N

Names in Vietnam are shown
without diacritical marks.

Before the Nguyen

The name Hue has its origin in the 14th century, when the Tran dynasty (1226-1400) of Vietnam took over the two territories of O and Ly from Champa, annexed them into what was then Dai Viet, and gave the land the two new names of Thuan Chau and Hoa Chau – Chau meaning territory. Later, under the Nguyen, the name Hoa was transformed into Hue to avoid it being one of the taboo words when pronounced, although in written Chinese characters – the official Vietnamese script until 1919 – it remains the same.

It is often said that the Cham territories of O and Ly were given to Vietnam as the bride price for one of the Tran princesses, Princess Huyen Tran, when she was sent to Champa to marry the Cham King Jaya Simhavarman III in the year 1306. Champa was the group of kingdoms once situated in the middle part of today's Vietnam, stretching from Quang Tri to Binh Thuan provinces. Historically, the annexation of the two Cham territories to Vietnam was much more complicated than a straightforward bride price. It happened as the result of the Mongol invasions of both Vietnam and Champa in the late 1280s. As a strategic piece of land crucial to the defence of Vietnam, the territories of O and Ly were put under Vietnamese control in January 1307, six months after Princess Huyen Tran was despatched to Champa. The arrival of the Vietnamese forces in O and Ly met with fierce opposition from local Cham inhabitants and the Tran court had to offer them a tax exemption of two years and other benefits to calm the situation. It is not known what happened subsequently, but, according to the Vietnamese annals, the territories were renamed Thuan and Hoa and, under Vietnamese administration, the region was governed from the Hoa-Chau Citadel, built on the location of present-day Hue.

The circumstances surrounding the cession of land in the 14th century have been shrouded in mystery, but the marriage between the Cham King, called Che Man in Vietnamese, and Princess Huyen Tran – his Queen Tapasi – did not last very long. The Cham king died only months after his wedding and the Vietnamese navy entered Champa soon after his death. They took the princess home, installed a new king on the Cham throne and placed Champa under Vietnamese 'protection' for 19 years. Even then, the situation was never clear-cut, for Vietnamese forces returned to Champa in 1311, took a Cham king back to their capital Thang Long, where he died the following year. His death was a defining event in Viet-Cham relations and thereafter the two realms never found peace. Many bitter wars were fought over succeeding centuries in the name of the 'O and Ly territories' with dire consequences for both and with the said territories being passed back and forth between the warring adversaries on many occasions.

The unstable situation attracted the attention of the Ming (1368-1644) who invaded and then occupied Dai Viet for 20 years in the

Po Nagar: Towers A and B seen from the southeast.

Opposite: Map courtesy of Hue Monuments Conservation Center.

early 15th century. In 1427, Le Loi-a wealthy landowner from Thanh Hoa-chased the Ming out of Dai Viet and established the Le dynasty who ruled for two long periods, 1428-1527 and 1533-1788. The early Le ruled until 1527 when the throne was lost to a usurper, Mac Dang Dung, who established the Mac (1527-1592) in the capital Thang Long. The remnant Le escaped to Laos and established a court in exile in 1533. The Le and the Mac were at war with each other for 65 years with the Le being supported by Nguyen Kim, his two sons Nguyen Uong and Nguyen Hoang, and his son-in law Trinh Kiem. The Le finally succeeded in 1592 in becoming the sole ruler of Vietnam.

When the Ming left Vietnam in 1427, the O and Ly territories remained with Vietnam and became definitively known as Thuan Chau and Hoa Chau. These two names were later combined into Thuan-Hoa. No matter who ruled in the then capital Thang Long (Hanoi), Thuan-Hoa remained a wild frontier land until the year 1558 when relations between the former allies Trinh and Nguyen soured. To avoid a potential conflict, Lord Nguyen Hoang, one of the two sons of Nguyen Kim, asked the more powerful Lord Trinh Kiem, his brother-in-law, to let him develop the inhospitable land of Thuan-Hoa and the Trinh Lord agreed.

Lord Nguyen Hoang arrived in Thuan-Hoa with his own entourage and his late father's army. He first chose to establish his residence in the Thuan part of the territory, today's Quang Tri province, north of Hue. Under his administration, Thuan-Hoa became a populated area with a strong army and a flourishing economy. Nguyen Hoang then began to search for a suitable location to establish a capital. Legend has it that in 1601, during one of these forays, Nguyen Hoang arrived at a high point by the Perfume River where he noticed that the formation of the land resembled a curving dragon, symbol of royal authority according to Chinese and Vietnamese Feng-shui principles. However, he was puzzled by the deep trench cutting through the spine of the dragon.

Dawn on the river at Thien Mu pagoda.

In fact, the trench had been dug several centuries earlier, on the order of Cao Bien, a Chinese governor of Giao Chau – Vietnam's name during the thousand-year Chinese occupation that ended in the 10th century. Realising that the auspicious dragon-shaped land would one day become a royal domain, Cao Bien decided to cut it in half to destroy its royal quality. The deep trench remained until rediscovered by Nguyen Hoang.

Unaware of Cao Bien's actions and while sitting pondering the mystery of the trench, an old lady suddenly appeared from nowhere and, before vanishing, told Nguyen Hoang that 'a master of the country will come to establish a capital here'. He interpreted this as a sign from above encouraging him in his quest for a capital and later built a simple temple on the spot to commemorate the prophecy, naming it Thien Mu – Celestial Lady Temple.

Nguyen Hoang's successor, Nguyen Phuc Nguyen, broke away from the Trinh in the north and established a southern independent region called Dang Trong in Vietnamese. The Nguyen then gave themselves royal status and began to expand southward at the expense of Champa and Chenla (ancient Cambodia) in a slow movement called the Vietnamese Nam Tien. At the same time, Lord Nguyen Phuc Nguyen cultivated relations with western powers and opened the port of Hoi An – 120 kms to the south of Hue – as a foreign trading post. At the beginning of the 17th century, Hoi An became a prosperous commercial centre where merchant ships from Europe, mainland Asia and Japan came to trade regularly. The Nguyen learned how to make bronze cannons from Portuguese engineers during this period, much to the Trinh's concern, and began to fortify their territory. The Trinh, meanwhile, ruled behind a weak Le Emperor in the north, now called Dang Ngoai to differentiate with the Nguyen's Dang Trong. The Trinh-Nguyen rivalry flared up into armed conflict in 1627 and after seven inconclusive wars, Vietnam was divided into two regions with the river Gianh as the boundary in 1672. From then on, the Trinh continued to rule behind the Le Emperor in the north and the Nguyen in the south.

The continuing rivalry and the bitter wars – albeit inconclusive – forced both sides to continue to modernise their arsenals and to build stronger fortifications. While the Trinh began to strengthen their relations with Europeans who possessed sophisticated arms, the Nguyen built walls near the demarcation line to keep the Trinh away from their southern region. Even after the two Trinh and Nguyen Lords agreed a truce in 1672, fortification of the south continued. The Nguyen's Citadel of Phu Xuan was built in 1687, near the original Hoa-Chau Citadel built under the Tran and at today's Hue location, as the result of this rivalry. Phu Xuan occupied the southeastern corner of today's Imperial Citadel of Hue.

By then, the Nguyen Lords had explored the geography of the location and believed that it was the best in feng-shui terms for a royal future: by the river bank, screened from bad air from the south by a flat-top mountain that they called Ngu Binh – royal

Thien Mu pagoda – view from the river.

screen, and with easy access to the sea via a good port – the Thuan
An, only 13 kilometres away. It was a kind of auspicious geomancy
that their predecessors – the Chams – recognised and exploited.
Indeed, dotted around the area and from local riverbeds, we can
still find remains of Cham buildings and artefacts.

The Trinh-Nguyen rivalry continued for another 100 years after
their truce, without any significant war occurring between the two.
However, the fragile peace broke down in 1774 when the Trinh
launched their attack on the Nguyen at Phu Xuan Citadel, taking
advantage of the fact that the Nguyen were busy fighting with
another armed group, the Tay Son from Binh Dinh province,
further south. The Nguyen was defeated by the Trinh and went to
take refuge in Gia Dinh, the area which later became Saigon and
today's Ho Chi Minh city. In 1776, the Trinh went back to the

Ngo Mon (Royal Gate).

north, leaving Phu Xuan to the Tay Son who pursued and killed most of the Nguyen clan, except for one Lord, Nguyen Anh, who managed to escape to Ha Tien province on the Vietnamese south coast and then to Siam, today's Thailand.

The Tay Son proclaimed their own dynasty in 1778, based at the Nguyen's Phu Xuan Citadel. From there, they entered into conflict with the Trinh and in 1786, they defeated the Trinh and unified Vietnam. The Tay Son Nguyen Hue became Emperor Quang Trung of Vietnam and established his capital in today's Hanoi.

Phu Xuan, meanwhile, remained a fortified citadel until 1802 when the last Nguyen Lord, Nguyen Anh, defeated the Tay Son in the north, returned to Hue area in victory and proclaimed himself Emperor Gia Long, beginning the 143-year-rule of the last dynasty of Vietnam, the Nguyen.

The Nguyen Dynasty

Thuong Tu gate.

The first Nguyen Emperor – Gia Long (r. 1802-1819)

The founder of the Nguyen Dynasty, Nguyen Anh, was the last surviving Lord when the victorious Tay Son took over central Vietnam, and pursued and killed the rest of the Nguyen Lords in an area further south of Gia Dinh in 1777. Aged 15, Nguyen Anh escaped to Ha Tien, a coastal province bordering the Gulf of Thailand. Here, he met a French missionary, Mgr. Pigneau de Béhaine, who was destined to play an important role in his life and in the struggle of the Nguyen against the Tay Son. The French missionary helped Nguyen Anh escape to the island of Phu Quoc, off the coast of Ha Tien. A year later, as head of the Nguyen clan, Nguyen Anh organised an army to fight the Tay Son. At first, he was successful in his campaign and took Gia Dinh, today's Ho Chi Minh City, from the Tay Son in 1780. There he established his headquarters and began to expand his power base.

From Gia Dinh, Nguyen Anh continued the Nam Tien movement to extend his territory further south and, at the same time, pursued the Nguyen war against the Tay Son. In 1782, the Tay Son launched a counter offensive and retook Gia Dinh. The defeated Nguyen Anh again escaped to Phu Quoc Island. From here, he regrouped and managed to regain Gia Dinh a year later, but was once more defeated when the Tay Son returned to dislodge him. After this defeat, Nguyen Anh took his family into exile in Phu Quoc and then to another island, the Poulo Condore – Con Lon Island or Con Dao in Vietnamese – where the Tay Son caught up with him. Fortunately for him, the pursuing Tay Son fleet was sunk by a storm and he was saved from being captured. Later, he went back to establish a base on Phu Quoc Island.

On Phu Quoc, the long entanglement between the Nguyen and the French began in 1783, when Nguyen Anh invited Mgr. Pierre Pigneau de Béhaine to come from Siam to see him and asked him to request the French Court of Louis XVI to intervene in Vietnam on his behalf. Nguyen Anh drafted a 14-clause-document and gave Pigneau de Béhaine total authority to negotiate with the French. As a gesture of trust, Gia Long sent his first son, Prince Canh, then only 4, with de Behaine to Paris. In the document, accompanied by a personal letter addressed to King Louis XVI, Nguyen Anh asked the French to give him soldiers, guns and ships to help him regain his land from the Tay Son. In return, he would cede to France the port of Hoi An, the island of Con Lon (Poulo Condore) and give France privileged status in its trade with Vietnam.

While preparations for the trip to France got underway, Nguyen Anh travelled to the new Siamese capital, Bangkok, to ask for more help. Siam had a new king, the founder of the House of Chakri, Rama I, who was more friendly to him than his predecessor, King Taksin, and Nguyen Anh was well received. King Rama I gave him 20,000 men and 300 ships to travel back to Vietnam to continue the

Emperor Gia Long.

Previous pages: The Nhon gate – symbol of achievement for the Nguyen.

Pigneau de Béhaine.

The Nguyen Dynasty 1802 – 1945

Emperor	Name at Birth	Reign
Gia Long	Nguyen Phuc Anh	1802–1819
Minh Mang	Nguyen Phuc Dam	1820–1840
Thieu Tri	Nguyen Phuc Mien Tong	1841–1847
Tu Duc	Nguyen Phuc Hong Nham	1848–1883
Duc Duc	Nguyen Phuc Ung Chan	3 days in 1883
Hiep Hoa	Nguyen Phuc Hong Dat	4 months in 1883
Kien Phuc	Nguyen Phuc Ung Dang	1883–1884
Ham Nghi	Nguyen Phuc Ung Lich	1884–1885
Dong Khanh	Nguyen Phuc Ung Duong	1885–1889
Thanh Thai	Nguyen Phuc Buu Lan	1889–1907
Duy Tan	Nguyen Phuc Vinh San	1907–1916
Khai Dinh	Nguyen Phuc Buu Dao	1916–1925
Bao Dai	Nguyen Phuc Vinh Thuy	1926–1945

Chart of Succession

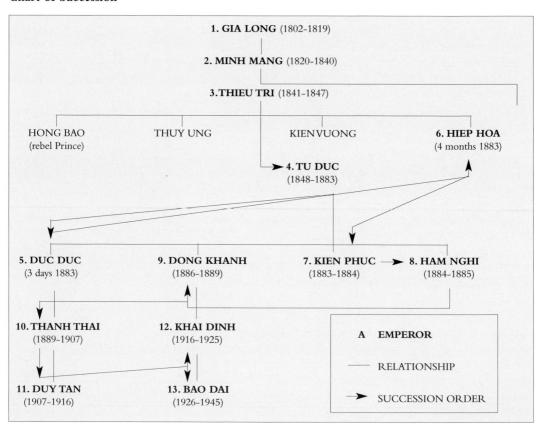

war against the Tay Son. The Siamese-Vietnamese army and navy under Nguyen Anh first took two provinces on the south coast, bordering the Gulf of Thailand, but were eventually defeated by the Tay Son under Nguyen Hue when they reached the well-fortified city of Gia Dinh. By 1785, most of the Siamese troops had been killed and Nguyen Anh's force fared little better. The remaining Siamese withdrew to their homeland with Nguyen Anh following behind. King Rama I again received Nguyen Anh cordially and allowed him and his entourage to settle in an area outside the capital. Nguyen Anh lived in exile in this village, his followers cultivated the land for their subsistence while he continued to organise an army to return to Vietnam. From Siam, Nguyen Anh sent words to Mgr. de Béhaine, urging him to set sail for France.

Unfortunately, the initially cordial relationship between Nguyen Anh and the Siamese court soon soured, after the Portuguese offered help to Nguyen Anh, an act the king considered as an insult since he had already assumed the role of Nguyen Anh's protector. Even though the Portuguese offer was not accepted immediately, relations between the Nguyen Lord and the king remained cool. Meanwhile, in Vietnam, internal conflict between the brothers had weakened the Tay Son; their war with the Trinh in the North of Vietnam did not improve the situation. Even though they were victorious over the Trinh, the Tay Son were exhausted. Taking advantage of this situation, and finding himself less welcome at the Siamese Court, Nguyen Anh left Bangkok at dead of night, leaving only a letter of thanks for the king, and took his army back to Phu Quoc island in 1787. From here, he moved inland to prepare for a campaign against the Tay Son in Gia Dinh. Subsequent relations with Siam, however cool, were carefully maintained.

Mgr. Pierre Pigneau de Béhaine arrived in France with Prince Canh in the same year, 1787. After initial reluctance from the French court, on 28th November 1787 he obtained an agreement from King Louis XVI and, together with the French Minister of Foreign Affairs and the Navy, Montmorin, signed the Treaty of

Prince Canh on his trip to France.

Signatures to The Treaty of Versailles, 1787.

Gia Long's ship shown in relief on a royal urn.

Model of the French ship La Thetis. c. 1813.

Nguyen Anh soldiers. c. 1800.

Versailles, a copy of which is still kept in the French National Archives. According to this treaty, France would send 1,200 infantrymen, 200 artillery troops, 250 African troops, guns and ammunition to help Nguyen Anh. In return, Nguyen Anh would cede to France the port of Hoi An and Con Lon island, give France exclusive trading rights with Vietnam, send men to help France whenever necessary and, lastly, give to France a ship each year, based on the model of the ships that France was preparing to send.

Dragon Motif on Thai Hoa Palace.

King Louis XVI then ordered the French Envoy in Ponchidery, India, to execute these terms, an order conveyed to him by Mgr. Pigneau de Béhaine on his return voyage to Vietnam. However, the French Envoy instead recommended that France should not get involved in Vietnam. Faced with his own internal problems during the pre-Bastille period, King Louis XVI did not insist and, as a result, no help came to Nguyen Anh. Pierre Pigneau de Béhaine and Prince Canh returned to Vietnam with a Treaty but no army and only the two French ships assigned by King Louis XVI to escort them back. However, the ship captains decided to stay and other French merchant ships came to join them soon after. They offered guns and ammunition for sale along with the use of their ships and their service. In 1789, with their help, Nguyen Anh managed to gain victory over the Tay Son and consolidated his power in Gia Dinh. The ship captains were later given court titles, Vietnamese names and prominent positions at the first Nguyen Court. Mgr Pigneau de Béhaine, however, died in 1799 without seeing the final Nguyen victory.

Even with his now well-equipped army and navy, it took Lord Nguyen Anh until 1801 to regain Phu Xuan Citadel. From there, in 1802, he travelled north and took control of that region from the Tay Son. He now effectively controlled the whole country and, proclaiming himself the first Nguyen Emperor Gia Long, named the country Vietnam with Phu Xuan as his capital. Envoys were sent to the Qing court in China to seek their assent, which was granted in 1804. To seal their approval, the Qing court bestowed on Nguyen Anh the title of King of Annam and a royal gold seal. This seal later played a pivotal role in the tricky triangular relationship between China, France and Vietnam in 1884 and 1885.

In Phu Xuan, with the country pacified and the Chinese having granted approval, Emperor Gia Long could start planning the royal city of Hue in 1804. When work was completed two years later, Hue became a shining example of East meeting West. It was, and still is, an exquisite combination of 19th century European construction skills and Vietnamese refined architectural design and decorative arts. Unfortunately, the same harmony would not prevail in relations between France and Vietnam.

Guns at The Nhon gate – the Nguyen's symbol of power.

Gia Long and the French

For seventeen years, Emperor Gia Long reigned over a court that welcomed the presence of his French allies who were called counsellors and given many special privileges. Each of the French counsellors was allocated 50 soldiers as personal guards and all were exempted from the most solemn rite: the traditional kowtow. The kowtow was a Chinese practice strictly observed at court, whereby each mandarin was required to prostrate himself several times in front of the Emperor at court assemblies before assuming their appointed places. The most influential of the French counsellors were Jean-Baptiste Chaigneau, known as Nguyen van Thang, the Vietnamese name Gia Long gave him to show his appreciation, and ship's captains Philippe Vannier, De Forsans and Despiau. Jean-Baptiste Chaigneau was given a Military Mandarin post called Truong Co in Vietnamese, his son Michel was given the Vietnamese name of Nguyen Van Duc and later became known as Michel Duc Chaigneau when he later served at the Nguyen court. In addition, Gia Long turned a blind eye to French and other European missionary activity. With the Emperor's tacit blessing, they built churches, openly practised their religion and converted ordinary citizens without any intervention from the court or local authorities.

Commercially, foreign ships continued to trade at Da Nang, Hoi An and Saigon with French ships accorded privileged status. However, according to Vietnamese records, Gia Long rejected diplomatic relations with England two or three times in 1804, on advice from the two French counsellors Chaigneau and Vannier.

The cordial commercial relationship changed somewhat in 1817 when King Louis XVIII sent an envoy, Baron Kergariou, to Vietnam

Jean-Baptiste Chaigneau.

Mandarins kowtow in front of Thai Hoa.

Some churches in Hue.

to demand Gia Long to respect the Treaty of Versailles signed by Mgr. Pigneau de Béhaine in 1787. The Vietnamese Emperor refused on the grounds that France had not fulfilled the terms of the Treaty. Nevertheless, French commercial ships continued to be received favourably at Da Nang port although there was no official trade agreement between the two countries. To rectify the situation, the French court asked Chaigneau to look after French interests. In 1819, Chaigneau went back to France on leave and was officially appointed French Consul to the Hue Court. However, when he returned to Vietnam in 1821, Gia Long had died in 1819, and his successor, Emperor Minh Mang had different ideas about the presence of foreigners. His courtiers also demonstrated a different attitude toward their French colleagues. While the Emperor himself ignored them most of the time, the Vietnamese mandarins did not hide their annoyance at the French presence. Emperor Minh Mang often refused to meet French envoys or to have anything to do with those already there. Disillusioned, both Chaigneau and Vannier left Hue in 1824.

In 1825, a French Envoy, Hyacinthe de Bourgainville, arrived in Da Nang with a letter from the French King but the king's letter was returned on the pretext that no one at court could read French. The next year, 1826, France appointed another Chaigneau, Eugene, to be the French Consul at Hue. However, he failed to obtain an audience with the Emperor and eventually left in 1829 after which time bilateral relations stagnated.

Hyacinthe de Bourgainville.

Funerary tablets – Gia Long and his Queen.

Right: Ballustrade of Ngu Phung Terrace.

The second Nguyen Emperor – Minh Mang (r. 1820-1840)

Minh Mang's reign was a period when European intervention in East and Southeast Asia was intensifying. By the end of his reign, British aggression in China had escalated into the full-scale Opium war of 1840 with the British eventually gaining the upper hand. During this period and the following years, the French also increased pressure on China and forced the Qing to open several ports to them by 1844. Other western aggressive acts followed and China signed treaty after treaty giving away yet more powers to the United States and European countries.

From Vietnam, it was inevitable that Emperor Minh Mang viewed events unfolding in China with alarm; if China, Vietnam's powerful mentor, had so much trouble with the West, surely Vietnam would have no chance? Eventually, he concluded that it would be safer to close all doors to foreigners – a decision that ultimately would cost Vietnam dear.

Throughout his reign, Emperor Minh Mang had to contend with external pressures, while internally general discontent occasionally flared up into organised rebellions that the court had great difficulty in subduing. Minh Mang believed that French missionaries were involved in some of these rebellions and ordered searches of churches and the interrogation and torture of European priests. The spread of Christianity was another cause of concern for him as the promotion of God went against the core of Vietnamese traditional belief that the Emperor was a Son of Heaven, chosen from above to govern the country with a clear-cut celestial Mandate. When European missionaries encouraged Vietnamese citizens to

Emperor Minh Mang.

serve a Christian God in Heaven, it was seen by the court as a direct challenge to the Emperor's authority, almost equivalent to a call for rebellion. That coupled with the perceived involvement of missionaries in actual rebellions prompted Minh Mang to ban Christianity altogether. However, French and other European priests continued working clandestinely and, when caught, a number were executed. In 1833 the Emperor issued several edicts ordering Christians to renounce their faith and imprisoned the missionaries.

The emperor's actions against the missionaries have been widely condemned and seen as the provocation that led to French intervention. However, although cruel and inhumane at times, his actions were a result of his Confucian upbringing and his belief in his status as the Son of Heaven. As a devoted classical scholar and emperor, Minh Mang saw the preaching of European priests as a rebellious act and a challenge to his celestial mandate.

Minh Mang died aged 50, after ruling for 21 years, during which time he built a firm base for an independent Vietnam, which he renamed Dai Nam (Great Realm of the South). He achieved many reforms and left a huge cultural legacy. His reign was a period when independent Vietnam under the Nguyen was at its strongest, but unfortunately, until his achievements were more widely recognised, for many, he would be forever remembered as the ruler who persecuted Christians and Christianity.

Minh Mang's stele.

Path to Minh Mang's Grave.

The Third Nguyen Emperor – Thieu Tri (r. 1841-1847)

Rigault de Genouilly.

Nghi Mon and Stele House, Tomb of Thieu Tri.

Thieu Tri, was the eldest son of Minh Mang. He ascended to the throne at the age of 31, on 12th February 1841. He was the most artistic of the Nguyen emperors as well as a prolific poet. Along with a rich legacy of poetry and calligraphic work, Thieu Tri left a set of 20 invaluable glass paintings that he commissioned from China to illustrate his choice of the 20 most beautiful locations in Hue. The glass painting entitled Cao Cac Sinh Luong ranks number 6 and can still be viewed at Dien Tho palace.

It depicts a pavilion built under Minh Mang in the middle of a lake within the Imperial Citadel. Thieu Tri's accompanying poem was engraved in a cartouche at the top. Apart from being a poet, Emperor Thieu Tri was a keen designer who built the Phuoc Duyen tower of Thien Mu Pagoda and left a remarkably subtle style of interior décor that we can still view and admire at the Museum of Royal Antiquity, formerly one of his palaces, or at his tomb.

Domestically, Thieu Tri continued to develop Vietnam into a well-organised realm and to uphold his father's traditional values. Externally, he followed his father's xenophobic policy, albeit in a less severe way. However, although he was mild in his attitude toward foreign interference, by then, Minh Mang's policy toward outsiders had fuelled an increasingly hostile attitude toward Vietnam in Europe that soon turned into a firm resolve for France to actively intervene. With China having provided rich pickings for western powers, the promise of another fertile, underdeveloped land immediately south of China served as an even stronger motive to propel French ships toward Vietnam under Thieu Tri.

From 1843 onward, French warships arrived at Da Nang port regularly to demand better treatment for French missionaries and citizens and for Vietnam to open their ports for foreign trading. Negotiations turned to hostility in 1847 when a French ship under the command of Colonel Lapiere and Lieutenant-General Rigault de Genouilly came to Da Nang with a letter from the French King. During this visit, the French commanders claimed to have found unusual activities among Vietnamese ships and port guards, and as a result they opened fire and sank five Vietamese ships. This incident made it impossible for Vietnam and France to reach any successful outcome in the on-going negotiation process. Indeed, it enraged Emperor Thieu Tri to such an extent that he gave an order to capture and kill all Christian missionaries in Vietnam. He also offered handsome rewards to anybody who could capture a foreign missionary. Emperor Thieu Tri died shortly after this incident aged 37, after a reign of only seven years. His body was buried in a modest tomb that was in ruins until recently. The prince chosen to succeed him was his second son Nguyen Phuc Hong Nham, the first prince having been passed over because he was the son of the second queen and as an alleged playboy, unsuitable to become king.

Thieu Tri's Glass painting *Cao Cac Sinh Luong*, no. 6th best sight of Hue.

Overview of the Tomb of Thieu Tri.

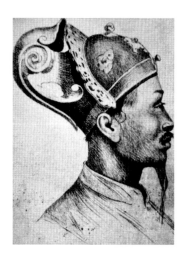

Emperor Tu Duc.

The fourth Nguyen Emperor – Tu Duc (r. 1847-1883)

Aged only 19, Nguyen Phuc Hong Nham became Emperor Tu Duc and inherited from his father a court cocooned in its Confucian values, a nation left behind by modernity, and on the brink of war with France. Under his reign, several petitions from the literati urging him to modernise were shelved by conservative mandarins who did not want anything to infringe on their privileged status in exchange for the unknown. The mid-nineteenth century Vietnamese court was insulated from reality outside the walled citadel, while Vietnamese ports endured constant harassment from French naval ships. European missionaries were banned, regularly persecuted or killed. By then, in Europe the Industrial Revolution was far advanced while countries like Vietnam remained entrenched in a conservative past. Nevertheless, both East and West still viewed each other as 'barbarians' who needed to be civilised. Under Tu Duc's reign, Minh Mang's anti-foreigner policy continued to be strictly enforced. Vietnam refused repeated trading requests from Britain, France and Spain and did not even allow their ships to enter Vietnamese ports when they arrived at Da Nang, Hoi An and Quang Yen. China, at that point, had been brought to its knees after the Opium War with the British and continuied aggression from the United States and European powers. Nevertheless despite this, the court under Tu Duc still considered China as a big brother who would be able to fend off any foreign intervention on their behalf.

While pressure from France increased, Tu Duc also had to deal with several domestic rebellions, the most infamous being from members of his own family. As a second son, Tu Duc faced constant opposition from his elder half-brother, Hong Bao, who felt he had been denied his rightful kingship. In 1851, he organised a plot to overthrow Tu Duc and when this failed, it was revealed that he had help from foreign priests. Hong Bao was imprisoned and committed suicide in captivity. The persecution of Christians was intensified after this failed coup and in the same year, 1851, Tu Duc issued a royal decree calling on all citizens to capture and kill European

Below left: Mandarins at Court Assembly.

Below right: Eunuchs and palace maids.

missionaries. Three French priests and many Christians were executed in 1851 and 1852, prompting both France and Spain to prepare for war against Vietnam. Another royal decree was issued in 1855 to reinforce the previous one issued in 1851. The scene was set for a Franco-Vietnamese confrontation.

Impresssion of the capture of Saigon, 18th February, 1859.

The French invasion

In 1855, the French envoy in Shanghai, De Montigny, was ordered to go to Thailand, Cambodia and Vietnam to establish political and commercial bureaux for Emperor Napoleon III. While De Montigny was busy in abroad, a French ship, the Catinat, under the command of Captain Le Lieur, arrived in Da Nang in September 1856. On arrival, Le Lieur gave the Vietnamese representatives a letter from the French Emperor and a message that a French envoy would arrive shortly to establish relations with Vietnam. The Vietnamese representatives opened the letter and then left it on the beach at Da Nang. Considering this an insult, the French captain ordered an assault on the town. Several barrages of artillery fire were launched on the port before the ship sailed, leaving a message for the Vietnamese court that they should expect the French envoy to arrive and negotiate terms. De Montigny arrived in January the next year, 1857, and gave the Hue Court a set of requests, including the establishment of a Consulate and a trading post in Da Nang, and a demand for Vietnam to open free trade and allow free missionary activities in Vietnam. Emperor Tu Duc refused.

The execution of another Spanish priest in 1857 in north Vietnam provided the excuse that France needed to intervene by force. 14 ships under Captain Rigault de Genouilly came to Da Nang in 1858 and occupied the port with the intention of proceeding to Hue. However, when met with strong Vietnamese resistance, the French captain left Da Nang and proceeded to the South instead.

The French invasion of Vietnam began in the South on 2nd February 1859. The French fleet entered the port of Vung Tau and travelled to the area north of Saigon. On 19th February, the French overwhelmed the Vietnamese forces and took Gia Dinh – Saigon. Captain De Genouilly then asked the Hue court to discuss terms but, again, Emperor Tu Duc refused. The French fleet returned to Da Nang for further bombardment before moving on to China to increase their pressure on the Qing.

The French Navy returned to South Vietnam in 1860, following a Franco-Chinese ceasefire. This time, they were reinforced by the French naval force in China. They arrived in February 1861 and the now expanded French campaign in South Vietnam began a few days later. Fighting continued until April 1861 when the Vietnamese asked for a truce. The French agreed and proposed a 12-point agreement. However, Emperor Tu Duc refused and war resumed. By June 1862, the French had won in most of areas of South Vietnam and proposed a new treaty, which was agreed. In this, among other concessions, Vietnam ceded to France three eastern provinces of South Vietnam for which Franche would return the western province of Vinh Long. Vietnam was also required to inform France of any foreign diplomatic activities and to pay a large sum in reparation. It was to be the first of several treaties that the Nguyen Court signed with France under heavy military pressure, opening up a sad beginning for Vietnam under French rule.

Unfortunately, peace did not return to Vietnam and popular resistance against the French continued in the South. After the signing of the treaty, Tu Duc sent a delegation led by one of his most trusted mandarins, Phan Thanh Gian, to Paris to ask for a renegotiation of the treaty terms. The French Emperor, Napoleon

Rain on Xung Khiem pavilion, tomb of Tu Duc.

III, agreed to give it his consideration, but, under pressure from pro-colonial quarters in France and in the now-occupied eastern provinces of South Vietnam, nothing happened to the Treaty of 1862. On his return, Phan Thanh Gian was appointed governor of the remaining three western provinces of south Vietnam.

By 1867, while the French court was still indecisive about what to do with Vietnam and on the pretext that Vietnamese forces could not maintain order in the three western provinces, the French army in Vietnam launched an offensive against these provinces. All three fell in the same year. Unable to defend his territory, the governor of Phan Thanh Gian committed suicide by taking poison. France had now succeeded in seizing all six provinces in South Vietnam and proceeded to turn them into a French overseas territory.

The French had begun looking to North Vietnam in 1866 when they tried unsuccessfully to open a route from southern Vietnam to Yunnan via the Mekong River. As the flow of this huge river was too unpredictable for safe navigation, they thought the Red River might be an alternative route to Yunnan from the South China Sea via the Gulf of Tonkin. With this in mind, French forces began pressuring the Nguyen Court once more. In 1873, a French fleet came to Da Nang to deliver a letter to Emperor Tu Duc, complaining about the way French missionaries and businessmen were treated in North Vietnam, stating that as a result France had to protect French interests there. The fleet then proceeded to Hanoi. After several months of heavy fighting, Hanoi fell to the French in the same year, 1873. The next year, a new treaty of 1874 was signed between France and Vietnam, formalising the French occupation of South Vietnam. According to this, France had total ownership of the South of Vietnam, known in French as Cochinchine, and Vietnam was to open the Red River Delta in the north for French trade and access to Yunnan.

The 22 clauses of the 1874 Treaty set out terms that, in essence, gave France total authority over military, trade and religious matters in Vietnam. It was formally ratified in Hue in 1875 after which the Nguyen court functioned in a surreal environment. The Emperor continued to rule and act as king of a Vietnam that had little sovereignty. It was a state of affairs that soon demanded attention.

One of the clauses in the treaty concerned the establishment of a French Legation in Hue and, in 1875, the first resident Chargé D'Affaires Pierre Paul Reinhart (1875-1876) was appointed. The French Legation was allowed to live outside the fortified Capital City, on the south bank of the Perfume River, and kept away from activities at court. It was a difficult existence that a French doctor described vividly in a journal article published in the *Bulletin de la Société de Géographie de Paris* in France in 1883, at the end of Tu Duc's reign. Dr. Auvray was a physician for the French Marine and lived for 18 months in Hue, from July 1879 to December 1880, a time that he recalled in his article:

Phan Thanh Gian, c. 1863.

Stele House, Tomb of Tu Duc.

'*At that time, no garrison existed and we lived in complete isolation among the Vietnamese, with no telegraph for communication. We only received irregular supplies and mail, whenever sailing conditions permitted, from the ship Antilope. We rarely went out because of the strict surveillance on our activities, except to the church at Kim Long, or some hunts, our lives were confined within the walls of the Legation…*
For Tu Duc, we were like a perpetual and living menace. We were constantly watched, everything we did was observed and commented on, sometimes, this led to fantastic suppositions….To the west of this was the Tu Duc Mausoleum, it was not that he had died, he was alive and reigned, or believed that he reigned over Annam…'

This uneasy cohabitation existed against a background of great division between the ruling class and ordinary citizens:

'*The rich continued to embellish their houses, their flowers, their final resting places… Meanwhile, the people were profoundly sad. It was such a pitiful sight in winter when we found the poor barely covered in their straw rain-capes, the only clothing they had, people literally died of poverty and hunger..*'

The criticism referred to Tu Duc and his tomb on the south bank of the river during this uneasy time of early Franco-Vietnamese cohabitation. Dr. Auvray's views were in line with the French stated objective in Vietnam, namely intervention would improve the life of the poor. In those early days, bilateral relations were distant but still cordial for, also according to Dr. Auvray, the emperor often gave the French Legation things to eat which he deemed inedible, such as various birds he had shot, local cakes, or an elephant foot that the Emperor's hunters had brought back from their expedition.

Emperor Tu Duc died in 1883 and, with him, the last pretence of Vietnam as an independent nation.

Emperors Duc Duc (r. 1883), Hiep Hoa (r. 1883), Kien Phuc (r. 1883-1884) and the French occupation

Emperor Tu Duc was childless and by the time of his death in 1883, he had adopted three of his nephews, and appointed three regents to oversee the succession process. Two of them, Nguyen Van Tuong and Ton That Thuyet, were more prominent, and both played important roles in the next chapter of Vietnamese history.

The first of Tu Duc's adopted sons was put on the throne as Emperor Duc Duc in June 1883 but dismissed three days later as unsuitable. Under Tu Duc's reign, the French legation had become friendly with a number of Nguyen princes and some members of the royal family in order to glean inside information. Duc Duc allegedly was one and, as such, was seen by the regents as someone who might give in to the French, or even turn Vietnam over to them eventually. At the reading-of-the-will ceremony, Duc Duc was officially found guilty of omitting certain sentences from Tu Duc's will; a grave offence of lèse-majesté, and was put in prison. He allegedly died from starvation sometime later.

The youngest brother of Emperor Tu Duc, also a son of Emperor Thieu Tri by a lesser queen, was crowned as Emperor Hiep Hoa. However, he did not rule for very long either. Hiep Hoa, allegedly, was also pro-French and favoured a peaceful solution by allowing Vietnam to become a full French protectorate, something the regents and the court were adamantly against. During this time,

Gate to Thanh Thai's burial area, Tomb of Duc Duc.

The signing of the Treaty of Hue 1883.

the French continued to pursue their war in North Vietnam to protect their trade route along the Red River to Yunnan. It was a chaotic period both at court and on the battleground in the north and culminated in the French taking over Hanoi and most of north Vietnam in 1883. After this victory, they moved to Thuan An port, outside Hue, and launched an offensive against the port. On 23rd July 1883, a new Treaty was signed between two Vietnamese mandarins Tran Dinh Tuc and Nguyen Trong Hop (or Hiep) on Emperor Hiep Hoa's order and representatives of France, the Governor Harmand and Chargé D'Affaires Champeaux, giving France total authority over the remaining part of Vietnam, including Hue. The South of Vietnam had become a French overseas territory in 1867. This Treaty of 1883 was not ratified by either side but became the legal basis for France subsequently to act as they wished in Vietnam, especially in the north where they were keen to consolidate their power. Needless to say, the treaty enraged the Hue court. Hiep Hoa was dethroned and forced to take poison in November 1883.

The 1883 Treaty was all the more controversial for being signed under an Emperor later condemned, and while the war of resistance was continuing unabated. To replace Emperor Hiep Hoa in 1883, the Hue court put the youngest of Tu Duc's three adopted sons, aged 15 at the time, on the throne as Emperor Kien Phuc. Within a short period of four months in 1883, the Nguyen court at Hue saw the comings and goings of three Emperors, an unprecedented upheaval. Nor was Emperor Kien Phuc to rule for long, dying eight months later, in July 1884, a month after France despatched another envoy to Vietnam to modify the previous treaty. The new treaty was

Grave of Emperor Kien Phuc, Tomb of Tu Duc.

signed in June 1884 between the French envoy Patenôtre and the two Vietnamese regents Nguyen Van Tuong and Ton That Thuyet. According to this one, known as the Patenôtre Treaty, except for the French-owned South of Vietnam, the rest of the country was divided into two regions governed by different authorities, the French in the north called Tonkin or Bac Ky, and the Hue Court in the middle part, called Annam or Trung Ky. Both regions were put under French protection. The French also had the right to enter the Imperial Citadel at will, their forces occupied Thuan An port, gateway to Hue, and any new Vietnamese Emperor would need French approval.

To protest against this definitive treaty that, in effect, gave France total authority over Vietnam, several mandarins left the court to take up arms against the French. Some remained in Vietnam, while others travelled to China and Japan seeking support. The two influential regents Nguyen Van Tuong and Ton That Thuyet stayed at court. After the death of Emperor Kien Phuc, another prince was chosen to be the next Emperor. Prince Nguyen Phuc Ung Lich was Tu Duc's nephew and blood brother of Kien Phuc but was not adopted. He became Emperor Ham Nghi at the age of 13.

Emperor Ham Nghi.

Emperor Ham Nghi (r. 1884-1885) and the resistance

With the choice of Emperor Ham Nghi, Vietnam and the Hue court opened a new chapter in the nation's history. His coronation met with fierce protests from the French Governor Rheinart, who demanded to exercise his right of veto and offered his own candidate, another Nguyen Prince that he had already approved, but the Hue court refused. Rheinart raised the matter with the French government in Paris but his request to use force to remove Ham Nghi and replace him with his choice was turned down. Even then, Rheinart ordered the French army under his command to aim their heavy guns towards the Citadel to express his displeasure. After a lengthy negotiation, Emperor Ham Nghi was recrowned by the Hue court, in the presence of French representatives, becoming the 8th Nguyen Emperor. The re-enactment of Ham Nghi's coronation was later described in Vietnamese documents as a celebration of Ham Nghi's coronation witnessed by French guests.

During the period leading up to Ham Nghi's coronation, relations between the Nguyen court and the French Legation in Hue were seriously strained with insulting incidents recorded by both sides. One of the most serious was the clash over Vietnam's relations with China. Following the signing of the Patenôtre Treaty, the French representatives demanded that the Nguyen Court should officially renounce China as their protector, and should hand over the royal seal that China had given the first Emperor Gia Long as a symbol of his authority. The regent Nguyen Van Tuong refused, proposing instead that the seal be destroyed. It was melted down in a solemn ceremony at court, in front of French representatives and Vietnamese courtiers. The event was a bitter experience for all concerned; for France who wanted to keep the seal for French museums, for Vietnam who did not want to relinquish China as an ally, and for China, who was by proxy humiliated by both. This incident was allegedly the reason why China abandoned the first Tientsin Treaty that they signed with France in 1884 and continued their war with France until 1885 when the two signed another treaty called the true Tientsin Treaty in June.

By April 1885, relations between France and Vietnam were almost at breaking point. The arrival of the French Marshall De

Courcy on 2nd July 1885 was the last straw. Following the signing of the true Treaty of Tientsin, in which, among other clauses, China renounced its alliance with Vietnam. De Courcy was appointed Commander in Chief of the French force in Tonkin and Annam and decided to travel to Hue to present his credentials to Emperor Ham Nghi. During the negotiation over protocols, De Courcy demanded that all his troops should enter the Imperial Citadel by the central entrance of the main gate, Ngo Mon, usually reserved for the Emperor alone, arguing that France was now the protector for Vietnam. He also demanded both regents to come to report to him. Ton That Thuyet excused himself and only Nguyen Van Tuong came. The ensuing arguments broke up the already fragile relationship. During the night of 4th July 1885, under the order of Ton That Thuyet and the Nguyen court, Vietnamese troops launched an attack on the French Legation and their garrison at Mang Ca fort but soon ran out of ammunition. At dawn, the French retaliated and launched an all-out assault on the Imperial Citadel in which a large part was burned to the ground and thousands of people perished. The regent Ton That Thuyet escorted Emperor Ham Nghi, the Queen Mother and some court members out of Hue, while, acting according to plan, the regent Nguyen Van Tuong stayed behind to negotiate. The fleeing royal group split up outside Hue: the Emperor and his entourage went to a secret base named Tan So in Quang Tri province, north of Hue, which had been held in readiness during most of Tu Duc's reign, while the Queen Mother's group returned to Hue to settle at Tu Duc's tomb, now that the Imperial Citadel was uninhabitable. Nguyen Van Tuong began negotiations with the French authority, on behalf of the court, from the Thuong Bac pavilion where he was imprisoned, while the French issued an ultimatum to the Queen Mother and the court, ordering them to bring Ham Nghi back within two months. When the deadline expired, Nguyen Van Tuong was tricked onto a ship and exiled to Tahiti where he died shortly after.

Ham Nghi's route of escape (After BAVH n. 3, 1929).

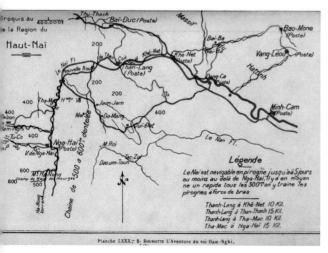

From the remote location of Tan So in the mountains of Quang Tri province, Ham Nghi launched an anti-French movement by issuing a decree calling on the people to fight against the French. This became known as the Can Vuong (Support the Emperor) movement. The response was positive throughout the country with many groups being formed to join the Emperor in exile and to stage ambushes against French forces. The resistance continued in varying degrees and strength even after Ham Nghi was captured and sent into exile three years later.

The storming of the Imperial Citadel was a devastating and tragic event that is still commemorated by Hue citizens today in the Fete of the Souls on the 5th moon of the Lunar calendar, June-July in our common era calendar.

When Ham Nghi did not return, the French Governor General put another of Ham Nghi's blood brothers on the throne as Emperor Dong Khanh in September 1885. Dong Khanh was the third adopted son of Emperor Tu Duc, and elder blood brother of Ham Nghi and Kien Phuc, but had earlier been overlooked.

The ninth Nguyen Emperor – Dong Khanh (r. 1885-1889)

While Emperor Ham Nghi conducted his anti-French resistance from Quang Tri and, later, further north in Quang Binh province, Emperor Dong Khanh ruled in Hue under French protection. In 1886 he did travel to Dong Hoi, Quang Binh province, to attempt to meet with Ham Nghi and persuade him to return, but failed to make contact and returned empty-handed. For the next three years, Vietnam had two Emperors: Ham Nghi who was actively resisting the French from Quang Binh province, and Dong Khanh who worked with the French in Hue. The country experienced an unsettled period with Eastern and Western values clashing regularly in the cities, and anti-French resistance continuing in the countryside.

Emperor Dong Khanh.

Whether or not Ham Nghi's resistance made any serious headway against the French, the French authority was alarmed at the frequency of attacks against their army posts and missionaries. Nor could they allow the existence of an alternative Emperor, so efforts to capture him were intensified. In the end, Ham Nghi was allegedly betrayed by a guard who captured and handed him over to the French in November 1888. He was immediately sent into exile in Algeria in January 1889 where he stayed, married a French woman, had three children with her and remained until his death.

Emperor Dong Khanh ruled until 28th January 1889 when he died unexpectedly at the age of 27, a mysterious death that was later described by his grandson Bao Dai in his Memoir of 1980 as arising from 'his sorrow at seeing his country being put under French tutelage, against his will'. His most memorable legacy for Hue was probably the construction of a new royal study decorated in fine mosaic art that we can still view today. For the Nguyen royal family, his notable legacy would be the creation of the Imperial Order of the Dragon of Annam, a medal that was not recognised by the Vietnamese government who took over from Bao Dai in 1945. This Order was re-instated in 2002 by the Nguyen Royal Family in exile. With the death of Dong Khanh, the Nguyen court at Hue, once again, searched for a successor and a ten- year-old boy was put on the throne three days later, under the regnal name of Thanh Thai.

Silhouette of the Court of Stone, Tomb of Dong Khanh.

Emperor Thanh Thai.

Thanh Thai returning to Hue, 1953.

The tenth Nguyen Emperor – Thanh Thai (r. 1889-1907)

Thanh Thai was the son of Duc Duc, who had been allowed to reign for only three days and allegedly died from starvation in prison in 1883. Under Thanh Thai's reign, the French completed their structural and political organisation of Vietnam and, especially, in Hue. The French Governor General in Hue now became the President of the Council of Ministers at Court. All decisions at court from then on had to be submitted to the French for approval. The Vietnamese Emperor remained simply as the Son of Heaven for his people, without having any power whatsoever. Even so, the

Grave of Thanh Thai.

Silver wash basin of Emperor Thanh Thai.

emperor was often accused of being mentally unstable and was considered as a threat to the administration. In 1907, at the age of 28, he was asked by the Hue Court to abdicate and in 1915, was sent to exile on the French island of Reunion. He stayed on the island until 1947 when he was permitted to return to Vietnam and lived in Saigon until his death in 1954.

After his abdication in 1907, Thanh Thai's youngest son was put on the throne at the age of 7 to become Emperor Duy Tan, the most militant king among the Nguyen under French occupation.

Coronation procession of Emperor Duy Tan.

Below left: Emperor Duy Tan in exile aged 30 as Prince Vinh San.

Below right: Bringing the remains of Emperor Duy Tan home to Hue

1003bis. ANNAM - Hué - Le jeune Empereur Duy-Than et son entourage

The eleventh Nguyen Emperor – Duy Tan (r. 1907-1916)

Emperor Duy Tan and his Court.

Duy Tan took over the Hue court at an interesting juncture in the politics of East Asia. Japan at that time was seen by the Vietnamese elite as a good example of a strong and developed country that beat Russia in the Russo-Japanese war of 1904-1905. The Japanese slogan of 'Asia for Asians' was taken to heart by the Vietnamese literati. Anti-French activities in Vietnam continued at an even faster pace than before. Secret societies were formed and got in touch with those in exile in Japan and China. Dr. Sun Yat Sen's success in China in 1911 fuelled even more anti-French activities in Vietnam with demonstrations regularly held in the cities while armed struggles continued in the countryside. The situation only became calmer in 1913 but again flared up in 1914 at the onset of the First World War. Thousands of Vietnamese citizens were drafted to fight for France in Europe. While French attention was elsewhere, demonstrations, meetings and agitation continued in the cities. The young Emperor Duy Tan who was 16 at the time decided to join the anti-French struggle. In 1916, he left the Forbidden Purple City with the intention of becoming a figurehead in the struggle for liberty for Vietnam. Unfortunately for him, he was captured almost immediately. After ten days of imprisonment in the French base at Mang Ca, on the northeast corner of the Imperial Citadel, he was also sent to exile on Reunion island in May 1916. As a citizen of this island, he became involved in the Second World War and died in an air crash in Africa in 1945.

Emperor Khai Dinh.

Senior Nguyen Mandarins attending a Tea Ceremony with the French Governor General,1924.

The twelfth Nguyen Emperor – Khai Dinh (r. 1916-1925)

The last but one Nguyen Emperor Khai Dinh was the son of Emperor Dong Khanh. He ascended to the throne in 1916 at the age of 32, a much more mature choice than the previous ones. He was a mild character who accepted the status quo and was friendly with the French protectorate authority. Under his reign, his court and the French Governor General were on excellent terms. Because of his appeasement, the Nguyen family became even more divided than before. While one Nguyen prince, Buu Loc, operated in Japan and Taiwan against the French in Vietnam, another prince, Buu Trac, considered himself as the rightful heir to the throne and actively opposed Khai Dinh.

Under Khai Dinh, while anti-French groups still operated in the countryside, Vietnamese ties with France became stronger, to the extent that Khai Dinh sent his son, Crown Prince Vinh Thuy, to school in Paris at the age of nine, in the care of the former French Governor General Charles. Khai Dinh's reign was relatively calm and without incident at court or with the French authority. The most significant act that the Emperor performed during his reign was probably his decree on the Vietnamese language, whereby from 1919 onward, Vietnam would cease to use Chinese characters in its official documents and romanised Vietnamese would become the only official written script. Khai Dinh himself had already been using this form in his private letters to his mandarins, but even though romanised Vietnamese had been popular and in use for several decades, only Chinese characters, until then, were used for Royal documents and decrees. With his decision to make romanised Vietnamese official, Khai Dinh signified a complete transformation of Vietnam from a Confucian realm to a Francophile society. Khai Dinh died in November 1925.

Emperor Khai Dinh and Crown Prince Vinh Thuy
(later Emperor Bao Dai), in France, 1922.

Emperor Khai Dinh in his study.

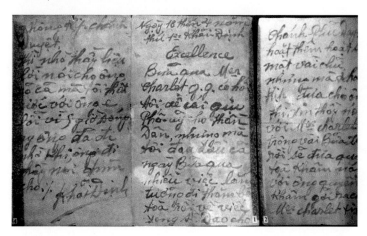

Khai Dinh's Decree and Seal.

Above left: Khai Dinh's letter in
Romanised Vietnamese.

Royal princes in a European-style horse-
drawn carriage.

Emperor Bao Dai. (Photo courtesy of Phan Thuan An)

The thirteenth and last Emperor – Bao Dai (r. 1926/1932-1945)

When Khai Dinh died, his heir, Crown Prince Vinh Thuy was considered too young to rule effectively so he stayed in France to continue his education while affairs at court were managed by the regent Ton That Han. At the age of 19, Prince Vinh Thuy returned to Hue for his coronation in 1932 and became Bao Dai, the last Nguyen emperor. His reign was no different from his father's in that he held only a titular post, with all state affairs in the hands of the French Governor General. In his Memoir, Bao Dai recalled the moment after his coronation, when he asked his mandarins what he was supposed to do and was astonished to learn that he was to do nothing, except 'uphold the traditional rites and rituals....everything else had been taken care of'.

Even then, to his credit, during the early years of his reign, Bao Dai tried to modernise his country and appointed forward-looking intellectuals to his court, including Ngo Dinh Diem, in the hope of winning over the younger, less conservative quarters of Vietnamese society. The attempt failed as in the eyes of many, Bao Dai was a king who danced to a French tune. Ngo Dinh Diem later left his court and, much later, became President of the newly-formed Republic of Vietnam after the partition of 1954. Frustrated by his failure, Bao Dai embarked on a pleasure-seeking life that earned him much criticism in and out of the country, and alienated the powerless Nguyen Court even further from the population.

Whether because he had been raised and educated in Paris as a modern man not encouraged to pay attention to his country's affairs, or because he was disillusioned after his failure to modernise Vietnam, Bao Dai became an absentee emperor, spending a lot of his time away from Hue, hunting at his estate in Quang Tri, to the north of Hue, sailing in Nha Trang on the coast of south central

Below right: Emperor Khai Dinh and Crown Prince Vinh Thuy in France, 1922.

Emperor Bao Dai after his coronation.

Vietnam, or resting and hunting in the highland city of Dalat. In each place, he built large estates complete with fine villas and stocked with his favourite game, which he hunted on elephant back. In the end, he was better known for his fine horsemanship and sporting activities, his luxurious cars, his mistresses, his yachts and airplanes, than for his politics. He only came to Hue irregularly to perform traditional rituals or to visit his aging mother. For many years, while the French ran the country and the people got by somehow, Bao Dai lived a rich and privileged life, married a devout Catholic, Queen Nam Phuong, and travelled mainly for pleasure.

Reality caught up with Bao Dai in 1939 when the world entered a new global conflict and Vietnam became involved in the war in the Pacific. Between 1940 to 1945, Vietnam was fought over by Japan and a weakened France. The tussle ended in March 1945 when Japan overthrew the French authority to establish a new Japanese protectorate. Bao Dai now headed a nation free of France but under a new Asian master, Japan. Forming a cordial relationship with the Japanese Ambassador Yokohama, he was allowed to form his own government. The Tran Trong Kim government under Bao Dai was welcomed by most in Vietnam, but it soon became obvious that it was an ineffective institution that could not cope with the fast moving pace of the last phase of World War II and proved too indecisive to steer Vietnam on a true course during the chaotic days of August 1945, when the Japanese 'protective' power was shown to be helpless and Japan surrendered to the West after the bombing of Hiroshima and Nagasaki. After that, according to recently released American classified documents, Japan was eager to disengage

Emperor Bao Dai's favourite concubine Mong Diep.

quickly from occupied lands such as Vietnam. A power vacuum developed and the resistance groups who had been fighting hard for independence seized their opportunity. On August 19th 1945, the Nationalistic Alliance (Viet Minh) under Ho Chi Minh emerged as the strongest party to succeed the Japananese, and a new government was formed in Hanoi. Six days later, on 25th August 1945, at the request of the new revolutionary government, Bao Dai signed his abdication statement thereby ending 143 years of Nguyen rule.

Bao Dai became a special envoy for the new government of Ho Chi Minh, but soon found himself in exile in Kunming and Hongkong. When the French came back to Vietnam in 1947, they needed a titular head for Vietnam and, after a period of indecision, invited Bao Dai to return as Head of State under a resumed French occupation. Still later, Bao Dai retained his Head of State status under the government of Ngo Dinh Diem in the South of Vietnam, after the 1954 partition. In April 1955, while he was in Cannes with his family, a meeting was held in Saigon between representatives of 18 political parties and 29 notable figures of the South to decide on the future of South Vietnam. After five hours of deliberation, the meeting decided on three main points, one to remove Bao Dai from the future government, while the other two were the setting up of a republic with Ngo Dinh Diem as president, and a referendum.

When Bao Dai was informed of this result, he remained in France, never to return to Vietnam. He died in Paris in July 1997 at the age of 83, survived by his fifth and last wife, a French woman who took his birth name and became known as Princess Vinh Thuy, and many children. Officially, he had five children with Queen Nam Phuong: the Crown Prince, Nguyen Phuc Bao Long, three princesses and the youngest prince, Nguyen Phuc Bao Thang. Then there was another son and two daughters by his other wives and mistresses that the Nguyen family acknowledged. Both Princes

Emperor Bao Dai and Queen Nam Phuong.
(Photo courtesy Phan Thuan An).

The Order of Dragon of Annam – Medal of The Nguyen.

Bao Dai's grave in Paris.
(Photo courtesy Phan Thuan An)

Emperor Bao Dai, his mother, his Queen and two children.

Bao Long and Bao Thang stayed away from politics, but different branches of the Nguyen Royal family in exile still claim the right to award the Nguyen's highest Imperial Order of the Dragon of Annam as a personal gift to those deemed deserving.

On Bao Dai's death, Crown Prince Bao Long succeeded him as head of the Royal Nguyen family. He lived quietly in Paris and died in July 2007 without children. The position of Head of the Nguyen Royal Family passed to his younger brother Nguyen Phuc Bao Thang.

Bao Dai's return to Hue from exile – Morin Hotel 1949.

A view of the Perfume river.

Hue Capital City:
Building an Imperial Capital
Eiffel's bridge over the Perfume River

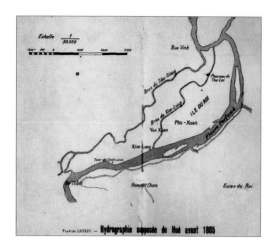

Hue location before 1805
(Source: Bulletin des Amis du vieux Hué)

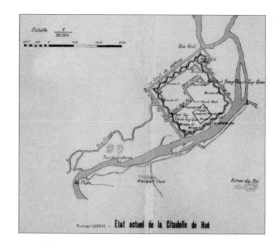

Hue location after 1805.
(Source: Bulletin des Amis du vieux Hué).

Public buildings.

Emperor's and royal palaces.

Map of Hue Capital City c.1885-1908.
(Source: B.A.V.H No.1-2 Jan-Jun 1933).

Rivers, lakes and moats.

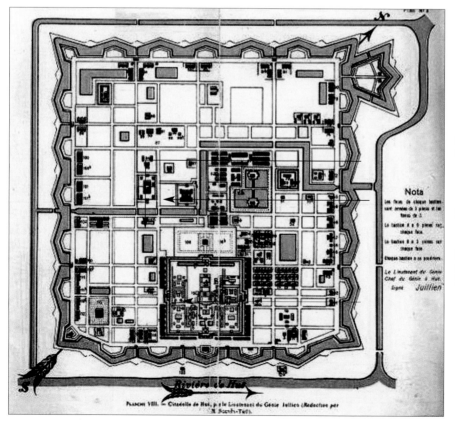

Long An Palace
(former location).

Tich Dien (Royal
planting Ceremony).

Imperial Citadel
and Forbidden
Purple City.

Building an Imperial Capital

A year after he came to power in 1802, with his authority now assured, Emperor Gia Long began to search for an auspicious spot to build his capital. Fortune-tellers and Feng-shui experts were called upon to offer their interpretation of the land and to identify the best location. Gia Long eventually chose an area that included the old Citadel Phu Xuan, a site that his ancestors had identified in 1687 as a dragon heralding a royal future for the Nguyen. The location settled, Gia Long now looked for a plan for his capital. For this, he consulted both his Vietnamese mandarins and his French allies who had come to help during the war against the Tay Son and now served at his court. They recommended a citadel plan in the style made famous by the French military engineer Sébastien Le Prestre, Marquis de Vauban (1633-1707), who in his time had been hailed as the most skilled architect in the art of building unbreachable fortifications.

The resulting plan for Hue as a royal capital was a large square citadel surrounded by high walls and deep moats, situated on the north side of the Perfume River, with the river acting as one side of the moat. Because of the particular flow of the river, in practice, the citadel was build like an even-sided diamond with one corner facing north. The total length of the four walls surrounding the citadel measured 10 kms, enclosing a total area of 5.20 square kilometres and incorporating eight existing villages, including Phu Xuan. The royal palaces were placed inside this fortified city, within their own walls and moats.

Hue Capital City had three distinct layers, one inside the other, with the Forbidden Purple City where the Emperors lived and worked-being the innermost. The next layer, the Imperial Citadel, was much larger and divided into squares, each square having a different function and purpose. The quarters for his mother and grandmothers occupied one square, while dynastic temples, landcaped gardens and official court buildings were placed in the others. Originally, there were over 100 buildings of all shapes and sizes in these two layers but not all of them survive to this day. Outside these two inner layers was a still larger area where mandarins, imperial guards, craftsmen and lesser people lived. Cutting through the middle of the Capital City was a man-made canal, the Ngu Ha, running east-west

Gates of the Imperial Citadel.

with a dog-leg around both the Imperial citadel and Forbidden Purple City. The spacious area to the north of this canal was kept for cultivation. Every year, at the beginning of the planting season, successive Nguyen Emperors came to this north bank to perform a symbolic ploughing ceremony to ensure a good crop for all.

The thick walls surrounding the Capital City were built like castle ramparts, in the style of a European medieval castle but on a much grander scale. Spaced evenly along the walls were 24 defence posts, watch turrets and guard towers armed with heavy artillery and controlled from a large base at the northeast corner called Mang Ca fort – *mang ca* meaning a fish gill, after the shape of this particular structure. Along the inside of these walls, there were many structures, including enclosures for valuable animals such as tigers and elephants situated next to guardhouses.

To access the city, there were four main gates, one on each side of the outer wall, with the Royal Gate being placed on the south wall, opening out to the Perfume River. Each of the main gates had its own name, such as Chanh Dong Mon (True East Gate), Dong Nam Mon (Southeast gate) etc. Several smaller gates were also placed along the walls for soldiers to access the defence towers. There were 10 gates of this type, built at different times during the first two reigns of Gia Long and Minh Mang. Over time, Hue residents gave the Forbidden

Plan of The Imperial Citadel and the Forbidden Purple City.

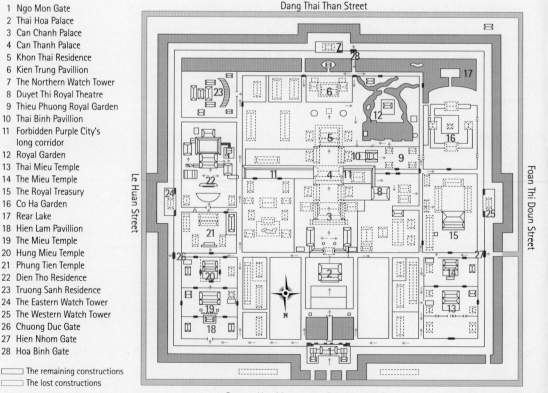

1 Ngo Mon Gate
2 Thai Hoa Palace
3 Can Chanh Palace
4 Can Thanh Palace
5 Khon Thai Residence
6 Kien Trung Pavillion
7 The Northern Watch Tower
8 Duyet Thi Royal Theatre
9 Thieu Phuong Royal Garden
10 Thai Binh Pavillion
11 Forbidden Purple City's
   long corridor
12 Royal Garden
13 Thai Mieu Temple
14 The Mieu Temple
15 The Royal Treasury
16 Co Ha Garden
17 Rear Lake
18 Hien Lam Pavillion
19 The Mieu Temple
20 Hung Mieu Temple
21 Phung Tien Temple
22 Dien Tho Residence
23 Truong Sanh Residence
24 The Eastern Watch Tower
25 The Western Watch Tower
26 Chuong Duc Gate
27 Hien Nhom Gate
28 Hoa Binh Gate

☐ The remaining constructions
⋯ The lost constructions

Dang Thai Than Street

Le Huan Street

Foan Thi Doun Street

Source: Hue Monuments Conservation Center

The Flag Pole – Ky Dai, viewed from Ngo Mon.

Purple City and the Imperial Citadel the combined common name of Dai Noi – The Great Inner Sanctum – that is still in use today. At the same time, the gates into the Capital City of Hue were also given their more common names that we still use, such as Dong Ba gate, Thuong Tu gate, Nha Do gate etc.

The plan included a system of waterways to provide easy navigation in and out of the capital by boat and to reach the Thuan An seaport 13 kms away for a quick escape in case of war. This navigation system maximised the use of existing smaller rivers, some of which were enlarged or modified by man-made canals to create an extensive water system flowing through all parts of the capital. The small horizontal river Kim Long, running parallel with the Perfume River was deepened and transformed into the Imperial Canal – Ngu Ha. The name was bestowed on the canal under Minh Mang in a solemn edict issued in 1830. Originally, the Imperial Canal was connected to the water of the surrounding moat only on the east. However, the canal was extended in 1825 under Minh Mang to link up with the moat on the west side as well, thus, creating the water system that was in constant use until the city was abandoned in 1945. The creation of the Imperial Canal and its extension were inscribed on two steles composed by Emperor Minh Mang in 1836.

A corner of the Citadel from outside.

Luong Y or Dong Thanh Thuy Quan bridge and moat.

Pavilions in front of Kien Trung Palace and their reflections on Ngoc Dich Pond.

The lesser rivers incorporated into the water system were either used as waterways, or enlarged into ponds and lakes. Over these rivers and canals, several bridges were built to connect the different quarters of the Imperial Citadel. Some of the bridges spanning the Imperial Canal were originally constructed in bamboo, but these were later replaced by stone bridges to accommodate the frequent comings and goings of people and animals, a fact carefully recorded by Emperor Minh Mang in 1836.

Tens of thousands of soldiers were drafted into the original construction work of the Capital City, under the direction of four mandarins specially appointed to oversee the project, and, possibly, an unknown number of French advisors and engineers. Construction began in 1804 with an extensive programme of modifying the ground to create an optimum landscape. The Imperial Canal was dug first and other ground modification works followed. By 1805, the groundwork was completed and the site was ready for building.

The outermost walls of the city were built first, initially made of packed mud taken from deepening the waterways inside the citadel and the construction of the surrounding moat. Each of the four walls was built to a height of 6.12 metres, and were 2 metres wide at the top increasing to 2.52 metres at the base. The military fort Mang Ca was built on the northeast corner of the walls at the same time.

Eight months were needed to complete the building of the fort and the outer mud walls, later lined with bricks on both sides in 1818-1819. Additional fortifications continued to be added under Minh Mang's reign until they were considered finished in 1822. Later Nguyen Emperors added yet more structures to the walls, such as gun emplacements and guard towers.

The gates on the outer walls were first constructed in 1809, with several of them being modified or embellished by successive Nguyen Emperors. The Garrison for the Emperor's Guard was constructed in the same year and continued to be reinforced until

Ky Dai from a corner of the Citadel.

Below left: Bamboo bridge over Tinh Tam Lake.

Below: Guard tower and moat at a corner of the Citadel.

1831. While the surrounding walls were being built, the royal palaces of the Imperial Citadel and the Forbidden Purple City were also taking shape within their own walls.

When completed under the second Nguyen Emperor Minh Mang, all royal palaces were exquisitely decorated with royal motifs of the dragon and phoenix created from the finest materials. The dragon is the highest symbol of royal authority, whether shown in profile or full-faced with a pearl in its mouth. The symbol of a five-clawed dragon was exclusively reserved for the emperor, while the lower ranking four-clawed ones were used either for princes or other members of the royal family such as the queen, queen mother and grandmothers. The symbol of the phoenix as the personification of grace and virtue is often seen as being associated with the female persona. In fact, the motif comes in both sexes and represents peace and stability. According to Sino-Vietnamese belief, the mythical phoenix dislikes conflict and goes into hiding at the slightest hint of trouble. Only when all is well again does the phoenix return. By displaying the phoenix as a royal motif throughout the city, especially under Minh Mang, the early Nguyen Emperors wanted to convey the message that all was stable and calm under their reigns. Another unusual symbol that the Nguyen used extensively for both

Dragon motif on Truong Sanh gate.

Opposite: Hien Nhon Gate.

Full-face dragon motif on Hien Nhon Gate.

Phoenix motif in the Imperial Citadel.

Phoenix, Grandmothers' quarter, Imperial Citadel.

Double phoenix on roof, Grandmothers' quarter.

A house in Truong Sanh quarter.

Bat motif, side roof, Grandmothers' quarter.

Roof drain hole, Dien Tho quarter.

Bat motif under roof.

Garden pavilions in front of former Kien Trung Palace.

the interior and exterior decoration of the Imperial Citadel was the bat. The motif is usually woven into strings of leaves or used as a corner piece that is often overlooked. The bat means good luck because the sound of the word 'bat' is similar to the sound of '*phuc*' meaning luck in Vietnamese. Once recognised as a symbol in its own right, we can see it almost everywhere and on several objects that the Nguyen cherished.

Each group of buildings in both the Forbidden Purple City and the Imperial Citadel was placed in its own garden, among specially created lakes and ponds to form separate quarters for each member, or each group of members, of the royal family. Each quarter had its own walls, differentiated from each other by their distinctive layout, architectural style and decorative materials. The arrangement of the quarters followed the strict principle of segregation of the sexes, with the male quarters being situated on the east and the female quarters on the west.

The quarter reserved for the emperor and his own family was in the middle, within its own high walls through which everyone except the emperor and his family was forbidden to enter without permission. Inside the Forbidden Purple City, the Nguyen Emperor lived in his own world, entertained by his concubines and his rare animals in his royal palaces and gardens, or dancers and actors in his private theatre. His food was served separately and exquisitely by a special kitchen. The emperor's residence was screened at the front by two long buildings, one for the queen and the other for the emperor to conduct the daily business of the palace. From around 5 years' old, the designated Crown Prince was assigned his

Recreation pavilion, Dien Tho quarter.

Corridor to Duyet Thi Duong Theatre.

Grandmothers' quarter – Dien Tho.

Inside Duyet Thi Duong.

own quarters, on the east side. The Queen Grandmothers and Great Grandmothers lived in their own residential areas in the northwest corner of the Imperial Citadel in two separate groups of buildings: Truong Sanh and Dien Tho.

Outside the Imperial Citadel were many buildings used as offices for the court, homes for mandarins and their families and for the army of servants waiting at court. Two distinct areas were reserved for dynastic temples and a Royal Academy on either side of the main gate. All along the inside of the outer walls were guard houses, stables, tiger cages, war elephants and stores of arms and equipments necessary for the defence of the Capital City.

It took 30 years for the city to be completed according to the Vauban plan. The construction went on throughout the reign of Gia Long and continued into the reign of the next emperor Minh Mang. The last major structure to be built, surprisingly, was the main gate, the Ngo Mon or Royal Gate, in 1833.

Hue Capital City was to be modified many times by successive emperors with more constructions added and some old buildings replaced by newer and more elaborate ones. Alas, the greatest change happened in 1885 when the French launched an assault on the Forbidden city, following an attempted coup against the French authority and the departure of Emperor Ham Nghi after the coup failed. During the French storming of the Imperial Citadel, many of the original buildings were destroyed or burned to the ground. Some of the remaining buildings were later modified, moved to new locations or replaced altogether.

Nevertheless, despite the modifications, Hue Capital City managed to retain its classical function of being a place where earth, water and foliage were brought together to enhance the harmony between Heaven and Earth, creating a peaceful conduit for the Nguyen in their communication between the power from above and the Son of Heaven on earth: the Emperor.

The Mieu or The To Mieu from Hien Lam Cac.

Ngoc Dich Pond – Looking toward Kientrung Palace.

The first French Luxury Hotel of Hue.

French products on sale at Hotel Morin.

The Old Headquarter of the French Legation.

During the early Nguyen reigns, from Gia Long to Tu Duc, the south bank of the Perfume River remained a wild area, with only few residents. It was here that Emperor Tu Duc gave the first French delegation a small concession of land by the river in 1876. At the time, there was no bridge and the French Resident lived in a simple Vietnamese house. Later, after the French reinforced their presence in Hue, they established a walled compound for the Legation on the same spot. From then on, the south bank of Hue began to be extensively developed with churches, convents, a luxurious hotel, shops and schools built in French architectural style along tree-lined avenues. French tourists began to flock to Hue to view their quaint overseas territory and experience the Vietnamese way of life within a typically French atmosphere surrounded by familiar French products. In 1930 a new Governor General's residence was built further along the bank of the river, on a spot opposite the Imperial Citadel on the North bank, to complete the picture of a mini French town, with all things French available within a short distance of each other. This fine French residence has recently been developed into a luxurious boutique hotel in Art Déco style to serve an exclusive clientele. Its presence

A church on the river bank.

Cyclos waiting for French tourists – Train station.

pushes the traditional and oldest hotel Morin to a second position in the league of luxurious historical hotels in Hue. The south bank of Hue was still called the French Quarter long after their departure from Vietnam, following the defeat of Dien Bien Phu and the partition of Vietnam in 1954. By then, though, the original French concession of land had been turned into a gated administrative and residential area, while the luxurious shopping centre and hotel across the road began to serve a different clientele. Even then, these former symbols of French authority and civilisation continued to guard the south end of the historical Truong Tien bridge, built by the best French engineering techniques of the 19th century to be the link between two contrasting ideals; the Confucian conservatism on the north bank and European modernity on the south bank.

Residence of the French Governor General, today's superb boutique hotel, La Residence.

Inside La Residence.

Eiffel's Bridge over the Perfume River

One of the lesser known facts about Hue is that the six-span bridge called Truong Tien or Trang Tien across the Perfume River was built by the French engineering company of Gustave Eiffel (1832-1923). It was commissioned ten years after Eiffel reached the zenith of his career with the success of the Eiffel Tower in Paris and his famous structural design for the Statue of Liberty in New York, and, ironically, following his spectacular failure at the Panama Canal. It was to be the first that Gustave Eiffel built in Vietnam. Later he also built smaller railway bridges in South Vietnam, an outright French colony from 1867 onward. Before the Truong Tien Bridge was built, the Truong Tien Ferry took passengers across the river. The name Truong Tien is derived from the name of the building where the ferry docked on the south bank, the National Bank.

Similar to his other constructions of the period, Gustave Eiffel favoured the use of wrought-iron lengths bolted firmly together into shapes to form an intricate pattern for the bridge spans. When it was finished, the bridge Eiffel created for Hue was a solid structure of six iron spans and a road surface lined with wooden planks. It was a graceful construction of just over 500 metres long and was painted in

Truong Tien Bridge after the storm of 1904.

Truong Tien Bridge in 1936.

Truong Tien Bridge in 1930.

his customary colour of silver, the colour that it has retained throughout its many repairs over the years. Thanks to this silver paint, Truong Tien has, in poetic fashion, often been compared to a silver comb adorning a long mane of flowing hair that is the Perfume River. As the bridge was built in 1897-99 during the two reigns of Emperors Dong Khanh and Thanh Thai, it was first named Thanh Thai Bridge. Then when Thanh Thai was forced to abdicate and sent to the Island of Reunion, the bridge was renamed Clemenceau Bridge, after the then French Prime Minister. This name endured until the partition of Vietnam in 1954 when the bridge was renamed after the original ferry: Truong Tien.

Not long after completion, the Thanh Thai bridge was heavily damaged in the severe typhoon of 1904, when two of its six spans broke and fell into the river. It was rebuilt with reinforced iron spans and the wooden road surface was replaced by a concrete road. Like the rest of the Capital City, the bridge was again damaged during the post-1945 war of independence against the French, but was repaired two years later when France re-established their control in Indochina. After the French departure in 1954, this bridge became known as the Truong Tien bridge. It was damaged yet again during the Tet offensive of 1968 and some spans fell into the river. The bridge surface was mended later but the broken iron spans were left unrepaired for many years. In 1991, the bridge was rebuilt extensively and in 1995 it was returned to its original shape albeit with a narrower road surface. It is now known as the Trang Tien Bridge and is used for light traffic during rush hour.

Trang Tien bridge at rush hour.

Inside An Dinh Palace.

Hue then and now: the Sites

For many years under the early Nguyen Emperors, Hue Capital City retained an aura of mystery and opulence, a great symbol of royal authority, and a place for the Emperor to exercise his divine mandate. Year after year, the palaces within the fortified citadel were further improved and embellished, the royal lifestyle further fine-tuned, each year more refined than the last. Alas, things began to change at the end of Tu Duc's reign with the arrival of the French armed forces. Suddenly, the fortunes of Hue changed dramatically. From being the seat of power for the Nguyen Emperors, Hue became a place where the Old and the New struggled to coexist, and where the values of East and West clashed regularly. Then in the first half of the 20th century along with the advance of modernity and the industrial revolution, a modern lifestyle became apparent at court. Royal palaces and tombs began to use European materials and show the influence of Western art, with European ceramic tiles and mosaic a particular favourite. By the end of the Nguyen dynasty, some parts of Hue had acquired a hybrid style with classical designs being marred, or complemented, by European modern arts.

Car going through Royal entrance of the Ngo Mon.

Opposite: Dawn on the Perfume River.

The greatest changes for Hue, however, came after the end of the Nguyen dynasty, when the city lost its royal status in 1945 and it seemed as if Hue was fated to be a battleground many times over. During these times, Hue went through three devastating periods when it was damaged in the fighting between the Japanese, the French and the Vietnamese. In his Memoir, Bao Dai recalled what happened to Hue after his departure:

> '...my family took refuge with the Canadian missionaries. The capital of Hue also went through terrible hours...The Queen and our children escaped from the Palaces to avoid being kept hostage. As for the Imperial Palace, it was completely ravaged. Many buildings were destroyed. The two bridges across the Perfume River, the road and the railway bridges, were both in ruins...'

Hue again witnessed death and extensive destruction during the Tet Offensive of 1968, when bombing and fighting was continuous in all areas for nearly a month. The fighting and destruction of many parts of the former Royal Capital City is still a sorry chapter in the history of modern Vietnam. The battle for Hue in 1968 also went down in the history of modern warfare as one of the longest and most destructive, both in psychological and material terms. Hue

Imperial modern transport.

A gate before restoration.

faced death and destruction once more in March 1975, during fighting for control of the city and the eventual reunification of the two parts of Vietnam.

Almost all buildings within the Forbidden Purple City and more than half of the 136 structures in the Imperial Citadel were destroyed during these times. The rest were damaged or left in a state of disrepair until the late 1980s, when renovation work began albeit slowly at first. By 1993, the year that Hue was placed in the list of UNESCO World Heritage Sites, several palaces and buildings in the Imperial Citadel were still covered with cheap corrugated iron sheets, their walls pockmarked by bullet holes. The extensive grounds – once beautifully adorned with lakes, ornamental bridges and rare fauna and flora – were overgrown with weeds, high grass and wild flowers with some areas transformed into agricultural fields. The brick-paved royal paths were covered in dark slippery moss and the interiors of many palaces were blackened with age and neglect. The former imperial domain exuded an air of deep sorrow, a sight made more poignant by valiant efforts in one busy corner of the citadel, where tiles and construction materials were being recreated in makeshift kilns so as to restore the imperial city to as close to its former glory as possible. It was a huge task that would have daunted the bravest architects and engineers but there was so much hope and optimism. Both the workers and the officials in charge of the renovation were looking forward to the rebirth of Hue. Many years later, the restoration is an on-going process with projects being planned for the years to come, but much has also been achieved.

Hue today has become a graceful but vibrant city. After years of meticulous restoration, some original palaces of the Imperial Citadel have regained much of their former beauty. There is still

The bombing of Hue in 1968.
(Photo courtesy Hue Monuments
Conservation Center)

Ornamental silver screen.

plenty of work to be done but on the whole, we can begin to picture the Royal Capital City as it once was, albeit on a reduced scale.

For Hue city itself, its former gentle lifestyle has undergone a transformation to catch up with a fast-moving modern market economy. The once common sight of barefoot street vendors, dressed in full length brown Ao Dai, their long hair twisted and braided in elaborate chignons, a wad of tobacco or a stubby cigar perched on their lips, has vanished. In those days, despite an Ao Dai being worn or patched, it would be full length for Hue was where good manners prevailed. Today, while some of the vendors retain a carefully groomed appearance, others wear practical Western dress.

Cyclo vendor.

The sounds of Hue have also changed dramatically. The typical songs of the Perfume River – thought to be an echo of its Cham past – are no longer spontaneously sung in the evenings to entertain visitors on the pleasure boats. Along the streets, instead of the melodious calls of street vendors touting their wares, are garish billboards. What remains, though, are the typically soft tones of Hue conversations, their particular accent emphasises certain words, peculiarly pronounced to avoid touching the Nguyen's decreed taboo words – of which there are many in Hue. Hue conversation is still an art, both in the way it is conducted and, for outsiders, in guessing as to what is being said.

Chilies – A staple condiment for Hue.

Since the year 2000, a Festival of Hue has been held every two years, on the years of even numbers. During the festivals, which last from one to two weeks in June, the entire city comes alive with activities, both in and outside the Imperial Citadel. Cultural events, such as the re-enactment of the Nam Giao Ritual, take place alongside more popular attractions such as fashion shows, court banquets, Royal music and dances for visitors and residents alike. During festival times, special displays and exhibitions feature paintings and photographs, records and photos of the Hue

Below left: Street vendor of today.

Dong Ba market.

Blue and White ceramic made in Jingdezhen.

restoration processes, courtly artefacts and everyday objects, along with arts and crafts demonstrations, at various locations throughout the city. At night, the Royal gate, Ngo Mon, is brightly lit to welcome visitors to one of the events in the heart of the Imperial Citadel such as Dem Hoang Cung, a spectacular cultural presentation of royal lifestyle, music, dance, drama and audience participation in royal games, ending with a sumptuous royal banquet. Over the years, each festival has become grander than the last. Odd numbered years see the Hue Crafts festival where visitors can marvel at the skill of the Hue artisans. Exhibitions of traditional arts and crafts, including talks and demonstrations by the artists, combine to create an enjoyable but cultured event for scholars and those who would like to study the different aspects of Nguyen arts.

Meanwhile, on Saturday nights in the summer, there are the events known as Dem Dai Noi, when, for the price of a ticket, visitors can re-enact the royal experience by being dressed like kings and queens to sit on gilded chairs and consume an elaborate banquet served by court attendants, while, at the same time, enjoying a spectacular royal musical variety show.

For permanent exhibitions, the Museum of Royal Antiquities presents a wealth of Nguyen treasure, from the unique royal Blue and White ceramics from Jiangxi, China, to English and French porcelain, and the exquisite textiles of court robes and embroidered shoes, royal furniture and drapes. The buildings housing the museum are themselves a work of art, having spent their previous lives as recreational palaces for Emperor Thieu Tri.

Even with such an extensive display of Nguyen treasures at the Museum and the Royal Palaces, the most remarkable art of the Nguyen Dynasty, arguably, lies in the architecture of their palaces and gardens, in their mausoleums in the Valley of the Tombs, and in the many temples around Hue. Away from the palaces and tombs, the Nguyen's most favoured sport took place in Ho Quyen – the Tiger Arena, where for much of the Nguyen Dynasty, tigers and elephants fought to the death for the Emperor's pleasure.

As the whole city is full of exquisite historical sites, it is impossible to describe all of them in one book. Here we feature the major sites and artefacts, leaving the lesser ones as welcome surprises for the more intrepid cultural visitor to discover alone.

Original Royal robe for daily court assembly.

The Sites

To visit Hue is to encounter surprises. One is that the Royal Capital City – the original Citadel – is so much bigger than expected. During the first 45 years of its existence, between 50,000 and 80,000 people, from mandarins to soldiers, peasants and artisans, lived and worked here. Visitors may be fooled into thinking that Hue Capital City begins with the Ngo Mon gate and can be explored on foot easily in half a day or so. The original Citadel that Gia Long built is, in fact, huge and looks so different from any map currently on offer. On the map, the Citadel appears as a walled square area with three layers, one inside the other. In reality, what most visitors see is only the two inner layers: the Imperial Citadel and the Forbidden Purple City, called by their combined name of Dai Noi.

Exploring the outer layer of the Citadel

The third and largest layer is a densely populated area that looks and feels like a separate town. In fact, this part still lies within the outer walls of the citadel. It is very large and comes complete with so many streets, canals, bridges, old and new houses, shops, and other structures that visitors can be forgiven for assuming that it is a separate town adjacent to the Imperial Citadel. Only when looking hard at the very edge of this bustling area can one discern traces of the old walls, now partly obscured by houses, gardens, shops or even animal enclosures. It takes stamina and determination to explore these outer walls, but it can be a rewarding experience, when the intrepid visitor can chance upon interesting scenes, such as a vegetable garden flourishing on top of the thick wall, modern solid houses nestling in former guard posts or a factory perching precariously on the high wall while busily producing timbers for yet more constructions. The road along the foot of the walls occasionally yields beautiful curving stone bridges, some still bearing former royal insignia. Standing on one of those bridges, we can see a part of the water system, once flowing freely inside the Citadel, now clogged with twisting strands of Morning Glory, a staple vegetable for the rich and poor alike. Here and there, a head or two of lotus blossom emerges

Road along the outer Citadel wall.

Road bordering the Imperial Citadel.

A street inside the Citadel.

Steps to the top of the outer Citadel wall.

Ngoc Dich lotus pond – Imperial Citadel.

Below right: Guard tower and a portion of the moat being turned into a field – Imperial Citadel.

Old wall forming part of a residential area.

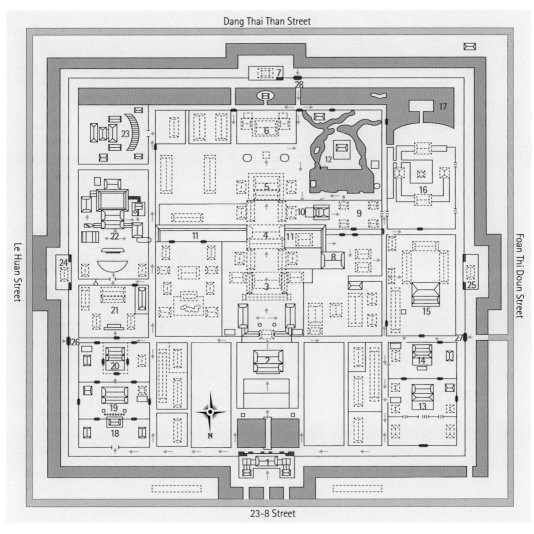

The general plan of Hue Citadel

Notes:
1. Ngo Mon Gate
2. Thai Hoa Palace
3. Can Chanh Palace
4. Can Thanh Palace
5. Khon Thai Residence
6. Kien Trung Pavillion
7. The Northern Watch Tower
8. Duyet Thi Royal Theatre
9. Thieu Phuong Royal Garden
10. Thai Binh Pavillion
11. Forbidden Purple City's long corridor
12. Royal Garden
13. Thai Mieu Temple
14. Trieu Mieu Temple
15. The Royal Treasury
16. Co Ha Garden
17. Rear Lake
18. Hien Lam Pavillion
19. The Mieu Temple
20. Hung Mieu Temple
21. Phung Tien Temple
22. Dien Tho Residence
23. Troung Sanh Residence
24. The Eastern Watch Tower
25. The Western Watch Tower
26. Chuong Duc Gate
27. Hien Nhon Gate
28. Hoa Binh Gate

	The remaining constructions
	The lost constructions

⟵ Suggested walk in the Imperial Citadel and The Forbidden Purple City.

through the thick foliage, as if to remind us of a not so distant royal past, when all the canals and ponds within the Citadel were covered with lotus blossoms, the Buddhist symbol of purity and a Nguyen royal favourite.

It is possible to walk all around the outer walls of Hue Capital City but it is not a pursuit for the fainthearted. Not only is the total length of the walls 10 kms, but the walk involves making several detours to avoid built-up areas and the large military installation at the northeast corner, the former Mang Ca fort. For most visitors, with little time and many sites to visit, Dai Noi is where the main attractions beckon. Although this area includes only the inner two layers of the Capital City, even that is large and can be a walk too far for some. Dai Noi occupies a large pedestrian square area with many paths crisscrossing its surface. Luckily, since April 2009, four golf carts have been operating inside this area to assist visitors who can't walk so far. They can be seen zipping around on the tree-lined roads surrounding the Imperial Citadel, and along the edges of the Forbidden Purple City. Their first and last stops are at the foot of the Royal Gate-Ngo Mon, on the inside. First, however, all visitors much pass through the Ngo Mon – Royal Gate – to enter Dai Noi.

Thai Hoa and Nghi Mon.

Ngo Mon – The Royal Gate

Ngo Mon was the last structure to be built in the initial construction phase of the Nguyen's Capital City. It was erected during the 14th year of the reign of Minh Mang – 1833 – when the court decided to review the original buildings of the city. During this review, a structure on the south side, called Nam Khuyet Dai, built under Gia Long, was replaced by a huge construction that resembled an open palace rather than a gate. This was to be called Ngo Mon – a south-facing gate for the Emperor to enter and exit the Imperial Citadel under the auspices of the Sun. Ngo Mon has been translated as the Sun Gate or the Noon Gate but this is not entirely accurate as it's difficult to make a straight translation of the words. While Mon means gate, Ngo implies much more than just midday or high noon. It signifies the sun's zenith, when it emits the best and brightest light possible according to Feng Shui principles. As such, it is considered as the most auspicious moment that the power from above bestows his grace on the Son of Heaven in order to guide him in the leadership of his people. By capturing the moment at the Ngo Mon, it was hoped that each time the Emperor passed through the gate, he would be blessed with maximum grace. In reality, because the Capital City was not built on a true north/south axis, this gate faces onto the Perfume River in a southeasterly direction, rather than true south.

Ngo Mon has two distinct parts, the substantial base and the Terrace of Five Phoenix – Lau Ngu Phung in Vietnamese – on top. The base is stone with an inverted U-shape, to accommodate five separate entrances. The largest, in the middle, was reserved for the

Emperor and the occasional Chinese envoys from Beijing, the two smaller side entrances were for the mandarins, that on the right for the military officers and on the left for the men of literature. The remaining two entrances were built discreetly inside the two arms of the U shape and reserved for the Imperial Guards and their horses. The length of the bottom of the base is 57.77 metres, with each arm 27.06 metres. The height of the base is nearly 5 metres.

The separate entrances of the Ngo Mon held such significance for the Nguyen court that it became a subject of severe contention between the Protocol Department and General de Courcy, the newly appointed Commander-in-Chief of French forces in Tonkin and Annam, who came to present his credentials to the Emperor in July 1885. The tense argument over which entrance(s) his entourage should use, while he went through the central one, was the last straw in the already fractious Franco-Vietnamese cohabitation. When de Courcy insisted that not only he but all his officers and troops would enter the Citadel by the central royal entrance, talks broke down. That night, 4th July 1885, the Vietnamese launched an ambush on the French Legation across the river and the French garrison at the northeast corner of the Citadel. When the attack failed, the Emperor left for the mountains to mount national resistance against the French, while the French unleashed a devastating bout of destruction in the Citadel on 5th July. Vietnamese history turned a decisive corner after that event and the whole of Vietnam became a full French protectorate from that day onward.

Hue Capital City has often been compared to the Forbidden City of Beijing, although visually only the base of the Ngo Mon bears any resemblance, as like the rest of Hue the Citadel has particularly Vietnamese features, with wood as the main building material for many structures. The wooden components gave the palaces a lighter,

Painting depicting activities inside the original Imperial Citadel.

Roof of Ngu Phung.

more graceful appearance and are distinctively Vietnamese in their
decoration. This Vietnamese style is clearly visible in the top
structure of the Ngo Mon, the Terrace of Five Phoenix. According
to ancient belief, the Phoenix represents femininity, and, as we will
discover in our exploration of Dai Noi, images of this fabled bird
appear very often, along with the supreme royal symbol of the
dragon – in the interior of royal palaces, on the roofs of royal
structures and embroidered on the clothing of Nguyen royals, both
men and women. It is typical of the Nguyen style to emphasise
peace and stability, and to ensure that harmony between the sexes
is maintained at all levels.

Lau Ngu Phung is called a terrace, or sometimes, by the generic
architectural term 'belvedere', because it is a huge building and has
an airy appearance when all the folding doors are fully open. It is
covered by a double tier of roofs, supported by 100 solid pillars of
ironwood. The central roof is covered by a special type of tile called
Hoang Luu Ly – Yellow tube tiles – yellow being the royal colour.
Under this roof is a set of eight smaller roofs covered in blue
tiles, now looking more green than blue. The roofs are decorated
throughout with phoenix shapes, creating a graceful appearance
of a flock of birds about to take off into the sky. The Terrace of
Five Phoenix is where the Nguyen Court conducted their most
important public ceremonies, such as the annual issuing of the
calendar, or the citation of the list of newly qualified Men of
Literature – those who have just passed the
imperial exams to achieve their Doctorate degrees.
It was also where the last Emperor Bao Dai
announced his abdication in August 1945.

Although they may be slippery when wet, it is
worth climbing the stone steps on either side of
the base to reach the first floor of Lau Ngu Phung,
a long hall of dark wood that appears empty at
first. However, upon inspecting the pillars and the
eaves under the roofs, one can discover several
original features often overlooked because of poor
lighting and dark wood. Here eight ancient poems
have been engraved, two of them identical to
those displayed in Thai Hoa Palace. One explains
that Lau Ngu Phung is an open terrace because

Yellow and blue/green tube tiles of
Ngu Phung.

Steps to Ngu Phung Terrace.

Interior of Ngu Phung Terrace.

there is nothing to hide inside, also, it is open so that it can exist in harmony with the Perfume River in front. It is also easy to miss a beautiful four-panelled picture, which provides an exquisite record of the Ngo Mon seen from inside out.

The top floor of the Terrace may sometimes be closed for maintenance. Both ends of the hall connect, at a 90-degree angle, to two side-terraces, built on top of the arms of the U-shaped base. The side terraces have the same style roofs and tube tiles as the main hall, but their sides are totally open, each with a fine set of solid pillars. Housed in the west side terrace is a huge drum and on the east side a giant bronze bell. These were sounded whenever Lau Ngu Phung was used for royal ceremonies. On the surface of the bell, an engraved text praises the quality of the metal, and the sound that it makes. According to this, the cheerful 'bong bong' serves to welcome those attending state ceremonies and makes the task of ruling the nation a more encouraging pursuit for the Emperor. From the side terraces, we can see the yellow and blue/green tube tiles on the central roofs at close quarters, and also, the clever drainage system, hidden under beautifully carved shapes of fish, frogs and other animals.

Bell on Ngu Phung Terrace.

View of Ngu Phung roof tiles from the bell wing.

A corner of Ngu Phung Terrace.

Ceremonial Drum on Ngu Phung.

Close-up of Ngu Phung balustrade.

Phap Lam panels of Nghi Mon.

Koi carp in a feeding frenzy.

A lotus bud finial on one of the gate posts.

Ngo Mon and Lau Ngu Phung were the subject of a detailed restoration programme under the auspice of UNESCO in 1993, funded by Japanese and Vietnamese governments. 50% or, in some places, 90% of the original tiles were replaced by new ones, the wooden pillars were coated with new lacquer and the surrounding wooden balustrade was consolidated for safety. The work was done by experts who drew on their experiences from the preservation of Sukhothai in Thailand and Borobodur in Indonesia, in 1991 and 1992 respectively.

From the long balcony running around the Ngu Phung pavilion, we can see the giant flagpole and part of the Citadel's outer moat – Ngoai Kim Thuy – to the south, and the front area of Thai Hoa Palace to the north, preceded by two ceremonial gates straddling a path running across a lotus and Koi carp pond. This path is called Trung Dao – True Path – bridge as it runs from the centre entrance of Ngo Mon, across the Lotus pond, to the Courtyard of Salutation in front of Thai Hoa Palace.

The best route for visiting Dai Noi is to follow a South-North direction, starting from Ngo Mon, a walk that takes longer than expected for it involves many stops to admire a variety of things, from the abundance of frangipani trees bordering the pond full of lotus blossoms in the summer, to the feeding frenzy of hundreds of golden Koi carp that vye with each other for a few morsels of food thrown to them by visitors. Small bags of fish food can be obtained from a glass box by the pond, at the price of a few thousand *dong*.

From this point on the True Path, we can examine the two ceremonial gates seen from Lau Ngu Phung, their decoration making them works of art in their own right. The slender bronze pillars supporting the gates sport royal motifs of dragons and clouds, with the Nguyen's favourite Buddhist symbol of purity, a lotus bud at the top. The horizontal section at the top of each gate is divided into panels, each decorated with a unique art called Phap Lam, similar to Cloisonné in appearance but using different techniques (discussed more fully later) that lived and died with the Nguyen Dynasty. Ceremonial gates decorated with the Phap Lam technique are replicated many times over in order to demarcate other quarters within Dai Noi, and at the Nguyen Emperors' final resting places – their mausoleums in the Valley of the Tombs, on the south bank of the Perfume River.

Passing under one of these gates we follow the paved Trung Dao path across the pond, once reserved for the Emperor alone, to the other gate and enter a large two-tiered courtyard leading to Thai Hoa Palace, the heart of the Nguyen court, where the 13 Nguyen emperors were crowned, royal birthdays were celebrated and important decisions were made.

Thai Hoa Palace on Emperor Khai Dinh's
40th birthday.

Thai Hoa Palace and pond.

Court of Salutation in front of Thai Hoa Palace.

Thai Hoa Palace

Thai Hoa Palace – The Palace of Supreme Harmony – was one of the first structures built under Gia Long, on a site originally slightly north of where it is now. It was moved to its new position under Minh Mang in 1833, without changing any of its original features. Construction started in 1805 and was completed in only eight months, just in time for Emperor Gia Long to celebrate his coronation officially in 1806. From then on, it served as the venue for the bi-monthly court assemblies. Here, in the Throne Room, the Emperor on his gilded chair, with the Crown Prince on a lower chair at his side, listened to his mandarins reviewing affairs of state. Only members of the royal family and the most important mandarins could enter the Throne Room on such occasions. Even then, the mandarins were not to look at the Emperor directly, being required to lower their gaze and prostrate themselves several times in front of him, before reciting their affairs. Lesser mandarins stayed in the Courtyard outside to show their respect, each standing at his appointed level, the nine levels of ranks being marked by rows of stone stelea. This formation of mandarins standing in attendance in the Courtyard of Salutation is reproduced in all but one of the Nguyen Tombs, each type of mandarin represented by a single stone figure, complete with their particular robes, hats, ranks and armour.

Phap Lam panel between the roofs of Thai Hoa.

Thai Hoa Palace follows the graceful architecture of the Terrace of Five Phoenix and sits on an elevation reached by mounting two tiers of steps. It is a long imposing building with three ornate roofs, one on top of another. The whole structure is supported by 80 ironwood pillars, painted in red lacquer and the Emperor's symbols of golden dragons and clouds. The roofs are connected to each other by copper bands decorated in the Phap Lam technique. Each band has many panels showing scenes of the four seasons, gentlemen's leisure pursuits, or poems written in Chinese characters. The yellow roof tiles are the same as on the Terrace of Five Phoenix. Each roof is decorated with nine dragons in different classic positions, nine being the auspicious number for the Nguyen royals. Some are in profile, while others are flying with their heads looking backwards. On the corners of the roofs, the dragons curve upward, while at the very top, two large dragons face each other across a flaming round object, in the classic position of Dragons Paying Homage to the Sun – Luong Long Chau Nhat, their claws sheathed out of respect to the Emperor, represented by the symbol of the sun. On the middle roof, another pair of dragons in profile pay homage to a third one in full face, its back supporting a wine bottle. Dragon pairs and their objects of respect, or dispute, is a motif often found on temple roofs, gates, stelea, and ritualistic monuments. Sometimes, the two dragons pay homage to the moon, in the Luong Long Trieu Nguyet posture, or show their open claws in a combat pose known as Two Dragons Fighting for a Flaming Pearl – Luong Long Tranh Chau. Like other structures in the Imperial Citadel, Thai Hoa Palace roofs do not curve up at the corners, unlike most temples seen in the north and in Chinese classical architecture. Rather the illusion of a curving roof is created by profile of the dragons soaring upwards. The three roofs give an impression of airiness and a more graceful appearance to the imposing building.

Stone mandarin at Minh Mang Tomb.

A group of mandarins, late 19th–early 20th century.

Side view of Thai Hoa Palace.

Stone stelea marking the positions of
the mandarins.

Ornate ironwood pillars inside Thai Hoa Palace.

The throne room inside Thai Hoa.

Inside Thai Hoa Palace before Khai Dinh's renovation in 1924.

The Emperor's throne and canopy with its underside of Phap Lam.

The two main roofs with dragon motifs, Thai Hoa.

Stepping inside the palace, one can feel as overwhelmed by the extensive use of red lacquer and gilded dragons on almost every surface, as by the sheer size of the huge hall. The floor area of Thai Hoa Palace is 40m x 30m, with the Throne Room occupying the largest part, the throne being placed at centre-stage. Originally, the interior of Thai Hoa Palace was completely open, with the front and the back parts screened by blinds and drapes that could be rolled up for court assemblies. In this way, such assemblies incorporated both the lesser mandarins in attendance outside, and the higher-ranking ones inside, to form one single court presided over by the Emperor.

In 1923, Emperor Khai Dinh added two sets of folding doors to the front and back of the building and two large motifs of long-life to the front wall, on either side of the folding doors, their corners supported by bats for luck. On this occasion, he also replaced the embroidered drapes over the throne by a solid structure, made of wood and decorated with nine dragons in Phap Lam. The renovation was in preparation for his 40th birthday and was the last time the interior was extensively modified under the Nguyen.

Once inside Thai Hoa Palace, although your eye will be drawn to the centre with its gilded throne, do not neglect the ceiling and supporting roof beams. On each panel of wood, no matter what their function, a poem is carefully carved and brightly gilded against a background of red lacquer. Altogether, 300 poems and couplets have been engraved and gilded on nine rows of panels displayed immediately under the roof. The most important row is placed centre-stage, opposite the gilded throne, and facing out above the sign with three large characters announcing the name Thai Hoa Palace. The 17 poems engraved on this row eulogise the importance of supreme harmony between a wise and just reign and the strength of the realm.

Character for 'long life' and bats on Thai Hoa Palace.

Dropping from the high ceiling are rows of oriental-style lanterns lit by electrical bulbs in a typical Nguyen mixture of East and West. When the dynasty was in power, precious ceramic and porcelain urns and vases, supported by ornate stools and stands adorned the rather sparse hall. Today, only a few royal artefacts are on display, intermingled with some new pieces to complete a replica of the former royal Throne Room. One of the remarkable original features of this hall are the acoustics, which were designed so that the Emperor could hear every word uttered around the room.

As with other structures in Hue Capital City, Thai Hoa palace was seriously damaged during the Tet Offensive of 1968 and was left unrepaired for many years, over which time rainwater and several typhoons contributed to damaging it further. Today, although it has recently been painstakingly renovated, Thai Hoa Palace has lost many of its finest original features. Even so, the interior of the Palace, as we see today, still manages to reflect some of its former glory.

If time allows, it is worth watching the orientation video prepared by UNESCO, shown at intervals at the back. It may help to make clearer some of the features of Nguyen arts within the Imperial Citadel and the Forbidden Purple City that we are about to visit.

Corners of roof and drain hole, Thai Hoa.

Backward-turning dragon motif, Thai Hoa.

The Forbidden Purple City

Leaving Thai Hoa Palace and continuing in a South-North direction, is the path into the Forbidden Purple City, a separate quarter surrounded by a high wall of 3.72 metres and covering an area of 324m x 290m. First is a courtyard decorated with a couple of large bronze vats, and flanked by two long buildings on either side – the Ta Vu and Huu Vu – offices where the military and civil mandarins used to prepare their paperwork before coming into the Forbidden Purple City to report their daily affairs to the Emperor. They now house periodic exhibitions and some theatrical props used to re-enact royal scenes during festival times. Beyond these are the remains of the former Can Chanh palace, where the Emperor worked and held his daily meetings with his officials, or presided over banquets for deserving mandarins and scholars. As such, it is translated as 'The Palace of Audiences' in the UNESCO's World Heritage Site list. Can Chanh was built in 1811 but was burned to the ground during the fighting of 1947. Its base is now used occasionally as a stage for the Dem Hoang Cung – Royal Palace Nights – one of the main attractions of the Hue festivals. Behind this is a large concrete screen marking the entrance to the private domain of the Emperor and his family.

A wall marking the boundary of the Forbidden Purple City.

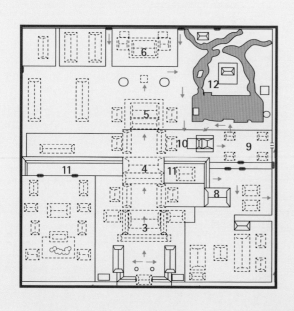

Notes:

3. Can Chanh Palace
4. Can Thanh Palace
5. Khon Thai Residence
6. Kien Trung Pavillion
8. Duyet Thi Royal Theatre
9. Thieu Phuong Royal Garden
10. Thai Binh Pavillion
11. Forbidden Purple City's long corridor

Plan of the Imperial and Forbidden Purple City *Dai Noi*.

Remaining constructions

Lost constructions

Kien Trung Palace under Bao Dai's reign.

The remains of Kien Trung Palace today.

The area behind the screen is the innermost sanctum of the Nguyen Emperors. Originally, 50 diverse buildings graced this quarter, but most, including the three main palaces, have been destroyed. What we see now are their peripheral structures, some of which have been almost completely reconstructed, such as the Truong Lang – Long Corridors – leading from the Forbidden Purple City to the Royal theatre on the east side, the female quarters on the west and, further out through a gate, to the Imperial Citadel where the Queen Mother and grandmothers lived.

Three main buildings once occupied the entire middle area of the Forbidden Purple City, behind the royal screen: Can Thanh, Khon Thai and Kien Trung Palaces. Can Thanh was where the Emperor lived before Khai Dinh's time. From here, he could walk down the long covered corridors to visit his Queen, his concubines, his mother and grandmothers, or his theatre. Khon Thai was the Queen's residence, while Kien Trung was a new palace built in European style by Emperor Khai Dinh in 1921. When completed in 1923, it became his own residence within the Forbidden Purple City. Khai Dinh died here in 1925 and a model of the palace in papier-mache was burned during his funeral ceremony, in the hope that it would become his residence in his afterlife. His son, the last Emperor Bao Dai lived here together with his Queen Nam Phuong, in a modern departure from the tradition of having separate residences for Emperors and Queens. All five of his children were born in this palace. Kien Trung Palace was also where Bao Dai drafted and signed his abdication statement of 1945.

All three buildings were destroyed in the anti-French struggle of 1945-1947. Can Thanh and Khon Thai palaces were razed to the ground and are marked only by two plaques over their barely visible foundations. Kien Trung Palace scarcely fared any better although more of its

Today's Kien Trung seen from a garden pavillion.

Workers repairing Truong Lang – The long corridor.

Above: A back gate of the Forbidden Purple City.

Above right: Steps and path leading to the back gate of Kien Trung Palace and out of the Forbidden Purple City.

Model of Kien Trung Palace for burning at Khai Dinh's funeral.

Royal screen at the back of the Forbidden Purple City.

foundations remain visible. The stone steps leading up to the base of the building are intact, flanked by two stone balustrades of dragons and clouds. Today, the base of the palace bears two marble plaques. One explains the origin of the site, as a moon viewing pavilion – Lau Minh Vien – built under Minh Mang, and twice destroyed and rebuilt under Tu Duc and Duy Tan being renamed Du Cuu. The other plaque details the construction of the Kien Trung palace under Khai Dinh. Although the building no longer exists, the garden in front of Kien Trung Palace continues to be kept as a lawn, with two ornate pavilions facing each other across the expanse of green grass and serving as welcome shelters from the occasional rain or the glaring sunshine. Luckily, these escaped the destruction of wars and were fully restored in 1990-1991. Similar to the entrance into the Forbidden Purple City, the back of Kien Trung Palace is also shielded from public eyes by a royal screen connected with two gates opening out to a moat called Noi Kim Thuy – the Inner moat. Two stone bridges cross the moat, one

Hieu Mon gate leading to Hien Lam Cac.

A roadside shrine.

connecting with a road leading to Hoa Binh – Peace Gate, a back exit from the Forbidden Purple City. Through this gate, the Emperor could enjoy boating or fishing in the moats, and, once a year, travel further north, to the northern bank of the Imperial Canal – Ngu Ha, to perform the annual ploughing ceremony – Tich Dien – thereby initiating a new planting season for the country.

Since 1994, the year after Hue was inscribed in the list of UNESCO World Heritage Sites, experts from the Hue Monuments Conservation Center and the University of Waseda (Japan) have been measuring the foundations of the ruined palaces of the Forbidden Purple City, and other sites in Hue, with the view to rebuilding some of the main palaces. The Can Chanh Palace will be the first and will be rebuilt exactly as it was, following surviving plans and documents.

Roof details of Thai Binh Lau.

Mosaic decoration on the front of Thai Binh Lau.

Thai Binh Lau – The Royal Library

From Kien Trung Palace, we go to the east side of the Purple City and come to Thai Binh Lau – the Royal Library/Study. In spite of the destruction of many palaces in the Forbidden Purple City and the Imperial Citadel, this building remains remarkably intact after the fighting of 1945-1947.

Thai Binh Lau was originally built in 1821, during Emperor Minh Mang's reign, in the eastern quarter of the City, next to a royal garden called Thieu Phuong and a beautiful pond called Ngoc Dich. Later, his son, Emperor Thieu Tri, modified it into a study to write poetry calling it Thanh Ha Thu Lau. In 1887, Emperor Dong Khanh replaced that building with this one, heavily decorated with mosaic, and gave it its present name Thanh Binh Ngu Lam Thu Lau which was later shortened to Thai Binh Lau.

Approaching from Kien Trung Palace, we arrive at the back door first. From here, we can see the ornamental pond at the back, decorated with a miniature rockery of mountains, woodland, bamboo houses and tiny figures. This landscape once entertained the royal scholar when he was tired of his books, the peaceful scene an inspiration for beautiful verses. The landscape was once linked with the back door of the Library by a wooden bridge, now broken.

Front of Thai Binh Lau.

Phoenix on Thai Binh Lau.

Above Left: Dragons and Phoenix on the top of Thai Binh Lau.

A corner of Thai Binh Lau, showing the Confucius mosaic.

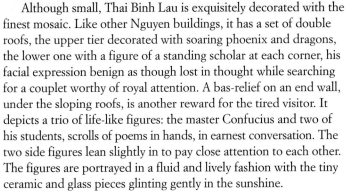

Although small, Thai Binh Lau is exquisitely decorated with the finest mosaic. Like other Nguyen buildings, it has a set of double roofs, the upper tier decorated with soaring phoenix and dragons, the lower one with a figure of a standing scholar at each corner, his facial expression benign as though lost in thought while searching for a couplet worthy of royal attention. A bas-relief on an end wall, under the sloping roofs, is another reward for the tired visitor. It depicts a trio of life-like figures: the master Confucius and two of his students, scrolls of poems in hands, in earnest conversation. The two side figures lean slightly in to pay close attention to each other. The figures are portrayed in a fluid and lively fashion with the tiny ceramic and glass pieces glinting gently in the sunshine.

The front of the building is also richly decorated with mosaic, the walls covered with images of seasonal flowers and plants, birds and deer, meticulously created from tiny pieces of china and glass. The building faces onto a topiary garden of tigers and elephants and is shielded by a heavily ornate screen, beyond which lies the former walled garden of Thieu Phuong. The once renowned royal garden is now a square of empty land with rough grass and broken bricks, surrounded by tall walls blackened with age. Nevertheless the visitor should persevere in order to see Ngoc Dich pond.

A scholar at a roof corner – Thai Binh Lau.

Royal screen and gateways to Ngoc Dich Pond – Thai Binh Lau.

Gate from Thieu Phuong garden to Ngoc Dich pond.

Right: Curving banks of Ngoc Dich pond.

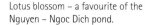

Lotus blossom – a favourite of the Nguyen – Ngoc Dich pond.

Ngoc Dich pond

This calm oasis was created by the royal architects as a curving pond that tapers into a canal connecting the Purple City with the inner moat. The pond is shaped by ornate high banks, broken by two sets of concrete steps leading down to the water's edge where, once upon a time, a boat might have been moored awaiting the Emperor's pleasure. An artificial island occupies the middle of the pond, connected with the far side by a wooden bridge. This islet was once a sanctuary for rare birds and animals and had a viewing pavilion built under Minh Mang in 1821. However, that structure was demolished under Thanh Thai in 1891, and, today, only a lone Queen Blossom tree remains. The combined features of water, flowers and trees invoke a deep sense of calm, harmony and well-being, inviting us to linger. However, there's still the western quarter of the Purple City and many more sites to visit. With this pond in front, we now move to our left and turn left again to follow the long corridor to the Royal Theatre – Duyet Thi Duong.

Thai Binh Lau from Ngoc Dich pond.

Island on Ngoc Dich pond.

Theatre equipment stored in Duyet Thi Duong.

A corner of Duyet Thi Duong.

Duyet Thi Duong – The Royal Theatre

Court music, dance and theatre were an important part of life under the Nguyen, and it is not surprising that the Forbidden Purple City. had a Royal Theatre. Built in 1826, under Emperor Minh Mang, it is a simple rectangular structure with greeny-blue tiled double roofs, the corners decorated with the royal symbols of dragons and clouds. It stands in a walled area some 11,740 m², with the building itself occupying an area of 1,182 m², and with a courtyard at the front. The surrounding area was once used to grow herbal medicines for the Royal Medical Department on its right, and the Royal Kitchen on its left. Both these buildings, separated from the theatre by high walls, have now been destroyed.

The intimate interior of the theatre is mainly wood, with tall pillars some 12 metres high. Today, the interior walls are adorned with many pictures depicting auspicious landscapes of Hue. The stage occupies a square area at the back, facing the entrance, and the two tiers of seating. The upper part, a U-shaped balcony facing the stage was once reserved for the Queen, Queen Mother and Grandmothers, concubines and other members of the royal family. The entire balcony was screened by slatted blinds that allowed the people behind to see out but kept outside people from looking in. Today, this part of the theatre stores costumes for actors and paying visitors, and other theatrical props.

The Emperor sat on the ground floor with his favourites and honoured guests, such as ambassadors, or the French Governor during the French occupation. After Bao Dai's departure in 1945, and the partition of Vietnam in 1954, Duyet Thi Duong became the Hue Music Conservatory in 1957. Under the auspices of UNESCO and the Hue Monuments Conservation Center, renovation began in 1995, a task interrupted in 1997 by a severe typhoon. Work resumed

in 1998 and in 2003, Duyet Thi Duong reopened as a theatre. Court plays are sometimes staged and it provides a backdrop for visitors wanting to be photographed as kings and queens.

Nguyen Court theatre and music were inscribed in the list of UNESCO's Intangible World Heritage in 2003 and some almost forgotten dances and plays have been researched and revived. Today, both streams of Court music, Dai Nhac – Grand Ensemble and Tieu Nhac – Small Ensemble, have been performed.

Stage inside Duyet Thi Duong theatre.

Dai Nhac to accompany grand ceremonial events such as the Nam Giao, and Tieu Nhac on more intimate occasions, such as royal banquets and concerts. In the same spirit of recreating an intangible heritage, eleven Nguyen Court dances have now been performed in the theatre, as well as several court plays, an art that reached its apogee under Emperor Tu Duc.

Nguyen court entertainment was subject to strict rules and regulations. On stage, the artists could not face the Emperor full on, the wording of the plays and song lyrics had to avoid prescribed taboo words, and the music had to use the correct instruments.

Duyet Thi Duong is the last structure in the Forbidden Purple City that we can visit as the other buildings have been destroyed. Leaving the Forbidden Purple City we continue along the east side to arrive at the eastern quarters of the Imperial Citadel.

A troupe from the South waiting to perform for Emperor Khai Dinh.

A gate in the Imperial Citadel.

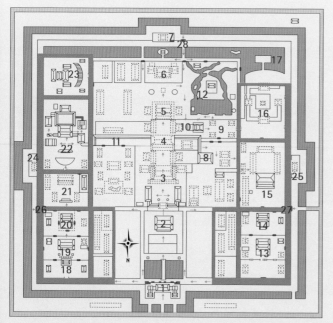

Notes:

1. Ngo Mon Gate
2. Thai Hoa Palace
3. Can Chanh Palace
4. Can Thanh Palace
5. Khon Thai Residence
6. Kien Trung Pavillion
7. The Northern Watch Tower
8. Duyet Thi Royal Theatre
9. Thieu Phuong
   Royal Garden
10. Thai Binh Pavillion
11. Forbidden Purple City's
    long corridor
12. Royal Garden
13. Thai Mieu Temple
14. Trieu Mieu Temple
15. The Royal Treasury
16. Co Ha Garden
17. Rear Lake
18. Hien Lam Pavillion
19. The Mieu Temple
20. Hung Mieu Temple
21. Phung Tien Temple
22. Dien Tho Residence
23. Troung Sanh Residence
24. The Eastern Watch Tower
25. The Western Watch Tower
26. Chuong Duc Gate
27. Hien Nhon Gate
28. Hoa Binh Gate

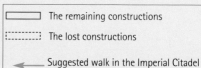

☐ The remaining constructions

┆┄┄┄┆ The lost constructions

⟵ Suggested walk in the Imperial Citadel
    and The Forbidden Purple City.

■ The 9 quarters of the Imperial Citadel

The Imperial Citadel

As we can see on the map, surrounding the Forbidden
Purple City is the middle layer of Hue Capital City,
the Imperial Citadel. This layer, in turn, is separated
from the outermost layer of the city by its own walls
and moats. There are many buildings in this layer,
grouped into nine square areas placed evenly and
symmetrically on both the east and west sides of the
Purple City. Each quarter has a different function
and status. The Imperial Citadel is separated from
the Forbidden Purple City by a square of tree-lined
roads and accessed by a number of gates, some simple,
others heavily ornate.

Overgrown garden of the eastern temple quarter.

The east side

The eastern part of the Imperial Citadel occupies a
sparse and almost wild area that houses a large garden,
an administrative building, ruins of royal factories
and a dynastic temple quarter, each section within its
own walls. The garden, called Co Ha, was once a play
area for the Crown Prince and other members of the
royal family, but today it resembles an overgrown plant
nursery, where greenhouses, potted plants and row
upon row of seedlings struggle for space among weeds
and rubble.

The next quarter to visit, as we continue in a
southerly direction back toward Ngo Mon, is the
Royal Interior Department – Phu Noi Vu, also called
the Royal Treasury.

A corner of the eastern temple quarter.

Phu Noi Vu – The Royal Treasury

Phu Noi Vu was an important department in charge
of all interior matters of the Nguyen Court. It also
had the function of overseeing all the royal factories.
The original building housing the offices has now been
replaced by a handsome structure built in European
style, in 1906-1908. The former royal factories which
were dotted around this area are all gone, with only
traces remaining in the form of broken-down walls
or rubble. It is hardly recognisable as the place where
many fine royal objects were once produced. The Royal
Treasury's main function was book keeping and looking
after all financial transactions for the Court. It also
had the duty to maintain and store old royal ceramic
and porcelain objects, carved ivories, bolts of silk

Another gate in the Imperial Citadel.

and brocade, tiger bones and chests full of royal robes and accessories. In this quarter, there was also an assembly house called Dien Tap Hien, where mandarins of literature gathered to discuss and draft their reports to the Emperor. There is no trace of this building today.

Temple in Phu Noi Vu quarter.

Middle: Temple of Thai Mieu.

The Temples of Trieu Mieu and Thai Mieu

Leaving the Treasury quarter and continuing south, we enter the quarter of dynastic temples, where two main temples are situated among the ruins of other smaller buildings. The one on the north side is called Trieu Mieu, the Temple for Nguyen Kim, the first ancestor of the Nguyen. It was one of the first structures to be built

Phu Noi Vu – the Royal Treasury – today.

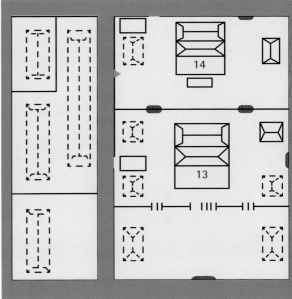

in Hue Capital City under Gia Long. Nguyen Kim was the general who supported the late Le to regain the throne from the Mac. He was the father of Nguyen Hoang, the founder of Dang Trong, land of the South, and father in law of Trinh Kiem, the powerful Lord Trinh who was seen by Nguyen Hoang as a dangerous rival.

The next temple, south of Trieu Mieu, is Thai Mieu reserved for Lord Nguyen Hoang and other Nguyen Lords. It was built at the same time as other ancestral temples in the Imperial Citadel, in 1805 in Gia Long's reign. Unfortunately, five original buildings in these quarters were destroyed during the anti-French war of resistance in 1945-1947, and Thai Mieu's roof was destroyed during a storm in 1956. The temple was restored in 1963 but was demolished and replaced by a smaller structure in 1971-1972, with a modern tiled roof. This is what we see today.

Unlike the rest of Dai Noi, the east side of the Imperial Citadel is still under developed and many walled areas are empty and overgrown. It is in complete contrast to the west side of the Imperial Citadel, where extensive restoration works have taken place and are continuing.

Gate into Trieu Mieu and Thai Mieu, eastern quarter, Imperial Citadel.

Hien Lam Cac, The Nguyen's Hall of Fame, Western quarter of the Imperial citadel.

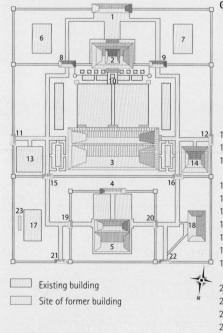

Existing building

Site of former building

N

GHI CHU : Legend

1 Mieu Mon (Temple gate)
2 Hien Lam Cac (Hien Lam Pavilion)
3 The To Mieu (The To temple)
4 Mieu Mon (Temple's gate)
5 Hung To Mieu (Hung To temple)
6 Ta Tung Tu (Right House)
7 Huu Tung Tu (Left House)
8 Tuan Liet Mon (Tuan Liet gate)
9 Sung Cong Mon (Sung Cong gate)
10 Cuu Dinh (Nine Dynastic Urns)
11 Khai Dich Mon (Sung Thanh gate)
12 Sung Thanh Mon
   (Sung Thanh gate)
13 Dien Canhy (Robing House)
14 Tho Cong (Soil God temple)
15 Hien Huu Mon (Hien Huu gate)
16 Doc Huu Mon (Doc Huu gate)
17 Than Kho (Divine steore house)
18 Than Tru (Divine Kitchen)
19 Chuong Khanh Mon
   (Choung Khanh gate)
20 Duc Khanh Mon (Duc Khanh gate)
21 Tri Tuong Mon (Tri Tuong gate)
22 Ung Tuong Mon (Ung Tuong gate)
23 Bia Ghi lich Su Xay Dung Khu Mieu
   (Slete inscribing contruction date)

The West Side

To reach this part of the Imperial Citadel, we leave the east side and cross behind Ngo Mon to enter another dynastic temple quarter enclosed by walls and lying symmetrical to Trieu Mieu and Thai Mieu on the east. Although several structures have been damaged, three main temples remain. From south to north, is Hien Lam Cac with its nine urns facing The Mieu, a large temple dedicated to the Nguyen Emperors and their queens and behind that building, Hung Mieu, the temple for Gia Long's parents set in a lovely garden.

Wine bottle on the roof of Hien Lam Cac –
one of the symbols of a gentleman's
leisure pursuits.

Drain Hole on the roof of Hien Lam Cac.

Hien Lam Cac

This three-story building was constructed in 1821-1822 under
Minh Mang with the specific function of glorifying the Nguyen,
and commemorating the most significant mandarins of their
court. As such, it could be aptly described as the Nguyen's Hall
of Fame rather than a temple. In the UNESCO list, it is called
the 'Pavilion of Radiant Benevolence from On-High'.

It is a long building built on an elevation reached by
climbing nine stone steps, flanked on both sides by stone
dragons and clouds. Compared to other structures within
the Imperial Citadel, the exterior of this building is simply
decorated with dragons, clouds, phoenix and carp, symbols of
achievement on all three roofs, while the top of the highest roof
bears a yellow wine bottle, one of the symbols of a gentleman's
leisure pursuits. The entrance is marked by a framed sign
identifying it as Hien Lam Cac, the frame decorated with nine
dragons, symbols of royal authority. The interior of the hall is
mainly wood and is highly decorated with curving dragons,
clouds, and garlands of leaves. Of all the buildings within
the Imperial Citadel, Hien Lam Cac is one of those most
meticulously maintained and regularly renovated. Outside, is a
row of nine giant bronze urns, the largest one standing slightly
forward to occupy a place of honour.

Hien Lam Cac and three of the nine bronze urns representing the Nguyen emperors. The middle one is the largest and most important – symbolising Emperor Gia Long.

Inside Hien Lam Cac.

Cuu Dinh – The Nine Bronze Urns

The Nine Bronze Urns were made in Minh Mang's reign to celebrate the power of the sovereign. They took four years to forge from 1835 to 1839. Each urn represents a Nguyen Emperor and has its own name: Cao Dinh represents Gia Long, Nhân Dinh is for Minh Mang, Chuong Dinh for Thieu Tri, Anh Dinh for Tu Duc, Nghi Dinh for Kien Phuc, Thuan Dinh for Dong Khanh and Tuyen Dinh for Khai Dinh. The biggest urn, standing in the place of honour is Cao Dinh for Gia Long, the last two urns, Du Dinh and Huyen Dinh, have not been assigned to any emperor, while six remaining Nguyen emperors are without urns.

Carved on each urn are reliefs of landscapes and products representing Vietnam, such as a bunch of rice stalks on Cao Dinh, or animals and landscapes on others. In all there are 153 such pictures. The urns are slightly different from each other in size, designs and the shapes of their handles, some are square, others are round, but all the urns are huge and supported by strong curving legs. The biggest urn is over 2.5 metres tall and weighs over 2.5 tonnes. The smallest is 2.1 metres tall and weighs around 2 tonnes.

Peacock on a royal urn.

Above Left: Beanstalks on the Urn for Emperor Gia Long.

Handles of the Nine Urns – Imperial Citadel.

The Mieu or The To Mieu

Opposite Hien Lam Cac, across a courtyard paved with Bat Trang tiles, is The Mieu, a large and long building. Within is an imposing line of red lacquer and gilded altars, dedicated to ten of the 13 Nguyen Emperors and their Queens, from Gia Long to Khai Dinh. Each Emperor is represented by a funerary tablet, or a portrait. Originally, there were seven dedicated to Emperors Gia Long, Minh Mang, Thieu Tri, Tu Duc, Kien Phuc, Dong Khanh and Khai Dinh. In 1959, three more royal tablets and altars of the anti-French Emperors Ham Nghi, Thanh Thai and Duy Tan were added. Currently, there are no tablets or altars for Emperors Duc Duc, Hiep Hoa and Bao Dai. While the temple was still in use, women were forbidden.

Quilin on side gate leading to Hien Lam Cac.

Hung Mieu – The Temple of Resurrection

Behind The Mieu is Hung Mieu, a new structure built in 1951 on the orders of Bao Dai after he returned to Hue as Head of State under French protection. Although new, this temple was built in a style similar to the rest of the Imperial Citadel. It stands in a garden of ancient pines, with some trees being so old that their knobbly branches need to be supported by wooden or concrete stakes.

Hung Mieu or Hung To Mieu is a temple for Gia Long's parents. His father, Nguyen Phuc Luan did not become a Nguyen Lord but was put in prison instead, after a dispute within the Nguyen family. He died at the age of 32, leaving six children. Gia Long – Nguyen Phuc Anh was one of them. The original Hung Mieu was built in the grounds of today's The Mieu in 1804 but was later moved to its present position in 1821, under Minh Mang, to make way for The Mieu. Sharing the same fate as other buildings within the Forbidden Purple City, the original Hung Mieu was burned down during the anti-French resistance of 1945-1947, and was not rebuilt until 1951.

Interior of The Mieu.

Ruins of Phung Tien temple, The Imperial Citadel.

Above: A gate in the western quarter.

As with other quarters within the Imperial Citadel, the western one is separated from other areas by tall walls and 12 ornate gates. The south wall of this quarter faces onto the main road running around the Imperial Citadel, which can be accessed via a highly ornate gate, itself a notable work of art. The gate on the north wall opens out to the next quarter, which once housed another large temple dedicated to the Nguyen Emperors and their queens: Phung Tien Temple.

Phung Tien temple

Unlike The Mieu, where women were not allowed to enter or to participate in the state ceremonies held there, Phung Tien temple was left in the charge of women, the royal spinsters or widows. In its heyday, this temple showcased the best treasures of the Nguyen, where royal seals, golden trees of gem fruits, precious Phap Lam objects, golden books and royal personal effects were put on show. During that time, the most interesting display was a collection of 33 bronze objects bearing poems and thoughts written

Bronze Pigeon cart. Minh Mang c.1839.

Rhino horn vase, modelled after a Thuong epoch tale. Minh Mang c. 1839.

by Emperor Minh Mang, in which he commented on his own Mandate of Heaven and other human virtues. No. 18 among these referred to an invasion by Siam of a Vietnamese city called Tan Long. Engraved on a three-legged urn, Minh Mang's poem declared that 'the invaders were repelled with a loss of many men and boats'.

According to documents contained in a book called Ngu Che Minh Van Co Khi Do (Text to explain about metal objects forged on order of the Emperor) written by the mandarins in charge of cataloguing this collection and dated 2nd August 1840, the bronze objects were made in 1839 after illustrations of Chinese models found in ancient books, ranging from the Thuong epoch (15th or 16th to 12th B.C.E) to the Han (206 B.C.E to 220 C.E). The objects were mainly vases and urns but they also included interesting items such as a cup in the shape of a buffalo head, or a little cart in the shape of a pigeon. All these artefacts were lost when Phung Tien Temple was burned to the ground during the fighting of 1947. Today, instead of an imposing temple, only a fragment of ruined doorway remains in the middle of a walled area overrun by wild grass, a haunting reminder of a glorious past. Phung Tien backs on to the next quarter, located to its north: Dien Tho, domain of the senior Queens.

Dien Tho – The Queen Mother's and Grandmothers' quarter

Carp motif on roof corner.

Royal Screen to shield the Emperor when he came to visit his mother at Dien Tho Palace.

Dien Tho occupies a surprisingly large area and includes an European-style house, where Bao Dai resided upon his return as Head of State in 1950. The whole quarter occupies a space equivalent to 1/20 of the entire area of the Imperial Citadel and Forbidden Purple City, on a rectangular plot measuring 126.4m x 138.5m. This was where the Emperor's mother, grandmothers and sometimes even great-grandmothers lived. The quarter was also one of the first areas to be built under Gia Long. It is surrounded by 2 metre high walls, each with a gate facing out to the four main directions. One of these gates opens onto a paved path linking Dien Tho with the Forbidden Purple City. Along this path and within the grounds of Dien Tho, a large ornate concrete screen shielded the Emperor from the public eye whenever he came to visit his mother or grandmothers.

When Dien Tho was first built under Gia Long it was called Truong Tho – long life, a name later changed to Tu Tho, Gia Tho, Ninh Tho and finally its present name, Dien Tho. There were 20 structures of all shapes and sizes within its walls, each connected or separated from the next by gardens and ponds. Many of the buildings have been remodelled or renovated during different reigns of the Nguyen dynasty but the general configuration of the area was kept intact over the years. A few, however, were damaged or destroyed during the wars, their skeletons still visible among the newly renovated structures.

The centrepiece of the quarter is a rectangular palace of several rooms and apartments connected by ornate corridors, occupying an area of 960m². This was the residence of the Supreme Queen Mother and was where she received her guests. Today, the palace shows how the last Queen Mother spent her days and displays her personal belongings. As she lived in a time when the last Nguyen emperors had embraced western values and culture, her residence shows a remarkable mixture of east and west, with European-style objects sitting alongside their traditional Vietnamese counterparts.

Some of the most noteworthy objects are the glass paintings hung on the two front columns, which are similar to those currently on display at Tu Duc's Tomb. Nguyen glass paintings are priceless works of art, with unique production techniques and subjects that are valuable on many levels, whether as records of lost structures or landscapes of Hue, or recording precious poems by the Emperors. Some were commissioned from China by Emperor Thieu Tri, others are of unknown origin. One showing Thieu Phuong garden in the Forbidden Purple City, is particularly well known. It depicts a dense garden with four covered corridors in the middle, shaped like

Thuong Mau Quan Canh. An important glass painting commissioned by Emperor Thieu Tri to illustrate his poem.

Bat motif on screen, Dien Tho Palace.

the Buddhist symbol of '*van*' – a swastika which symbolises good luck. Currently the garden is in ruins but there are plans to rebuild it according to the image shown on the glass painting.

The next interesting object is the ornate screen of glass panels surrounded by a carved wooden frame, on the left when entering the palace. On the frame, carved flowers, birds and bats are strategically placed to create an elegant frame worthy of a lady occupying the highest female position at the Nguyen Court. The symbol of the bat means 'happiness' because the character 'bat' when pronounced sounds the same as the character for 'good luck'- *phuc*. The bat was a favourite decorative motif under the Nguyen, although it is not always easily recognised. The motif can appear as a single bat, in a group of five representing perfect happiness, woven into the design with tendrils of leaves, or as corners marking devices, as in the large 'long life' characters at Thai Hoa Palace. Sometimes, the bat motif includes something the bat is carrying in its mouth, which symbolises a good wish for happiness. In the middle of the room is a seating area where the Queen Mother met and discussed important affairs with State visitors.

Lady Tu Cung – Wife of Emperor Khai Dinh and mother of Emperor Bao Dai.

Glass screen, Dien Tho Palace.

130

Leaving the palace and walking to the left of this building, ducking under a low gateway, we reach the next significant building in this quarter, Tho Ninh palace, reserved for the Queen Mother of second rank. This building tends to be overlooked for visitors are immediately drawn to the elegant wooden pavilion opposite, built on a small island in the middle of a pond adorned by a miniature landscape. This is Truong Du

Lady Tu Cung receiving French governor Paul Reynaud.

pavilion, built in 1849 in a 530m² pond. As befits a pavilion built for a lady, light wood was used throughout and every detail is graceful. The interior has thin wood panels carved in intricate lacy patterns, the roof was supported by 16 slender columns and the whole structure was surrounded by a wooden balcony. Today, the pavilion and the pond it stands in still exude an air of elegance and finesse. Truong Du pavilion was connected to a shrine on one side of the pond by a tiny wooden bridge, from where the path leads back to the main palace at the centre. The Queen Mother, Grandmothers and Great Grandmothers came to pray regularly at this shrine. On the opposite side of the ornate pond is a teahouse where visitors waited for their turn to have an audience, a building which is now in a skeletal state awaiting its turn to be renovated.

Wood panels, pavilion interior, Dien Tho palace.

On the southwest corner of the Dien Tho quarter, there was once a private theatre called Thong Minh Duong, reserved for the senior queens, but in 1927, it was replaced by a modern building called Tinh Minh. In 1950, that building was enlarged to become a residence for the last Emperor Bao Dai who, by then, had returned to Vietnam from France to assume his new status as Head of State.

Tinh Minh villa where Bao Dai lived as Head of State, in 1950.

General view of Truong Sanh quarter.

The Truong Sanh quarter

Truong Sanh was to the north of the Dien Tho quarter and had a less defined function. It was originally built in 1821 under Minh Mang as a landscaped garden where the Emperor and his mother could walk and relax. Several houses, ponds and bridges were added in 1846, under Emperor Thieu Tri, who listed it as the seventh best landscape of Hue. The following year, the quarter was again modified to provide an extra residence for the Queen Mother and grandmothers such as Lady Le Thien, Emperor Tu Duc's queen, Lady Tu Minh, Emperor Duc Duc's queen and Lady Tien Cung, Emperor Dong Khanh's queen. Under Emperor Khai Dinh, in 1923, the layout was altered to add two garages for his carriages and vehicles. Unlike its sister quarter Dien Tho, Truong Sanh quarter has been neglected until recently when it too became the subject of an extensive renovation. Even though, for now, the buildings and landscape within this quarter are overgrown with wild plants and long grass, the east gate, facing onto to the main road running around the Imperial Citadel, is a beautiful work of art and deserves a few minutes of quiet admiration.

This area is the last main quarter to be visited within the Imperial Citadel.

Apart from this, however, there are some significant objects dotted around the citadel that are worth seeing. The most noteworthy are the Nine Bronze Canons, known as Cuu Vi Than Cong, and the huge Bronze Vats of unknown function, seven of which can be found in the grounds, with the others being at the Nguyen tombs and the Museum of Royal Antiquities.

Paved path inside Truong Sanh quarter.

Gate of Truong Sanh – The Queen
Grandmothers' quarter.

Ceramic mosaic on gate into Truong Sanh quarter.

A corner of Truong Sanh quarter.

The four canons guarding The Nhon gate, representing the four seasons of the year.

Details of reliefs on the canons.

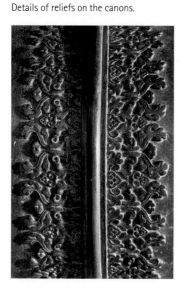

Cuu Vi Than Cong – The Nine Bronze Canons

Emperor Gia Long ordered the forging of nine, huge canons in 1803 to commemorate his victory over the Tay Son the year before. They were made by melting the bronze objects that Gia Long's army seized from the Tay Son and it took nearly a year for all nine canons to be completed. Each is 5.10 metres long and weighs between 17,000-18,000 kilogrammes. They were awarded the rank of 'Champion General' under Gia Long in 1815 – a fact still inscribed on each gun. Each sits on its own intricately carved base, supported by wooden wheels reinforced with iron girdles, and lined up side by side in two groups. One group of four was placed inside the The Nhon gate and the other group of five behind the Quang Duc gate. The group of four represents the four seasons: Spring, Summer, Autumn and Winter. The group of five represents the five elements: metal, wood, water, fire and earth.

Throughout the Nguyen dynasty, the Nine Bronze Canons were revered as symbols of royal power and national pride, and worshipped as the great protectors of the Nguyen. A platoon of soldiers was assigned to look after them day and night. Under the early Nguyen, each year, the Court held a ceremony and a feast to celebrate them. During these times, animals such as buffaloes and goats were sacrificed to prepare a feast for all. This ceremony was abandoned after French forces took over the Imperial Citadel, and the Court was left with only a nominal status in 1885. The Nine

Bronze Canons narrowly escaped from being destroyed following this event.

According to documents kept in the French Archives, after the takeover, a Captain G. Gilbert compiled an inventory of arms found in the Imperial Citadel, and proposed using dynamite to blow up all the guns and canons captured from the Nguyen, including the Nine. Although what happened next was not documented, a negotiation must have taken place between the Court and the French Governor General over the following months and years, for, in a letter to the Nguyen Privy Council, dated 8th July 1887, the French Governor General agreed to return the Canons to the Emperor, in exchange for 500,000 Francs, and to allow the Emperor to move freely within the Citadel. Subsequently, according to a French official document dated 18th February 1888, the French Artillery Service in Vietnam handed the Nine Bronze Canons over to the Nguyen Emperor Dong Khanh. Since then, they have been guarding the east and west side of the Imperial Citadel in the positions that we see today.

Royal decree on one of the canons.

Handle of one of the nine canons.

A bronze vat.

A boar on one of the vats.

A bird on one of the vats.

The Fifteen Vats

Two of these huge vats may have already been seen behind Thai Hoa Palace, on the walk toward the Forbidden Purple City. They appear to have no other purpose than decorating the courtyard in front of the mandarin offices Ta Vu and Huu Vu.

The 11 large bronze vats were made at different times between 1631 to 1684, according to inscriptions on their rims. Explanations vary as to their history before entering the Imperial Citadel. One version says that they were made by the Nguyen Lords in the south as a show of strength, while another maintains that they were made in Hanoi by the Le Emperor during the Trinh-Nguyen conflict. According to this latter theory, when the first Nguyen Emperor Gia Long succeeded in defeating the Trinh and uniting the country in 1802, he brought the vats to Hue from Hanoi, on large junks. The argument to support this explanation relies on two facts: the dates inscribed on the vats, and the political situation during the eighteenth century, when the Tay Son defeated the Nguyen Lords in the south. If the vats had been built by the Nguyen to show off their power, surely they would have been destroyed by the Tay Son when they were victorious. Also, the dates correspond to a period when the Nguyen Lords were engaged in constant warfare, first with the Trinh and then the Tay Son, making their manufacture unlikely. The first theory, does, however, propose a more likely manufacturing location, namely the Forge Quarter – Truong Duc, where the Nguyen later made their functioning bronze canons.

Today, seven of the original vats sit inside the Imperial Citadel, three in front of the Museum of Royal Antiquities and one in Dong Khanh tomb. Each is extremely heavy, weighing from a few hundred to a few thousand kilogrammes, with a height of over 1.5 metres. Most are carved or decorated with fine reliefs depicting garlands of leaves and flowers, animals such as deer, bird or wild boar, and dot-like motifs grouped together in square, star or circle formations, all the motifs being evenly placed in between ornate lines. Compared with the Nine Urns (page 124), the vats have handles, from two to four or even eight, but only very short legs, and in some cases none. Four more vats were made under Minh Mang, in 1825 and 1828 according to their inscriptions, and are now in the Tu Duc mausoleum. These are smaller and lighter, each weighing around 400 kilogrammes and all have four handles.

The durability of bronze, the huge size and the heavy weight of the Nine Bronze Guns, the Nine Urns and the Bronze Vats combined to deliver a message that the Nguyen Emperors were powerful, their dynasty was long-lasting and their authority was weighty. Although the Nguyen Dynasty is gone, these magnificent bronzes are still in place, perhaps not as symbols of a long-lasting power but nevertheless as objects for us to marvel at.

The Gates of the Imperial Citadel

As we have discovered during our walk, both the Imperial Citadel, and the Forbidden Purple City within today's Dai Noi, were built on the south side of the Imperial Canal – Ngu Ha – and connected with the rest of the Capital City by four gates constructed at different times under different Nguyen Emperors. One gate already visited is the Ngo Mon, but the other three may have been overlooked from concentrating on other structures within the Citadel. Before leaving it is worth looking at these gates for each one of them is a work of art in its own right.

Hien Nhon gate.

The two most significant ones are the Chuong Duc gate on the west side, parallel with the western Temple Quarter, and Hien Nhon gate, on the opposite side, parallel to the eastern Temple Quarter. Chuong Duc was originally built under Gia Long and went through several alterations in the following reigns, with the most dramatic being under Emperor Khai Dinh, in 1921. Under his order, the original Chuong Duc gate was destroyed and rebuilt as a large concrete structure of two stories, completely decorated in mosaic ceramic and glass tiles, similar to the style seen in his mausoleum in the Valley of the Tombs and in Emperor Dong Khanh's Study – Thai Binh Lau. On this gate alone, there are 148 tiles, 50 panels and friezes depicting flowers of four seasons, or precious birds and animals such as phoenix, pheasant, tiger, elephant and deer. Some panels contain a full set of pictures depicting a fable or traditional story.

Two years after the completion of this gate, the opposite one on the east side, Hien Nhon, was also rebuilt in the same style and decorated with similar ceramic and glass tiles. Unfortunately, like the rest of Hue, both gates were left in disrepair until 1977 when the Hien Nhon gate was renovated followed by the Chuong Duc gate in 2003. At that time the art of decorative mosaics was extensively researched. Each tile and panel was carefully studied and catalogued. It took a year for the Chuong Duc gate to be returned to its former state, albeit with some tiles and panels missing, or damaged beyond repair. Both gates are now considered the best examples of late Nguyen mosaic work. The south gate, as we have seen, is the Ngo Mon and the north gate, Hoa Binh, is the back gate to the Forbidden Purple City.

An inner gate inside the imperial citadel.

Mosaic on Hien Nhon gate.

Outside Dai Noi is the residential and light commercial quarter of Hue Capital City, a noisy and busy area, in contrast with its original function as a spill-over quarter for Dai Noi. Here, were court buildings and residences for mandarins and those who served at court. Scarcely any traces of these structures remain. However, although most have been destroyed, a few remain such as the National Archives Building.

Tang Tho Lau – The National Archives

Tucked away behind trees on a side street east of Dai Noi and obscured by modern buildings is the former National Archives, an important building where Court papers were stored for posterity. It is located in an area once reserved for the Ministries of Rites and Protocols and other courtly departments.

Tang Tho Lau was built in 1825, under Minh Mang, in the middle of a rectangular pond, called Hoc Hai – the Ocean of Study. It was connected with the main waterway system flowing through the Capital City, via a large lake and a canal. The building was placed on an island to protect the contents from a possible fire in another part of the Citadel, as well as keeping insects and moths at bay. In Nguyen times, Hoc Hai pond was by the Path of Mandarins, along which court officials walked to their offices and to Tang Tho Lau to deposit their papers by way of a stone bridge. This path has now beecome a road and the bridge has been enlarged.

One thousand soldiers were drafted into building Tang Tho Lau, under the direction of a general. The brick and stone building had a large ground floor with 11 rooms and an upper floor of seven rooms and two wings. After the abdication of Bao Dai in 1945, the archive building fell into disuse and the books and documents were lost or destroyed. After 1975, the main building was used for relief housing, the interior divided by partitions to create private rooms for several families. The pond was turned into a vegetable plot, its waters polluted by rubbish from the dwellers. The Archive has not fared any better. Years of neglect and misuse have turned this fine building into a sorry state, its walls blackened by dirt and damp with water seepage. A plan exists to restore this area to its former beauty but it is unclear how long this might take, as the relocation of residents is a huge task.

Tang Tho Lau, The National Archives today.

Road into Tang Tho Lau today.

Tinh Tam Lake

Tinh Tam is the most symbolic of the Nguyen royal gardens and still retains its original shape, albeit in a rundown and weed-ridden state, the wild plants vying for space with the thousands of lotus blossoms. Tinh Tam lake was created during the reshaping of the Kim Long river to build the Imperial Canal, in the initial phase of the Capital City, under the reign of Gia Long. In this phase, all buildings within Dai Noi and the outer layer of Hue were surrounded by gardens, ponds and lakes, connected by stone bridges and adorned by little ornamental islands, rare flowers, precious trees and bushes.

All that is left of the Tinh Tam lake pavilion.

Tinh Tam lake was incorporated into a large royal garden laid out under Minh Mang's reign and the whole, constructed by some 8,000 soldiers, was known as the Tinh Tam lake garden, once the largest and most beautiful royal garden of Hue. Emperor Thieu Tri placed this lake garden in his list of 20 best sites of Hue and left a poem singing its praise.

The elaborate water park was surrounded by high walls (long since gone) pierced by four gates. The circumference of the lake is 1.5 kms and it has three linked islands on which there were various structures. Emperor Minh Mang often relaxed in the main pavilion on the largest island. According to Michel Duc Chaigneau, one of the French members of his court:

Steps to the base of the old pavilion, Tinh Tam lake.

'It was a small but beautiful pavilion in the middle of a lake, on a man-made little island full of bushes and flowers. It was small but graceful. The pavilion was richly decorated with ornaments but in a simple style.'

Bamboo, weeping willow and rare flowers once adorned the lakeshore and were planted throughout the garden, but today all is in disarray and the island pavilions have been destroyed. A plan currently exists to restore Tinh Tam lake garden to its former glory but it is not known when, or if, it will be implemented.

Tinh Tam lake today.

Outside the walls

Replica of a dragon boat in front of the boat house Nghenh Luong Dinh.

Apart from the high walls enclosing Hue Capital City on all sides, the Citadel is also surrounded by deep moats with the Perfume River acting as one side of the moat.

The Nguyen Emperors often left their walled Capital for boat trips on the Perfume River, to visit temples along the north bank, to cross over to the south bank for the Nam Giao ceremony, to visit royal tombs or to watch a tiger and elephant fight at the Tiger

Arena – Ho Quyen. To board their boats, the Emperor and his
entourage travelled a short distance from the Ngo Mon Gate to the
river bank, stopping for a rest at the royal boathouse Nghenh
Luong Dinh before embarking on their dragon boats. On the way
to the river, they would pass two structures lying on a straight line
from Ngo Mon to the river bank: the flagpole – Ky Dai and the
Pavilion of Royal Edicts – Phu Van Lau, symbols of royal authority.

Ky Dai from a corner of the Citadel.

Ky Dai – The Flagpole

The Royal Flagpole is an enormous structure built during the sixth year of Gia Long's reign – 1807 – as a symbol of royal authority. It dominates the north bank, towering over the Ngo Mon Gate and is visible from almost anywhere in Hue city. The height of the entire three-tiered base is over 17 metres, and the concrete pole is 37 metres tall. Each tier of the base is like a large terrace, laid with fine Bat Trang tiles and enclosed by ornate iron fences. During the Nguyen epoch, there were gun emplacements on the top tier of the base but this is now left empty.

The Flagpole in 1913.

Originally, the pole was made of two pieces of wood joined together to form a single 30-metre-high pole. In 1846, this was replaced by a single wooden pole 32 metres high.

After this pole broke in the typhoon of 1904, an iron pole was installed, which, in turn, was broken during the fighting of 1945-1947. The 1948 concrete replacement of 37 metres tall is what we see today. The flagpole is the first structure visible outside the Capital City long before the Citadel is reached. The pole flew the yellow Royal flag of the Nguyen Dynasty until 1945, when the flag was raised for the last time at Bao Dai's abdication ceremony in August 1945, before being replaced by that of the Vietnamese Revolutionary Government.

View from Thai Hoa Palace to the Flagpole in 1924.

Phu Van Lau.

Phu Van Lau – Pavilion of Royal Edicts

This structure is a graceful two-story building situated between the flagpole and the boat house, Nghenh Luong Dinh, on the riverbank. It was built under Gia Long as a small hall to display royal edicts, lists of people passing exams and other orders from the Emperor, but in 1819, the modest hall was replaced by the pavilion that we see today. Later, under Minh Mang, it became a ceremonial place. Once the Emperor passed a decree, the scroll containing his orders was carried out of the Imperial Palace in a parade, read out to the assembled public and then placed ceremonially on a board in the pavilion for all to see and obey. The heavy roof and upper storey is supported by strong wooden pillars. In front of the building, two canons face each other. As the pavilion symbolised the power of the Emperor, throughout the Nguyen period, anyone passing the pavilion would have to get off their carts or horses to pay their respects.

Nghenh Luong Dinh – The Boat House

To embark on a boat trip on the Perfume River, the Nguyen Emperor and his royal entourage would travel through the layers of the Capital City, exit through the Ngo Mon gate, pass the Flagpole and the Pavilion of Royal Edicts before reaching a third structure on the river bank called Nghenh Luong Dinh. Here,

Nghenh Luong Dinh – The royal boathouse.

they could rest and enjoy the fresh air from the river, or board the Dragon boats via a set of steps leading down to the edge of the water. Although Nguyen Emperors often travelled on the Perfume River, each time they went on a boat trip was an occasion of commotion and disruption for ordinary people. Not only was the path from Ngo Mon to Nghenh Luong Dinh screened off from the eyes of common people, but river traffic came to a standstill as people had to get out of the way quickly and shelter from the whips of the Imperial Guards. No one dared show their faces as the Royal boat glided past, as any violation would result in severe punishment. One of the French residents in Hue, Dr. Auvray, witnessed one such royal outing when Emperor Tu Duc went out for a hunt upstream. He described the scene vividly in his article published in the Bulletin de la Société de Géographie de Paris in 1883:

> '..Each time the Emperor went out, he left the Citadel to get to the riverside via a covered corridor, there, he embarked on one of the huge boats of many stories that awaited him, as always. These are like floating houses towed by 7 or 8 warships..the river traffic was interrupted to make way for the royal fleet...While the sound of drums announced the approach of the Emperor, the sampans scattered to take refuge among the reed beds by the river banks...'

Thuong Bac Pavilion

Under Emperor Tu Duc, relations between the Nguyen Court and the French Representative were severely strained. European envoys were no longer received inside the Capital City. Under the Emperor's order, in 1875, a group of buildings was built on the North bank of the Perfume River as a venue for court members and the Protocol Ministry to receive visiting Europeans. This group of buildings was given the name of Thuong Bac and placed on a piece of land facing the compound of the French Governor General across the river, on the south bank. Over the years, the original structures of Thuong Bac were severely damaged before being destroyed altogether. In 1936, to commemorate the existence of this venue, a single European-style pavilion was built on its former location, in the middle of an empty space on the north bank, and this is what we see today.

Thuong Bac pavilion.

The Valley of the Tombs

Nguyen Tombs – Palaces of the Afterlife
Thien Tho Lang – The Tomb of Emperor Gia Long
Hieu Lang – The Tomb of Emperor Minh Mang
Xuong Lang – The Tomb of Emperor Thieu Tri
Khiem Lang – The Tomb of Emperor Tu Duc
An Lang – The Tomb of Emperor Duc Duc
Tu Lang – The Tomb of Emperor Dong Khanh
The Tomb of Prince Kien Thai Vuong
Ung Lang – The Tomb of Emperor Khai Dinh

Map labels:

- Hue Capital City
- Thien Mu Pagoda
- Temple of Literature
- Voi re temple
- Tiger Arena
- Tu Duc Tomb
- Hon Chen temple
- Minh Mang Tomb
- Duc Duc tomb
- Nam Giao Platform
- Dong Khanh tomb
- Thieu Tri Tomb
- Khai Dinh Tomb
- Gia Long Tomb

Previous pages: A view from Du Khiem
Pavilion, Tomb of Tu Duc.

The Valley of the Tombs

The building of tombs – *lang* in Vietnamese –
as the palaces of the Afterlife was a uniquely
Nguyen practice. No other Vietnamese Emperor
had bothered with such a grand gesture before
and either made do with small tombs in
the places where they were born or came from,
or had modest temples built and dedicated to
them by local people or family members of later
generations. The Nguyen, on the other hand,
began to search for a suitable location for their
tombs as soon as they came to power. If the
Emperor died too soon to supervise or complete
the building of his tomb, it was the task of the
first son or grandson to finish them. Sometimes,
it took years to find the right location that offered
a combination of elements necessary to ensure
a harmony between Heaven and Earth, or to
complete the modification of the landscape to
achieve this harmony artificially. Emperor Minh
Mang took 14 years and many geomancers to find
the location for his tomb. Emperor Tu Duc did
not take that long to find his location but the
construction process was so hard that the three

thousands soldiers he mobilised to build his tomb revolted against him in the middle of the work in 1866. The rebellion was quickly suppressed, and the construction was finished 16 years before his death. This meant that during his lifetime, Emperor Tu Duc often travelled to his tomb to relax, fish and compose poetry.

There were 13 Nguyen Emperors but only seven grand tombs were built. Two Emperors, Ham Nghi and Duy Tan, were exiled to French overseas territories after they joined the anti-French resistance and were captured. A third, Emperor Thanh Thai was also exiled as he was deemed mentally unstable. Two of these short-term emperors, Thanh Thai and his son Duy Tan, were later re-buried in the An Lang tomb of their father and grandfather, Emperor Duc Duc. Ham Nghi and Bao Dai died in Algeria and France respectively, and were both buried in decent but ordinary graves in France. There have been plans in Vietnam to bring Emperor Ham Nghi's remains back to Hue for reburial either in the same An Lang, or in a separate tomb more worthy of his position in Vietnamese anti-colonial history, but his family has so far refused.

In the spirit of making the royal afterlife comfortable, the Nguyen built their tombs as citadels complete with palaces, gardens and lakes, surrounded by high walls or hills and mountains. The landscape plays a large part in the spiritual defence of the tomb and combines the most auspicious Feng Shui elements to ensure a continuation of the dynasty. The burial site within the tomb is in a walled area, behind solid gates, to keep potential enemies away, a necessary precaution in view of the practice in ancient China and

Dragon motif, Thieu Tri's Tomb.

Mountains on the way to Gia Long tomb, upstream on the Perfume River from Hue.

Civil mandarin, Minh Mang's tomb.

Central path and temple, Minh Mang's tomb.

Court of stone, Tomb of Gia Long.

other Sinicised countries, whereby victorious rivals would dig up their enemies' bodies to wreak revenge on them so that the afterlife of their enemy would be as unsettled as possible. In classical Sinicised cultures this was the worst possible insult.

The Nguyen tombs may differ in architectural style or in the arrangement of buildings, but all strictly followed the design principles of the Imperial Citadel on the north bank of the Perfume River. The tomb began with a royal gate and a body of water, over which, a bridge leads into a grand courtyard, Bai Dinh – Courtyard of Salutation – modelled on the one in front of Thai Hoa Palace in the Imperial Citadel. Here, instead of a full court assembly, similar to those held twice a month in the Imperial Citadel, only two or four rows of stone figures, representing both civil and military mandarins, stand facing each other across the courtyard, backed up by their guards, horses and elephants. Each of the figures was carved from rare stones, with a individualised facial expressions, each different from the next. The clothing of each figure was also meticulously presented in great detail. The men of literature wear long-sleeved robes – their Court attire – adorned by ivory badges of rank and hats with wings, their eyes half-closed in an expression of respect, as no one should look directly at the Emperor during the Court Assembly. The military stone mandarins wear shorter tunics or simpler clothing for ease of movement and all carry weapons. Their eyes, however, are almost fully open, on the look out for trouble. As with a real court assembly, the highest-ranking mandarins were nearest to the Emperor, and the military ones furthest away because of their weapons.

The Terracotta Army of the late Chinese Emperor Qin Shi Huang (c.210 BC) has been greatly admired throughout the world for the uniqueness of each of the 8,000 pieces so far found. Much has been written in praise of their particular facial expressions, different postures and clothing. The Nguyen Courts of Stone, although much smaller in number, possess the same admirable qualities, and arguably more so, for each of the figures was made of stone quarried from a particular mountain, hand carved without a mould. Unlike the Terracotta Army though, the Nguyen stone mandarins are closer to life-size and their numbers are kept to the minimum, one or two of each type, to create a solemn and dignified essence of a royal court, more befitting to a tomb setting.

The next area in the tomb usually has many buildings serving different functions. A House of Stele displays a large stone inscription, which is, in effect, the late Emperor's biography and list of achievements. It is usually erected by the first son or grandson, but in the case of Emperor Tu Duc who did not have a birth son, he composed the text himself. Facing the House of Stele is a temple to house the altar displaying the royal funerary tablet – a plaque bearing the name and Buddhist alias of the late Emperor. This plaque is a symbol of the Emperor's presence in his afterlife. The altar and the temple would be looked after by the late Emperor's concubines who moved to the tomb as soon as the Emperor passed away. They lived there with the sole duty of maintaining the temple and lighting incense sticks to worship the ethereal form of their late master. By tradition, the private effects of the late Emperor would also be on display. Some of these are extremely valuable both in cultural and materialistic terms. The late Emperor's concubines and the soldiers guarding the tombs lived in retirement in several buildings behind the temple and continued to serve the late Emperor until their deaths.

Some of the Nguyen royal tombs have extra buildings designed as imperial palaces in this middle part, which were for the emperors to reside in while overseeing the construction of their tombs. In the case of Emperor Tu Duc, his tomb was where he lived for months on end, to work, rest and get away from the official court in the Imperial Citadel which was subject to constant pressure from the French. The last area of a tomb complex is where the late Emperor and his queen were buried. It is usually at the back of the tomb, well protected in a walled enclosure and behind locked iron gates.

All the tombs were placed in a hilly area on the upper reaches of the Perfume River, the furthest is the tomb of Emperor Gia Long, 16 kms from the Capital City of Hue and the nearest is the tomb of Emperor Duc Duc, almost across the river from the Imperial Citadel. The placement of these tombs, on a stretch of hills running along the Perfume River, is comparable to the Valley of the Kings along the Egyptian Nile and, as such, inspires an apt name for this area in Hue: the Valley of the Tombs.

Tu Duc's tablets.

Gate to Khiem Cung, Tu Duc's living quarters, Tu Duc's tomb.

The seven grand tombs are:

Thien Tho Lang belonging to Emperor Gia Long
Hieu Lang belonging to Emperor Minh Mang
Xuong Lang belonging to Emperor Thieu Tri
Khiem Lang belonging to Emperor Tu Duc
An Lang belonging to Emperor Duc Duc
Tu Lang belonging to Emperor Dong Khanh
Ung Lang belonging to Emperor Khai Dinh

In addition, there are a number of tombs for lesser royals, almost as grand in architecture and design, which were built near or within the grounds of the grand tombs. One such example is that of Prince Kien Thai Vuong, Tu Duc's favourite brother and birth father of two of the three boys that Tu Duc adopted as sons, and who later became Emperors Kien Phuc and Dong Khanh. Prince Kien Thai Vuong was also the birth father of another Emperor, Ham Nghi, who was not adopted by Tu Duc but was later chosen by the Court.

When Emperor Bao Dai abdicated in 1945, one of the terms he requested and had accepted was that the new government would look after the royal tombs and temples. However, bad weather, several wars and many battles over the decades has meant that the tombs inevitably fell into disrepair, with some buildings razed to the ground, and others damaged beyond repair. Since the late 1980s and early 1990s, efforts have been intensified by the Hue Monuments Conservation Center, in conjunction with Japanese, French, Polish and German initiatives and other institutions, to restore the tombs to their former glory. At the same time, archaeological work has taken place at several sites. Some of the tombs have regained much of their former beauty, such as the elegant Khiem Lang, Tu Duc's Tomb, the dignified Hieu Lang, Minh Mang's tomb, or the opulent Ung Lang, Khai Dinh's Tomb, while restoration works are still ongoing at those most damaged by time and war, such as Gia Long's Tomb. All the tombs are included in the UNESCO World Heritage list for Hue.

Gia Long's tomb is in the most ruinous state.

Today, for historians, as well as for discerning scholars and cultural tourists, a visit to the tombs is just as important as one to the Imperial Citadel itself, as, from their layout and architectural style, we can learn much about the Nguyen Dynasty and, more surprisingly, the state of affairs between Vietnam and France at the time the tombs were built. By looking at the tombs chronologically, we can almost see how the Nguyen were feeling against the background of French intervention in Vietnam. The symmetrical, scholarly style of Minh Mang's tomb displays an obvious hankering for a more orderly past, while the enemy was beating at the door and classical values were severely threatened. The romantic beauty of Tu Duc's tomb represents a desire to sidestep a turbulent period when the French were exerting heavy pressure on Vietnam and the court. The Europeanised style and building materials of the Dong Khanh and Khai Dinh tombs signify an acceptance of the new order and the embrace of modern values. Whatever the style, however, the Nguyen Tombs were meant to be not the final resting places for the Emperors but their palaces of the Afterlife.

Dong Khanh's tomb.

Nguyen Tombs – Palaces of the Afterlife

As all the tombs were built on the upper reaches of the Perfume River, visitors can travel by boat from the centre of Hue to their nearby piers, and continue the journey on foot to reach these tombs. The pleasant and leisurely journey on the river can take up to the best part of a day, even just to visit a few of them. A road journey is easier, although much less enjoyable. Either way, it is only possible to visit some, not all seven in one day, for each one has many groups of buildings spread over a vast area and each building, in turn, contains so many decorative details that it would be remiss not to linger to absorb their unique beauty and execution. The best times of the day to visit the tombs are at dawn and at sunset when the soft light adds a dreamy quality to the ethereal atmosphere.

A boat journey back to the centre of Hue at sunset allows visitors to reach the area around Trang Tien Bridge just as the river comes alive with night-time activities and the little boats moored along the Perfume River and its canals light their lanterns to await their visitors. It is the moment when, once upon a time, a Hue lady of the night would start singing her enticing songs to invite guests aboard for an evening of feasting and pleasure on the river. In the more recent past, the boat songs might come from the radio or other electronic device but the lyrics would still be the same, either a praise for the many facets of Hue's beauty or a lament for a long-gone past. Today, the singing does not always mean an invitation for pleasure; it is merely a cultural performance for those visitors who have discovered the delightful experience of a night boat trip.

Thien Tho Lang – The Tomb of Emperor Gia Long

This is the furthest, the most damaged and the hardest tomb to reach, although it is only 16 kms from the centre of Hue. Situated in a pine forest, with trees lining the long winding path from the riverbank to the gate of the tomb, Thien Tho Lang occupies an extensive area of 28 km² and encompasses a group of 42 hills. It is a complex of many structures that includes smaller tombs of royal family members. Unlike many later Nguyen tombs, Gia Long's tomb does not have a surrounding wall. The geomancers decided, instead, that the hills would form a natural wall of 11,234 metres in circumference to protect the hilly land within. The Emperor's grave

Pier for the 'ferry' to Gia Long's Tomb.

Dawn on Huong (Perfume) river.

Damaged obelisk at the Gia Long Tomb.

and that of his queen occupy the top of the biggest of these inner hills. Queen Thua Thien Cao was not just his First Spouse but a faithful companion who accompanied him for many years, first into exile and then in his many campaigns against the Tay Son. She was the mother of his first two sons, the first of whom died young and the other, Prince Canh, once travelled to the French court in Paris on his behalf at the age of four, but died in his late teens. Emperor Minh Mang was his son by another queen.

It took six years to build the tomb, from 1814, the year Queen Thua Thien Cao died, to 1820, when the Emperor himself died. The tomb was completed by his fourth surviving son and successor, Emperor Minh Mang, who also composed the biography engraved on the royal stele. According to court documents, Emperor Gia Long rode an elephant to inspect the location and selected it on the recommendation of his best Feng Shui expert, who suggested that the harmonious landscape would ensure that the late Emperor would benefit from the good air purified by the pine forest, and that the Nguyen family would be blessed with good fortune for ten thousand years. Emperor Gia Long and some of his sons came to stay at the site several times to supervise its construction.

Time, typhoons, flood and wars contributed to turn this once fine complex into a sorry ruin which was left abandoned until 2007, when the Hue Monuments Conservation Center began an extensive restoration programme to make the tomb accessible to visitors. However, at the time of writing, access was still rather difficult. At the moment,

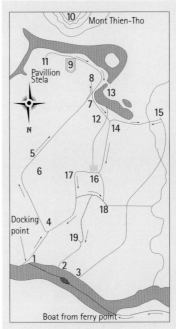

Gia Long Tomb
(Source: BAVH No. 3 Jul–Sept 1923)

1. Nearest point into the Tomb
2. Alternative docking point
3. Alternative docking point
4. Former guard-post
5. Direct route to Gia Long's Temple
6. Tomb of Prince Quang Hung
7. Cross-roads
8. Minh Thanh temple
9. Thien Tho: Burial ground of Gia Long and his Queen Thua Thien Cao
10. Court of Stone
11. Stele House
12. Royal Grave
13. Temple for Grandmother
14. Temple for Gia Long's 2nd Queen
15. Royal Grave
16. Grave of Gia Long's mother
17. Royal Grave
18. Royal Grave
19. Royal Grave

The landscape surrounding the Gia Long tomb.

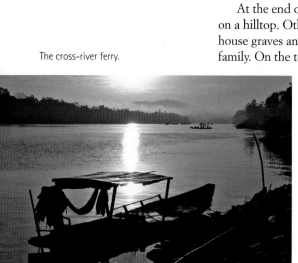

The cross-river ferry.

Ruins – Tomb of Gia Long.

it is only possible to arrive by boat, either as a single journey of 18 kms from Hue along the river, or by travelling 16 kms by road and then taking a boat, or two depending on the mood of the boatmen. If they are agreeable, one boat can take you to near the beginning of the path to the tomb, otherwise you need to take a so-called ferry, not much bigger than a canoe across the river, and then negotiate for a second boat to travel a few kilometres upstream. At the point nearest to the tomb, the boatman deposits his client on a patch of sand, next to a large concrete pier, now in ruins, and then, the visitor must walk, or grab a lift on the back of a motorbike along a bumpy road through a dense pine forest to the tomb complex some 1.5-2 kilometres away. The path was once lined by two rows of 85 obelisks but today only two survive. It is important that you negotiate with the boatman to wait for your return for there is no other way to travel back. Until the way into the tomb is more accessible, Gia Long tomb, although hauntingly beautiful, should only be attempted by those who are reasonably agile and have a strong sense of adventure.

At the end of the road, the main part of the tomb lies on the left, on a hilltop. Other parts of the complex, extensive, but still in ruins, house graves and temples dedicated to other members of the royal family. On the top of the hill, we come first to the Minh Thanh temple dedicated to the Emperor and his Queen. This is where Emperor Gia Long's belongings – such as his saddle, his belt, the hat that he wore into battle against the Tay Son, and his court robes he wore at court later – were once on display but have now vanished. Today, it has only the two funerary tablets of the late Emperor and his Queen.

From the temple, we go down some steps, through a newly decorated ornate gate and turn left toward the burial area and the stele house, and arrive at the side of the Courtyard of Salutation. Here, a court of 10 stone mandarins stands to attention, backed by their horses, elephants and imperial guards. These stone figures were placed in the tomb in 1833, two years after Emperor Minh Mang approved their design and ordered the artists to begin. He was so satisfied with the quality of the work that he rewarded the carvers handsomely, according to court documents. Unfortunately, five years later, it was reported to him that a piece of rein on one of the stone horses was missing. A court inquest was opened and the two mandarins responsible for guarding the tomb were severely caned in punishment, one receiving 60 strokes and the other 40, regardless of the fact that the missing piece might have been caused by lightning damage during a storm. Today, only a few of the original stone mandarins remain, their number made up by newly-carved figures, who look somewhat similar but lack the fine lines and patina of the older ones.

Minh Thanh Temple.

In front of the Courtyard of Salutation is a pond in the shape of a half-moon that can be reached by a set of steps, flanked on both sides by stone dragons. From the court of stone, we ascend six tiers of terraces, heavily decorated with the royal symbols of dragons and clouds, to the royal burial site at the top of the hill. Here, the graves of the late Emperor and his queen were placed side by side in the shade of two adjoining houses with sloping roofs. As we will see again at later royal tombs, the graves of Emperor Gia Long and his queen were housed within a walled area, shielded by ornate royal screens, and locked behind heavy bronze gates. These were originally wood but, on the orders of Emperor Thieu Tri in 1845, they were replaced by the bronze ones that we see today. In 2009, while renovation work was going on, it was seen that the two doors and the inside of the walls were still pockmarked by bullet holes, an eloquent testimony to a disturbing past when wars showed respect for no one.

Corridor of Minh Thanh Temple.

Emperor Gia Long's remains were interred in this walled area on 28th May 1820, after a long funeral lasting three days. A Nguyen royal burial ceremony was an elaborate affair with many pauses to perform certain rituals, or to wait for the next auspicious moment. The last set of rituals began with the writing of the funerary tablet, a solemn occasion with many stages, from the preparation of the ink to the placing of the tablet on the altar, and, finally, the untying of a length of white silk to symbolically release the soul into its new dwelling. Each stage was performed according to the royal Rulebook, at a precise time.

The two royal graves sit on top of the largest of the 42 hills, with 14 hills visible to the left, 14 to the right, and six more hills behind. On top of two of these hills are the Minh Thanh temple and the Stele House. The stele that Emperor Minh Mang erected to record his father's biography is housed in a simple pavilion with a wooden roof, a new construction remade according to the original design.

Stone animals, Gia Long Tomb.

Gia Long's funerary stele.

The inscription on the large stone stele recalls the hard years that Emperor Gia Long spent in exile while struggling against the Tay Son and the stages in the campaign that eventually brought him to the throne. Interestingly, it describes specifically the time he spent in Bangkok, when he felt 'similar to a black leopard being kept in a cage, or a dragon existing at the bottom of a deep well'.

Within the grounds of Gia Long's Tomb, are six other tombs belonging to his second queen, Emperor Minh Mang's birth mother, the late Nguyen Lords and some of their wives, as well as his mother, Queen Mother Hung To Hieu Khuong. The whole site is huge and difficult to walk around in places, although in some areas the path is beautifully paved with red bricks. In the section belonging to other members of the Nguyen family, most of the buildings are still in ruins, the ground littered with shattered pieces of ceramic. Though broken, the pieces show a high level of craftsmanship, with colours as vivid as when they were made. The square pond and large lake remain almost inaccessible due to the flooded ditches or muddy fields. The pond currently serves as a watering hole for a herd of cows grazing in the fields nearby. A walk around the area reveals some more delightful surprises, such as hidden steps leading to beautiful but tarnished screens or intimate courtyards. However, for some, scrambling over the rough ground may be too arduous and one must save energy for the journey back, which is no less difficult than the journey in.

Detail of stone carving on a screen.

Graves of Gia Long and his Queen.

Steps up to the burial area.

Minh Thanh Temple roof, Tomb of Gia Long.

Thien Tho Huu tomb, Tomb of Gia Long.

Ceramic fragments, Tomb of Gia Long.

A ruined wall.

Nevertheless, a visit to Gia Long's tomb is a unique and delightful experience that is not to be missed if you have the time and the stamina. To see how the founder of the Nguyen dynasty created his palace of afterlife is to understand how the last surviving Nguyen Lord managed to win through in the end. To experience the solemn but dignified environment of his final destination is to appreciate how he came to build such a controversial but remarkable dynasty that lasted almost a century and half, and, at the same time, left an entrancing cultural heritage that we can still enjoy to this day.

Rooftop of Minh Thanh temple.

Gate into temple area, Minh Mang's tomb.

Hieu Lang – The tomb of Emperor Minh Mang

Situated in the Hieu Son hills, upstream of Hue on the left bank of the Perfume River, this is the best example of the Sino classical style of Nguyen tombs in Hue. Seven years after Emperor Minh Mang ascended the throne in 1821 to succeed his father, the late Emperor Gia Long, he appointed mandarins from the Ministry of Astronomy and the Ministry of Rites to look for a favourable location for his tomb. It took years for them to complete this task, until finally in 1840, mandarins from the Ministry of Astronomy pinpointed the place, and drew up a plan according to the directions of the Mandarins of Rites. They then signed a petition and presented the plan to Emperor Minh Mang who approved their choice and ordered the Ministry of Works to begin construction. Unfortunately, he did not live long after that and the completion of the tomb was left to his son and successor, Emperor Thieu Tri, a fact which gave the tomb its name Hieu Lang, which can be loosely translated as 'the Tomb by the Loyal Good Son'. Emperor Thieu Tri conscripted 10,000 soldiers for the task and the tomb was ready less than one year later. The body of Emperor Minh Mang was interred in his tomb in 1841 but it took another two years for all the other structures within the grounds to be completed.

From an aerial perspective, it can be seen that the layout of Minh Mang's tomb resembles the shape of a womb. This deliberately created shape probably symbolised that the tomb would be a nurturing place to await a good rebirth, according to Feng Shui principles.

Although Minh Mang's tomb is the second furthest royal mausoleum in the Valley of the Tombs, unlike Gia Long's it is possible to get to its gate by road. Once there, it is easy to walk around and enjoy the breathtakingly beautiful scenery.

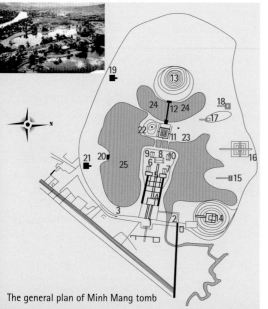

The general plan of Minh Mang tomb

1. Great Entrance
2. Left Gate
3. Right Gate
4. Stele House
5. Hien Duc Gate
6. West cult temple of Military mandarins
7. East cult temple of Civil mandarins
8. Sung An Temple
9. Lodging for royal concubines
10. Servants' quarters
11. Minh Lau-Pavillion of Light
12. Thong Minh Chinh Truc Bridge
13. The Grave & the underground part of grave
14. Truy Tu House
15. Quan Lan House
16. Linh Phuong Pavillion
17. Tame deer compound
18. Left lodging for the royal followers
19. Right lodging for the royal followers
20. Hu Hoai waterside bower
21. The storehouse
22. Fishing Pavillion
23. Nghenh Luong Bower
24. Tan Nguyet Lake
25. Trung Minh Lake

Source: Hue Monuments Conservation Center.

Hieu Lang is a symmetrical citadel with a wall of 1,750 metres surrounding a spacious area that includes a vast lake, several landscaped gardens and 40 buildings. The latter are arranged on the typically classical principle of three on both sides of a straight 700-metre-long path, running from the gate to the rear walled enclosure, where the graves of the Emperor and his queens were housed. Halfs of the length of this path was built like a bridge over the lake. To access the tomb complex, we first go through the Great Entrance – Dai Hong Mon built as a classic three-door gate covered by 24 small roofs arranged in tiers, and decorated with the royal symbols of dragons and clouds. The Great Entrance is a brick construction 9 metres high by 12 metres wide and divided into three sections. The central entrance was, as is usual, reserved for the Emperor, or in this case, his coffin and it was sealed up after the funeral. The gate leads to a long straight path spanning a pond of lotus blossoms, a configuration replicating the route to Thai Hoa Palace in the Imperial Citadel. Following the central path, before we get to the main lake, we reach the Stele House. Here, a large stone inscription of 2,500 characters records the biography of the late Emperor. The stele measures 3m x 1.60m and was erected by Emperor Thieu Tri to inform later generations of Emperor Minh Mang's achievements, as well as recording the layout and the history of the tomb.

From the Stele House, we descend the steps, through a ceremonial gate identical to those seen at the Imperial Citadel. The columns supporting the horizontal band on top of this gate have carved reliefs of dragons and clouds. The horizontal band is divided into panels richly decorated in Phap Lam enamel with the typical royal motif of dragons, and symbols of a scholar's leisure pursuits: wine bottles and flowers of the four seasons. From here, we continue on the path across Trung Minh lake. The beginning of the bridge across the lake is one of the best places to enjoy the overall sense of beauty and tranquillity. Like a vivid painting executed with the utmost skill, the lake extends gracefully on both sides of the path, surrounded by pine and frangipani trees, its blueish green water reflecting the landscape like a faithful mirror. On the far side, an ornate viewing pavilion completes the picture of serenity.

Pavilion, Minh Mang's tomb.

Lake at Minh Mang's tomb.

Temple house, Minh Mang's tomb.

Temple, Minh Mang's tomb.

Temple interior, Minh Mang's tomb.

Minh Mang's daybed.

Ahead on the path is the Courtyard of Salutation where two rows of stone mandarins stand to attention. They are flanked by two temples dedicated to the Emperor's own military and civil mandarins. Beyond this is Sung-An temple, housing funerary tablets of the late Emperor and his Queen. In the early 20th century, some of Emperor Minh Mang's personal effects were on display here, including a silver tea service on a tray inlaid with ivory, his two jade sceptres, several vases and Phap Lam incense burners. There were also some oddly out-of-place European ceramics that might have been added at a later date by the Europeanised Emperors. None of these artefacts remain today except for a day bed that Minh Mang was said to have used in his life time. On the other side of Sung-An temple are the two quarters reserved for the former concubines and the servants; the concubines had the duty of lighting incense sticks on the Emperor's altar in the temple, while the servants had other duties around the tomb.

Roof Dragon – Minh Mang's tomb.

Further along the centre path is the Minh Lau – Pavilion of Light, a moon-viewing pavilion embraced by a crescent lake representing a new moon. A bridge leads across the lake to a set of 33 steps, at the top of which is the entrance to the resting place of the Emperor's earthly remains. Here, the graves of the Emperor and his Queens are protected by a large circular walled structure resembling a walled citadel and locked bronze gates. After his funeral, Minh Mang's coffin was carried into this circular citadel through a tunnel, buried deep inside the mound, and the tunnel was sealed.

Phap Lam panels – Minh Mang's tomb.

Over time, some smaller structures along the central path have been damaged or destroyed but many still remain scattered throughout the extensive grounds. Some have extraordinary Phap Lam decoration, Emperor Minh Mang's favourite medium. The Phap Lam panels often carry poems in Chinese characters or both poems and motifs. There are 600 panels of this kind at the tomb.

Doors, Minh Mang's tomb.

As a strong Emperor who had organised Vietnam into an orderly nation with a clear legal system, while maintaining a firm stance against foreign intervention, Minh Mang's earthly remains rest securely in the walled citadel, while his ethereal being enjoys the exquisitely beautiful landscape of the tomb. Unfortunately, while Minh Mang was and still is appreciated by most Vietnamese as a nationalistic king, to the rest of the world, his reputation remains somewhat tarnished by a Eurocentric perception of him as a King who did little except inflict great harm on missionaries and Christianity in Vietnam.

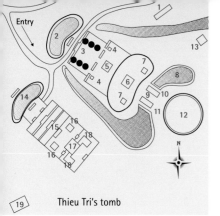

Thieu Tri's tomb

1. Guard House
2. Lake
3. Court of Stone
4. Lions
5. Stele House
6. Duc Hinh Pavilion
7. Obelisks
8. Lake
9. Bridge Chanh Trung
10. Bridge
11. Bridge
12. Thieu Tri's Grave
13. Pavilion
14. Lake
15. Gate
16. Temple
17. and 18. Houses
19. Queen's Grave

Xuong Lang – The tomb of Emperor Thieu Tri

This tomb was built entirely by his son and successor, Emperor Tu Duc, who was also responsible for his own tomb, the most elegant of all Nguyen Tombs in Hue. Xuong Lang is located on the right bank of the Perfume River, in the village of Cu Chanh, Thuy Bang commune, Huong Thuy district, about 8 kms from the centre of Hue City. The most remarkable feature of the tomb is that it was built facing Northwest, an unusual choice according to Sino-Vietnamese Feng Shui principles.

Emperor Thieu Tri reigned for only seven years and did not have enough time or, according to some historical documents, was not so interested in building his tomb. Before he died at the age of 41, he allegedly told his son and successor, Emperor Tu Duc, not to spend too much money or to subject the people to too much hardship in its construction. These last words were engraved on the royal stele that his son erected at this tomb, along with his confirmation that he had indeed kept the tomb simple. Perhaps, thanks to this instruction, the tomb looks more relaxing and blends in better with the surrounding landscape.

The architects of Xuong Lang followed the same plan as Minh Mang's tomb, but modified it to suit the location. Like the Gia Long tomb but different from Minh Mang's it does not have a surrounding wall, relying instead on the natural landscape to define the outer limits of its grounds. As dictated by the Nguyen

Overall view of the tomb.

Temple, Tomb of Thieu Tri.

Rulebook, Thieu Tri's tomb layout followed that of all royal tombs, beginning with an ornate gate leading to a Court of Stone, a Stele House, temples, gardens, lakes and ponds, and ending with a walled citadel to house the graves of the late Emperor and his Queen. All were to a more modest scale than the tombs of Gia Long and Minh Mang. One example is the Court of Stone, where only six stone mandarins, two horses and two elephants, stand at attention in two rows facing each other across the Courtyard of Salutation. As at Minh Mang's, Thieu Tri's tomb also has a crescent lake embracing a circular walled citadel called Buu Thanh where the late Emperor's remains were kept. To access the citadel, three ornamental bridges span the crescent lake and a set of steps leads up to Buu Thanh. Like his father Minh Mang, and his son Tu Duc, Emperor Thieu Tri was a poet who composed many famous poems, some of which are recorded in Phap Lam on the 450 panels incorporated into the structure of the buildings dotting the site. Others were carved, gilded and inlaid with mother-of-pearl on wood in the interiors of the tomb buildings.

Burial area at Thieu Tri Tomb.

The entire construction took only three months to complete and the remains of Emperor Thieu Tri were buried in his tomb eight months after he died. Later, Thieu Tri's tomb also housed the graves of his mother, his queen and several of his children. To make up for the relatively simple tomb, Emperor Tu Duc composed a lengthy inscription of 2,500 characters, engraved on a large stele, to record his father's life and achievements. In this inscription, Emperor Tu Duc also listed the 10 collections of essays and poems that the late Emperor composed during his life, with each including hundreds of essays and poems.

Top of stele – Tomb of Thieu Tri.

Although small, Thieu Tri's tomb has a natural, majestic beauty. Its smaller scale allows the visitor to obtain an excellent overview of how the structures integrate with the landscape. The less fussy decoration also earns praise for showcasing the most original Vietnamese art forms of the 19th century – Phap Lam. Today, Thieu Tri tomb is less known than those of his predecessor Minh Mang and successor Tu Duc, probably because it has not been fully renovated. The still half-ruined state of the tomb, however, imparts a haunting and melancholy beauty that will appeal to those who value originality and authenticity over well-polished grandeur.

Court of stone, Tomb of Thieu Tri.

Bat, dragons and Phap Lam panels, Tomb of Thieu Tri.

A stone madarin, Tomb of Thieu Tri.

Faded door, Tomb of Thieu Tri.

Khiem Lang – The Tomb of Emperor Tu Duc

This is perhaps the best known of all the Nguyen tombs for its unique beauty and unashamed romanticism. It was also the place to which Tu Duc escaped whenever the pressure at court became too much. Here, for 16 years after its completion, the Emperor lived for long periods of time to work, relax and compose poetry, surrounded by his concubines and court entourage.

Khiem Lang – *khiem* meaning modesty – is located 8 kms from the centre of Hue City on the right bank of the Perfume River, in Thuong Ba village, Thuy Xuan Commune. It is the second tomb that Tu Duc supervised from conception to completion, the first being that of his father, Emperor Thieu Tri. Unlike Thieu Tri's, Tu Duc's tomb was elaborately executed in every detail, and designed to be a peaceful, relaxing place set in a forest of pine and frangipani trees, a perfect environment to encourage an escapist frame of mind

As the longest-serving Emperor, reigning for over 36 years, Tu Duc had plenty of time to plan and design his tomb with the result that all details of the tomb complex were made according to his own specifications. As it was also his occasional residence away from the Imperial Citadel, Tu Duc's tomb carries more traces of the Emperor than anywhere else in Hue, apart from the Forbidden Purple City. Tu Duc took over from his father Thieu Tri at a difficult point in Vietnamese history, when French pressure was mounting and internal discontent reached an unusually high level. He was also considered a usurper in some quarters of the Royal Family, being a second son who was appointed king instead of his elder brother, Hong Bao, a traditional inheritor by primogeniture succession rules. The resentment boiled over in 1851 when Hong

A gate in Tu Duc's tomb.

Roof pediments, Tomb of Tu Duc.

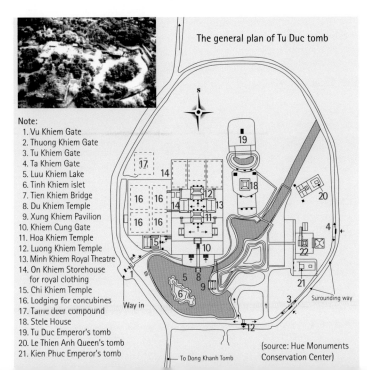

The general plan of Tu Duc tomb

Note:
1. Vu Khiem Gate
2. Thuong Khiem Gate
3. Tu Khiem Gate
4. Ta Khiem Gate
5. Luu Khiem Lake
6. Tinh Khiem islet
7. Tien Khiem Bridge
8. Du Khiem Temple
9. Xung Khiem Pavilion
10. Khiem Cung Gate
11. Hoa Khiem Temple
12. Luong Khiem Temple
13. Minh Khiem Royal Theatre
14. On Khiem Storehouse
    for royal clothing
15. Chi Khiem Temple
16. Lodging for concubines
17. Tame deer compound
18. Stele House
19. Tu Duc Emperor's tomb
20. Le Thien Anh Queen's tomb
21. Kien Phuc Emperor's tomb

Way in

Surounding way

To Dong Khanh Tomb

(source: Hue Monuments Conservation Center)

Ceramic art between roofs, Tu Duc's tomb.

Bao staged a coup against Tu Duc, an event later known as the Hong Bao rebellion. Failing to dislodge his brother from the throne, Prince Hong Bao committed suicide. Royal resentment lingered in some quarters throughout Tu Duc's reign at a time when hundreds of small rebellions were taking place across the country and relations with the French were deteriorating at an alarming rate.

Against this turbulent background, Emperor Tu Duc began to build his tomb in 1864 with an army of 3,000 men, much less than the number that Emperor Thieu Tri used to build his father Minh Mang's tomb. However, the men were made to work relentlessly hard while some secret societies in Hue actively encouraged them to express their resentment. In 1866, their anger exploded into another coup against Emperor Tu Duc, this time with a plan to put another of his brothers on the throne. The rebellion was quickly suppressed, the coup leaders were executed and building work resumed at the tomb.

When the tomb was finished, it was named Khiem Cung – the Palace of Modesty, the entire tomb complex being renamed Khiem Lang after Tu Duc's death. The name Khiem Cung was kept for one area, the palaces where Emperor Tu Duc lived whenever he came to visit. With modesty as the theme, all the main buildings in the tomb grounds had names beginning or ending with *khiem*, such as Khiem Cung Mon – Gate to the Palace of Modesty, or Xung Khiem Pavilion looking over lake Luu Khiem, where the Emperor came to fish and compose poetry. There were 50 different structures scattered asymmetrically throughout the extensive grounds, some of them built on high terraces, others facing sideways such as Y Khiem and Tri Khiem palaces in the concubine residential quarter, now in ruins.

Today, crossing the modest Vu Khiem gate into the tomb is like entering a different world where time stands still and troubles are left behind. The first spectacular tableau spreading out in front of the visitor is the shimmering Luu Khiem lake, accompanied by the elegant Du Khiem and Xung Khiem Pavilions. The calm blue-green water of the lake reflects the sky in its ever-changing moods,

Xung Khiem pavilion, Tomb of Tu Duc.

A bridge, Tomb of Tu Duc.

Khiem Cung Courtyard.

while the wooden pavilions cast trembling soft shadows over the water. Pine trees by the lakeside and flower bushes on the little island in the middle gently complement the picture to create a scene of utter tranquillity. Before reaching the lakeside and the way into the main area of the tomb, there is an interesting group of ruins on the left, namely the former Chi Khiem temple, once dedicated to the lesser queens, today only jagged walls and broken doorways.

Further along the path, opposite the lake and on the left is an imposing gate at the top of some steps – the entrance into Khiem Cung, the former royal residence. This spacious area houses many buildings that Emperor Tu Duc used as his own living and working space. Two long buildings facing each other across a courtyard behind this gate served as offices for Tu Duc's mandarins, who accompanied him here to continue their courtly affairs. Next comes Hoa Khiem Palace, the Emperor's former office and now a temple displaying the funerary tablets of the late Emperor and his Queen. Behind this building is another spacious courtyard leading to Tu Duc's private palace, Luong Khiem, with one side of this quarter opening onto a set of steps leading down to the concubine quarter of Tri Khiem and Y Khiem, adjacent to a garden where the Emperor kept deer and other animals.

Ruins of the Concubines' quarter, Tomb of Tu Duc.

After Tu Duc died and the tomb became his final resting place, Khiem Cung was still maintained as a residential area. This was a fortuitous, or carefully calculated, decision, as not long after Tu Duc's death, Hue and the Nguyen court were

Hoa Khiem Palace, Tomb of Tu Duc.

plunged into conflict with the French that resulted in Emperor Ham Nghi leaving the Imperial Citadel in July 1885 to form an anti-French movement in the mountains. The Citadel was burned and plundered immediately after that and many royal residences were destroyed or damaged. Suddenly homeless, the Queen Mother and grandmother, along with their entourage, came to live in Khiem Cung for several months while their palaces were being rebuilt.

Even before then, somewhat incongruously for a tomb, opposite the concubine quarter and forming a connection between Hoa Khiem and Luong Khiem palaces was a working theatre – Minh Khiem Duong. This provided necessary entertainment for Emperor Tu Duc who occasionally lived and held court here for 16 years. Today, Minh Khiem Duong is a large hall panelled in dark wood with the stage occupying one end and the royal seating area the other, raised up on a balcony covered by embroidered drapes. The ceiling of this theatre is most unusual and fascinating, bearing as it does a map of the night sky, complete with the sun, the moon and the stars, all deeply carved and painted white against a background of dark blue. Minh Khiem Duong is now used for plays and dance performances, and as a store for theatrical costumes, which can be hired by visitors who want to be photographed as kings and queens in a royal setting.

Some personal items belonging to Tu Duc are still displayed in his Luong Khiem palace, now used as a temple for his mother, Lady Tu Du. In this palace, and also in Hoa Khiem, hanging high on the wooden pillars supporting the roofs are 24 unique glass paintings. Some are part of the priceless collection of 20 original glass paintings that Emperor Thieu Tri commissioned from China to illustrate his famous poems praising the beauty of 20 locations in

The Theatre, Tomb of Tu Duc.

Royal seating area in the Theatre, Tu Duc's Tomb.

Theatre ceiling, Tu Duc's Tomb.

Hue, such as Thien Mu Pagoda, Tinh Tam lake, or the Thieu Phuong royal garden in the Imperial Citadel. The glass panels were painted on the back with the details and characters painted first and in reverse, so that from the front, the paintings and their poems read correctly. Each of the glass paintings contains both a landscape and a poem and is displayed in a thick gilded frame, with the title of the painting or the accompanying poem engraved in gold characters at the top. These glass paintings are priceless work of arts in many ways, not just for their technique and artistry but also for preserving a record of sites in Hue and the Imperial Citadel, many of which no longer exist.

The paintings displayed at Tu Duc's tomb are part of sets which have been broken up and are partially displayed at The Museum of Royal Antiquities, at Dien Tho, the Queen Mother's quarter in the

Glass painting, Tu Duc's Tomb.

Glass painting, Tu Duc's Tomb.

Imperial Citadel, and other royal tombs. Among these, those from the set of 20 poems by Thieu Tri are the most valuable as they were specially created for the Nguyen court, whereas the others are ready-made paintings by Chinese 19th century artists depicting classical Chinese stories, without accompanying poems, brought back by Vietnamese embassies from their travels in Qing China. Some of the glass paintings are thought to have been created in Vietnam by Vietnamese artists but this has not yet been proven.

In 2005, archaeological excavations in the now-ruined concubine quarter, discovered that there might have been four groups of residences, instead of two as previously thought. Thus it appears that the groups of houses were separated from each other by tall walls. During their study, the Vietnamese archaeologists also found that the concubines' houses were connected with each other and the rest of the tomb by paths and walkways, but that all exits from the area to the outside were sealed up after the Emperor died, thereby restricting the concubines to living the rest of their lives confined to their quarter.

Retracing our steps back to the main path by the lake, and proceeding left as we face the lake, we find the customary Courtyard of Salutation and the House of Stele. This stele is the largest of all the Nguyen stele and bears a long inscription of 4,935 characters written by Emperor Tu Duc himself on the completion of his tomb in 1867. On it, he recounted that he was a feeble child who was not looked after very well by his nurse after his mother fell ill for many months following his birth. During childhood, he was often ill and his life was threatened more than once by these bouts of ill health. Even so, he acknowledged that he had enjoyed a privileged life with a serious mother and a kind and doting father. Discussing the later part of his life, Tu Duc lamented the fact that he was too weak to achieve anything remarkable in his lifetime and that his nation had been conquered with him unable to regain it because of his weakness. Tu Duc also explained that he had no birth son and that he chose to adopt three sons so that there would be someone to manage the affairs of the State and to carry on his plans for the nation. To end this long autobiography, Tu Duc argued that people have passed harsh judgment on certain ancient kings because they expected someone in such a supreme position to possess certain superhuman qualities. Instead, he reminded the reader that it was for the celestial being(s) in heaven to choose on whom to bestow such virtues, and that successes were not entirely the result of human

Gateway from Concubines' quarter to Luong Khiem Palace.

Inside the ruins of the Concubines' quarter.

Close-up of stele, Tu Duc's tomb.

Tu Duc's grave.

efforts. His knowledge was too limited to achieve any grand project, his feeble physique did not allow him to adequately complete the important and considerable duties that he was required to carry out, but he insisted that he had done everything with sincerity and honesty in order to achieve peace for the country. What he had done was, in his own words, to accept voluntary humiliation in order to bring peace to his kingdom. Tu Duc concluded with an explanation that, in order for him to express this humiliation, he had chosen to place his tomb in a solitary location in the village of Duong Xuan.

At the back of the Stele House is the burial quarter for the Emperor, his lone grave placed within a walled enclosure behind bronze gates. Unlike the practice of his predecessors, his queen was buried separately in another walled enclosure, across a stream feeding into the main lake Luu Khiem. It is rumoured that when he died, Tu Duc was taken into his tomb by a secret tunnel and that he was buried with a treasure but this has never been verified. Also buried within the grounds of Tu Duc's Tomb was Emperor Kien Phuc's remains, one of Tu Duc's adopted sons who reigned only for a short time in 1884. His tomb was placed on the far side of the grounds, on an elevation, next to a temple housing his funerary tablet and marked by a plaque.

Detail of screen, Tu Duc's tomb.

An Lang – The Tomb of Emperor Duc Duc

An Lang is a small tomb built by Emperor Thanh Thai to house the remains of his father, the late Emperor Duc Duc who reigned for three days in 1883 and allegedly died from starvation in prison. Duc Duc was the first adopted son of Emperor Tu Duc and was supposed to be his heir. However, only three days after he was proclaimed Emperor, Duc Duc was accused by the regents of having committed a serious crime against the late Emperor Tu Duc by omitting a sentence from his will when reading aloud its contents in front of the court. Duc Duc was put in jail even before he had time to choose a regnal title. He was later called Duc Duc after the name of his residential palace. Duc Duc died three months later in prison. According to one version of events, as a condemned prisoner, Duc Duc's body was wrapped in a humble straw mat and taken to be buried in a common grave. On the way, his body

Boi Lang, the tomb of Emperor Kien Phuc.

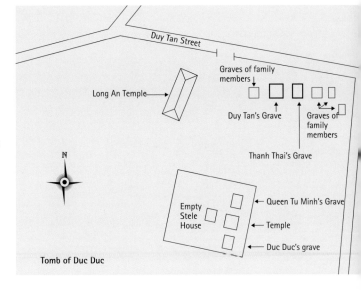

Side view of the gate to Thanh Thai's burial area, Tomb of Duc Duc.

Above right: Empty Stele House, Tomb of Duc Duc.

Thanh Thai's grave stone.

was said to have slipped out of its wrapping and he was buried where he fell. Another version holds that Duc Duc was not allowed to become Emperor because the regents found that he was too close to the French and had passed them vital information while still a prince. They feared that if he became Emperor, he would turn the country over to the French and decided to trump up a lèse-majesté charge. According to this version, he was well treated under house arrest and died much later. Whatever really happened, six years later, by a quirk of fate, Duc Duc's son became Emperor Thanh Thai after Emperor Ham Nghi left Hue to set up his resistance base in Quang Tri and Quang Binh provinces, and Emperor Dong Khanh, Ham Nghi's successor, died young. One of the first acts that Thanh Thai performed was to build his father a royal tomb in 1890.

Within the grounds of Duc Duc's tomb there are many other graves belonging to members of his family such as his queen, Emperor Thanh Thai's queen, his grandnephews and grandnieces. It is a crowded tomb of only 3,445 square metres, situated in the middle of a built-up area. To access the tomb complex, we pass under a concrete gate to enter an area marked by many tombstones, with a temple standing in the middle of the ground in the shape of an ornate building called Long An Pavilion.

As a tomb celebrating the life of a short-lived Emperor, An Lang is modest in every way and does not have a Courtyard of Salutation or a stele. In the customary Stele House, there is only a stone table used to prepare the incense sticks and offerings to be placed at the late Emperor's grave.

Long An pavilion was built in 1899 to house the funerary tablets of Emperor Duc Duc and his Queen. Today, it serves as temple for three blood-related Emperors: Duc Duc, his son Thanh

Thai and his grandson Duy Tan, each occupying a high altar displaying his funerary tablet and photographs. Emperor Duy Tan's area displays a number of photos in an alcove at the back of his altar, the photos showing Duy Tan as a middle-aged man, not a child-Emperor, and his two wives. The first wife was Vietnamese who chose to return to live in Hue after he went into exile, and the second was a French woman that he married abroad.

Eight years after his coronation in 1907, Emperor Thanh Thai was exiled by the French to Reunion island, allegedly for being mentally unstable. He was allowed to return to live in Saigon in 1947 and died there in 1953, soon after his last visit to Hue. His remains were reburied in Duc Duc's tomb in 1954. Emperor Duy Tan was also sent to join his father in exile in 1916 and died in 1945 in a plane crash in Central Africa. His remains were brought back to Vietnam and re-buried next to his father's grave in 1987. In front of Duy Tan's grave, stands a simple stele naming the grave, giving his dates of birth and death and a few lines of his life story. His stele is the only one composed in today's Romanised Vietnamese.

Compared with other Nguyen tombs, An Lang is small and somewhat insignificant in terms of arts and architecture. However, in historical terms, it is a tangible testament to a turbulent period of Vietnam's past, when all three of its main occupants shared the misfortune of being emperors at a time that the French were asserting their dominance and would not tolerate any dissent.

Interior of Long An temple, Tomb of Duc Duc.

The funerary tablets of Duc Duc and his queen.

Duy Tan's stele, Tomb of Duc Duc.

Tu Lang – The Tomb of Emperor Dong Khanh

Emperor Dong Khanh took over the Nguyen throne at a highly volatile period in Vietnamese history. Of his four predecessors, three died in tragic and suspicious circumstances, either by starvation in prison or by poison: Duc Duc, Hiep Hoa and Kien Phuc reigned for only three days, 4 months and 8 months respectively. The fourth, his younger brother, Emperor Ham Nghi, escaped into a jungle base to conduct anti-French resistance and was still active when Dong Khanh was crowned by the French protectorate authority. The escape of Ham Nghi and his subsequent anti-French activities sparked off a state of war between the French authorities and the court at Hue. First, the French attacked the Imperial Citadel on 5th July 1885, and then took over the running of the Court, including the appointment of a new Emperor, thereby effectively assuming control of Vietnam. Dong Khanh was nominally appointed Emperor by the Hue court under pressure from the French Governor in September 1885. In this capacity, before his coronation, he travelled first to the French Governor General's Office on the South Bank of the Perfume River to perform his 'act of vassality'. It was the first time in Vietnamese history that a Vietnamese King was chosen – albeit seeming indirectly – and put on the throne by a European power.

Dong Khanh's reign was notable for several things – his failed attempt to persuade his brother Ham Nghi to surrender to the French, the building of the Royal Library Thai Binh Lau in the Forbidden Purple City, and the construction of a tomb for his birth father, Prince Kien Thai Vuong. His own tomb – Tu Lang – was not built by him, but by his successor, Emperor Thanh Thai, and later enlarged by his own son, Emperor Khai Dinh. Tu Lang was thus built in two stages, in 1889 and 1916, and had two distinctive architectural styles. Here, East meets West in a somewhat awkward co-existence, a mirror reflecting the accelerated transformation of Vietnam from a Sino-classical to a modern Europeanised realm.

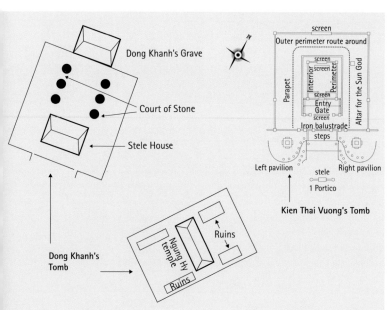

Gate and grave, Tomb of Dong Khanh.

Left: Stele house – Tomb of Dong Khanh.

Below left: Grave, Tomb of Dong Khanh.

Dragons and Phap Lam panels on roof.

Columns of Ngung Hy temple.

Dong Khanh's tomb is located in a beautiful hilly area of Thuy Xuan commune, near the tomb of Tu Duc and almost next to the tomb of his birth father, Prince Kien Thai Vuong. Unlike other Nguyen tombs, Dong Khanh's is currently in an early stage of renovation so many original features are still visible, albeit in a ruined or damaged state. Following the Nguyen's principles of tomb building, the tomb is divided into two areas, the temple space and the burial space, standing 30 metres apart. In the temple space, still largely in ruins, only the main temple – Ngung Hy – stands fully restored as a shiny gem.

The temple was originally built by Emperor Dong Khanh to house his birth father's funerary tablet and was named Truy Tu. However, Dong Khanh died unexpectedly young, before the building work was finished. Emperor Thanh Thai then developed it into a temple to house Dong Khanh's funerary tablet and renamed it Ngung Hy. Ngung Hy temple was again renovated in 1923 under Khai Dinh who had finished the rest of the tomb seven years earlier, in 1916. During the second building phase, Emperor Khai Dinh added a Courtyard of Salutation, a Stele House and many other structures, making it the grander tomb we see today.

In the middle of an area littered with broken houses, ruined gardens, half standing walls and rubble, Ngung Hy temple is adorned with glittering royal motifs of dragon and clouds, two decorative bands on top of the roof and vivid panels of Phap Lam between the double roofs. Solid stone pillars supporting the roofs are carved with dragons and clouds and have been newly coated in a sheen of varnish. The interior of the temple houses many remarkable examples of Vietnamese lacquerware, such as landscape panels with rare beasts and flowers of the four seasons, some inlaid with mother-of-pearl and precious gems, or carved as mythical scenes in bas-reliefs. The most notable group comprises 24 panels depicting scenes from Chinese fables with examples of children's good deeds to their parents – the same theme that Dong Khanh used in Prince Kien Thai Vuong's tomb. Although renovated by Khai Dinh, an Emperor who favoured European culture, European art and materials only appear in a restrained manner in Ngung Hy temple, such as in the stained glass panels on the doors and windows.

In contrast to the temple area, the burial section of Dong Khanh's tomb is an unbridled display of modern construction materials and motifs, a prelude to the full-blown eulogy to European arts found in Khai Dinh's tomb. The most notable feature of Dong Khanh's burial area is the use of concrete, rather than the bricks, stone or wood of his predecessors' tombs. The decorative motifs are also different, representing greater diversity

A corner of Ngung Hy temple, Tomb of Dong Khanh.

Above left: The ruined temple quarter.

and a departure from formal subjects that classicists tended to favour. The Court of Stone is present but the figures have different shapes, are taller and are executed in stronger lines with more angular features, said to reflect European influence.

The next remarkable feature of this area is the breathtaking view. It is a landscape that has to be seen in order to experience its full beauty, especially in the early morning, when the sun's rays compete with the mist rising from the valleys, and the grassy paths still sparkle with the morning dew. From here, we can see several tombs dotting the landscape. Belonging to lesser members of the royal family, some are very grand, while others are more modest. Sadly most are in varying states of disrepair. Well hidden among tall pines and obscured by Dong Khanh's temple space is a grand tomb that can be reached by retracing our steps, down the side of the temple space and over a grassy path. Here we find a surprisingly glorious tomb, dedicated not to an emperor but to a Prince, Kien Thai Vuong, the birth father of three Nguyen Emperors: Kien Phuc, Ham Nghi and Dong Khanh, and grandfather of Emperor Khai Dinh.

Court of Stone, Tomb of Dong Khanh.

The tomb of Prince Kien Thai Vuong

This remarkable but little-known tomb lies slightly outside the main route to the royal tombs. It is obscured by Dong Khanh's tomb, also little known, and by the many pine trees. Although the tomb of a prince not an Emperor, architecturally it displays some of the finest features of the Nguyen decorative arts.

Kien Thai Vuong was originally Prince Nguyen Phuc Hong Cai, the 26th son of Emperor Thieu Tri and a favourite half-brother of Emperor Tu Duc. When Tu Duc decided to adopt, he chose two of his sons, Ung Sy and Ung Dang, and a third son of another brother, Prince Nguyen Phuc Hong Y, to take to court and raise as potential Emperors. Prince Hong Y's son later became Emperor Duc Duc for

Tomb of Kien Thai vuong.

Plates, Tomb of Kien Thai Vuong.

Tomb of Kien Thai Vuong.

three days. Prince Hong Cai's two sons became Emperor Kien Phuc, and Emperor Dong Khanh. The third son of Prince Hong Cai who later became Emperor Ham Nghi, after Kien Phuc and before Dong Khanh, had not been adopted by Tu Duc. When Dong Khanh became Emperor, he gave his father the title Prince Kien Thai Vuong, *vuong* meaning royal, and began his tomb, on behalf of all three Emperor sons, Kien Phuc, Ham Nghi and himself. This fact was engraved on one of the stele standing in the two pavilions flanking the entrance into the tomb.

Dong Khanh was an Emperor who favoured mosaic, as we have seen on the royal library, Thai Binh Lau, in the Forbidden Purple City. Accordingly he adorned this tomb with many mosaic features symbolising classical Vietnamese sentiments such as the characters for happiness, motifs of dragons, the Buddhist flaming wheel, bamboo, fans, lotus blossoms, vases and flowers of the four seasons. All were executed with fine detail and a careful choice of ceramic and glass pieces to create intricate but not over fussy motifs.

On the walls of the two pavilions at the entrance of the tomb were 24 tableaux depicting examples of good behaviour by loyal sons toward their parents, taken from Chinese scholarly books. One such story is that of a poor scholar who was invited to dine at a rich man's house and was found to have hidden a tangerine in his sleeve, a thieving act that was usually condemned by Chinese society, but, in this incident, was praised because he said he wanted his mother to experience the same good food that he had enjoyed. Another story featured a son whose parents could not afford a mosquito net. So to protect his parents, the son slept naked, thereby offering his blood to the mosquitoes instead. The stele inside the two pavilions, dated 1888, expresses the same sentiment of filial love, namely the love and respect felt for their father by the Prince's three sons, Kien Phuc, Ham Nghi and Dong Khanh. An inscription on the left pavilion has an eulogy by another Emperor, Khai Dinh, Dong Khanh's son and Kien Thai Vuong's grandson. This gives a biography of Prince Kien Thai Vuong and dates to the second year of Khai Dinh's reign (1917), when he finished enlarging the tomb of Dong Khanh nearby.

Inside, the Prince's burial enclosure was similar to a royal tomb, with ornate screens shielding both the front and back. The front screen is perhaps the most interesting feature of this tomb, for on its surface, complemented by similar décor on the gateposts, are many blue and white ceramic plates of all shapes and sizes. Some clearly show their British origin by sporting one of the best known oriental designs: the willow pattern, depicting a Chinese castle, a willow tree by a stream and a bridge with three figures and two birds fluttering above. This type of china came to Asia with sea captains who lived in ports near Vietnam, such as Bangkok, Guangzhou or Singapore. They were later imported directly and were highly valued as rare and interesting objects. It was perhaps because of this that they were used by Dong Khanh to decorate Kien Thai Vuong's tomb. Mixed with such pieces are ceramics made in China, also in blue and white, and in Long Tho, near Hue, the royal ceramic factory under the Nguyen.

Quilin motif, Tomb of Kien Thai Vuong.

Close-up of a story panel, Tomb of Kien Thai Vuong.

A pavilion, Tomb of Kien Thai Vuong.

Left: Dragon motif, Tomb of Kien Thai Vuong.

Façade of Temple house, Tomb of Khai Dinh.

The last but not least Nguyen tomb belongs to Emperor Khai Dinh, son of Dong Khanh and father of the very last Emperor of Vietnam, Bao Dai. As a Europeanised Emperor, Khai Dinh was not shy in displaying his taste, whether at the Forbidden Purple City or at his palace of afterlife – the Khai Dinh Mausoleum.

Ung Lang – The tomb of Emperor Khai Dinh

Of all Nguyen tombs, this one is the most unusual, embodying the final stage in the Europeanization of a Sino-classical realm. Khai Dinh's tomb was built entirely in concrete, a material that appeared earlier in the burial part of Dong Khanh's tomb built by Khai Dinh. It was also the main material for his two personal palaces, Kien Trung in the Forbidden Purple City and An Dinh, on the south bank of the Perfume River. In his tomb, Emperor Khai Dinh used this new material unreservedly, from the huge Stele House which dominates the entrance to his temple space to the dragon balustrades flanking the steps up to the terrace with the temple building, and the decorative details of the temple façade. The latter was built in the style of a European palace. The result is distinctive but slightly sinister as time has blackened the concrete of the Stele House and many decorative details. This dark exterior is in total contrast with the opulence we find inside, where ceramic motifs gleam brightly everywhere, from floor to the ceiling and from the altar to the throne area. It was a dizzying display of Khai Dinh's personal taste, which must have been admired by some, but horrified others.

Khai Dinh's tomb is the third furthest from the centre of Hue but is easily reached by road. It occupies the top of a hill, called Chau Chu or Chau E, overlooking a panorama of mountains, streams and forests. To enter the tomb, we mount the first tier of high steps and pass under a three-part ornamental gate to the first level, the Courtyard of Salutation, where four rows of mandarins, horses and elephants face each other in front of the imposing Stele House.

It took Khai Dinh several years after he ascended to the throne to find the location for his tomb and to finish enlarging and renovating his father's tomb first. The construction of Ung Lang began in 1920 and took 11 years to complete, long after he passed away. It was a small tomb, occupying an area of only 117m x 48.5m, but the time was probably spent on the

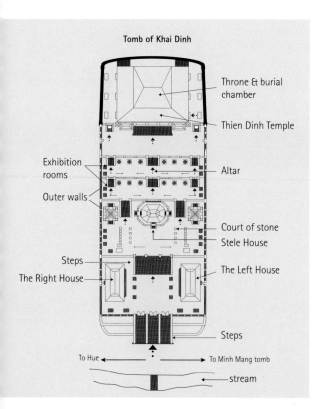

Tomb of Khai Dinh

Throne & burial chamber

Thien Dinh Temple

Exhibition rooms

Altar

Outer walls

Court of stone

Stele House

Steps

The Right House

The Left House

Steps

To Hue

To Minh Mang tomb

stream

Entrance to tomb of Khai Dinh.

Top of obelisk, Tomb of Khai Dinh.

General view of Khai Dinh's tomb.

Detail of the temple house.

interior decoration where no expense was spared to make it as opulent as possible. Envoys were despatched to France, China and Japan to buy materials such as cement, iron, and French tiles for the building, or ceramics and glass for the mosaic motifs. Khai Dinh also commissioned French sculptors to make a bronze statue of himself which was later gilded in gold, no doubt at enormous cost. State tax was raised a hefty 30% to provide funds, an act for which he had to ask the approval of the French authority, according to archive documents, and which was highly condemned by his contemporaries and later generations.

Nevertheless, Ung Lang was built according to Khai Dinh's wishes and completed under his son, Bao Dai. The place that shows most clearly his penchant for showiness is the Thien Dinh Palace, perched atop the hill, his funerary temple and throne room in the afterlife. This palace is divided into three areas, the front room is Khai Thanh hall where his altar occupies a prominent position in the centre, inlaid with ceramic and glass, similar to its four walls and ceiling of dragons and swirling clouds. Behind this is the throne room, where his huge bronze statue, in full Emperor's robes, sits on an imposing throne, under an equally large canopy of concrete. It is said that the Emperor's body is buried under the throne. The entire room and everything in it were inlaid with ceramic and glass to create oriental motifs of dragons and clouds, flowers of the four seasons, the characters for 'long life' and birds of all descriptions. All these shared this crowded space with European motifs such as alarm clocks and tennis rackets.

Below right: Court of stone.

A military mandarin. Tomb of Khai Dinh.

The throne room.

Ceiling detail.

Behind this hall is the third room, partly visible but closed to visitors, displaying the funerary tablet. All three rooms were decorated with mosaic to within an inch of their lives. Strangely, although unusual, the colourful spectacle is not as overwhelming as one might imagine, perhaps because all the concrete pieces were designed to look as if they were made of softer materials. Thus the canopy above Khai Dinh's statue gives the impression of being made from a rich fabric embroidered with royal symbols, rather than solid concrete weighing over a tonne

Adjacent to these three halls are two large rooms, one on each side, the right one being where we first enter the building. Here, a small seating area has a television showing an audio-visual guide to the tomb. On the opposite side the other much larger room, is divided into two display areas. The main display in the front part is another huge bronze statue of Khai Dinh, this time standing in European attire and sporting French medals on his chest. This statue originally stood in his private residence – An Dinh Palace, outside the Imperial Citadel, where he lived until he became Emperor and moved to the Forbidden City. Sharing space with this statue is a large glass case showing his royal scholarly objects: his royal seals, inkpad, inkwell, a number of pages showing his own handwriting and a decree bearing his seal and signature. On the walls are many photographs of his family, his visit to France in 1922, his life at the Imperial Citadel, his 40th birthday celebrations and his funeral. The back of the room displays many of

Motifs of flowers and clock.

Motifs of birds and flowers .

his personal effects, from his tea sets, his European dinner service, his fancy clock to his silver belt and European-style chairs.

Without the natural features characterising Gia Long's tomb, the orderly calm of Minh Mang's, or the romantic beauty of Tu Duc's, the tomb of Khai Dinh stands apart in its own league, a subject of awe, admiration and, sometimes, criticism. Like it or hate it, the Tomb of Khai Dinh is a place that invites comment. It was the last Nguyen tomb as the Emperor's son, Emperor Bao Dai, died in exile in France in 1997 to be buried in an ordinary grave in Paris.

When Bao Dai drafted his short abdication statement in 1945, one of the terms he included and had accepted was that the new government would look after his ancestors' tombs. After experiencing several bouts of fighting over the years, and the ravages of time and bad weather, the Nguyen tombs have now been restored, some fully, while works are still in progress in others. Since 1993, all seven of these magnificent sites have been included in the list of UNESCO's World Heritage for Hue.

Khai Dinh's cortege enterring the tomb.

View of Stele house from the back.

A belt given to Khai Dinh on his 40th birthday, by the Crown Prince of Ethiopia in 1922.

Standing statue of Khai Dinh, Tomb of Khai Dinh.

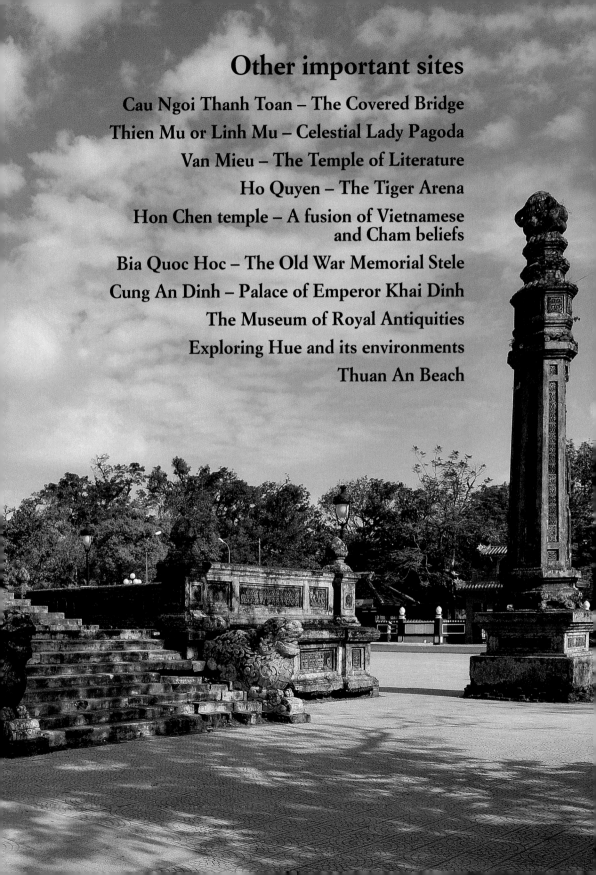

Other important sites

Cau Ngoi Thanh Toan – The Covered Bridge

Thien Mu or Linh Mu – Celestial Lady Pagoda

Van Mieu – The Temple of Literature

Ho Quyen – The Tiger Arena

Hon Chen temple – A fusion of Vietnamese
and Cham beliefs

Bia Quoc Hoc – The Old War Memorial Stele

Cung An Dinh – Palace of Emperor Khai Dinh

The Museum of Royal Antiquities

Exploring Hue and its environments

Thuan An Beach

Other important sites

Above and below: Thanh Toan covered bridge.

Outside the Imperial Citadel and the Valley of the Tombs, there are a number of notable sites which have special connections with the Nguyen, or have played a role in Nguyen history.

Cau Ngoi Thanh Toan – the Covered Bridge

This site, often talked of in Hue, lies 8 kms to the east of the city, in Thanh Thuy village. It is a wooden bridge similar to the better-known covered bridge of Hoi An, and was built during the first phase of Lord Nguyen Hoang's migration to the south in the 16th century, using funding from the wife of a former mandarin of the Le court in order to cross a stream that ran through village land. The bridge is covered by a tiled roof and its interior includes an altar and seating benches on both sides, a favourite place for today's villagers to catch a cooling breeze. The bridge has been granted two royal decrees, in 1776 by a Le Emperor, and in 1921 under Emperor Khai Dinh. Over the years, the bridge has been damaged by bad weather and repaired several times. The latest renovation dates to 1991, the year it was listed as a national heritage.

Thien Mu/Linh Mu – Celestial Lady Pagoda

Thien Mu main temple at dawn.

All the Nguyen Emperors were Buddhists and were educated according to Confucian teachings. Under the dynasty, hundreds of temples and pagodas were built, many dates in the Nguyen calendar celebrated Buddhist occasions, and many objects in their daily life displayed Buddhist motifs. Some of the precious Blue and White china has Buddhist themes, inscriptions uphold Buddhism as the national religion, and bells were forged to celebrate important Buddhist or national religious events. Of all the temples in Hue, Thien Mu or Linh Mu Pagoda is the most original and the most important to the Nguyen.

The pagoda occupies a beautiful spot on the north bank of the Perfume River, 3 kms west of the Imperial Citadel, at a point where the river veers east to reach the sea. It is known by two names, the original Thien Mu which is also its official name today, and Linh Mu, its name under Emperor Tu Duc, who changed it in 1862 to avoid committing an act of contempt toward the Power in Heaven by naming something earthly *thien*, meaning Heaven. The new name Linh Mu was changed back to Thien Mu in 1869 but in just seven years that name became equally familiar to Hue residents as Thien Mu and the pagoda is known by both names to this day.

Thien Mu Pagoda is the symbol of the Nguyen and of Hue, their capital. It was built in 1601 by the first Nguyen Lord, Nguyen Hoang, who arrived at this spot and was told by a mysterious lady who appeared from nowhere that this part of Vietnam would be an

Top: Close-up of bell.

Right: Inscription on bell.

Far right: the bell.

auspicious land for the Nguyen Dynasty. Nguyen Hoang then built a simple temple to commemorate the site and named it Thien Mu. In 1613 the pagoda was completed by his successors, who continued to develop it as an important centre for Buddhism in the then Dang Trong. In 1710, Lord Nguyen Phuc Chu gave the pagoda a huge bell, on which he engraved an eulogy praising the beauty and the qualities of the site. Thien Mu was embellished over the years, with extra structures, bell towers and stone stelea added to its grounds. By the reign of Emperor Thieu Tri, Thien Mu pagoda had become a place of such exquisite beauty, commanding one of the best views of the Perfume River and displaying some of the finest structures and decorative arts, that it was included in his list of 20 most beautiful sites of Hue

In 1846, Emperor Thieu Tri erected two stelea at the site, one to record the history of the pagoda and the other inscribed with his poems celebrating the building of an octagonal tower on the forecourt. On one of the stelea, he stated that he built the tower to celebrate the fact that the realm was prosperous and peace reigned supreme in the capital and throughout the land. Thieu Tri stated that he had drawn up the plan and construction began in 1844. It was completed in the year of the Dragon (1846) and he named it Tu Nhan tower. This name was later changed to Phuoc Duyen, by which we know it today. To mark its completion, Emperor Thieu Tri ordered a grand celebration that lasted seven days.

Phuoc Duyen tower is 21 metres tall, the tallest building in Hue at the time, and has seven stories connected by a narrow internal staircase. The first six floors house a statue of the Buddha. The top storey can only be reached via a trapdoor from the sixth floor and once housed several small golden statues of the Buddha, all now lost. Originally, one could access the top floor of the tower to see the statues and enjoy the best view of Hue, but over time, the structure became unsafe and the tower was closed to visitors.

Thieu Tri's stele.

Tourist boat at Thien Mu.

Detail of Phuoc Duyen tower.

As a group of buildings existing over several centuries, Thien Mu has been damaged many times by natural disasters, with some structures completely destroyed during the severe storm of 1904. In 1999, along with many other historical sites in Hue, including the Imperial Citadel and the Nguyen tombs, Thien Mu pagoda was severely damaged when Hue experienced one of the largest floods in its history. Most of the flood damage has now been repaired and Thien Mu once again stands proud by the Perfume River.

Thien Mu pagoda can be reached by boat or by road, with boats stopping at the bottom of the steps. Either way, we ascend to the site via two tiers of steps. We first reach Phuoc Duyen tower, flanked by stele houses displaying some of the most ancient Nguyen inscriptions. The oldest, a stele with Nguyen Phuc Chu's inscription, is on our right as we enter, sitting on top of a stone turtle. His large bell is housed in a small pavilion on the left, but the bell that emits the pure sound for which Thien Mu is famous is a little bit further in on the right, in a small pavilion by the gateway to the main temple. This bell still tolls everyday to remind people of Thien Mu's role as the symbol and the spiritual keeper of Hue

The main temple is a beautiful wooden structure housing many valuable artefacts, including ancient statues of the Buddha and panels with poems and couplets in Chinese characters, some composed by the Nguyen Emperors themselves. One of the most notable features of this temple is the decorative band under its front roof. Here several panels were carved in exquisite detail illustrating the many stages of the Buddha's life and his long progress toward enlightenment.

In the grounds behind the temple, is a tranquil garden displaying many pots of bonsai, each one carefully shaped and nurtured by the resident monks. To the left of this garden is a garage displaying the car that Venerable Thich Quang Duc used to travel to Saigon in 1963 to perform his self-immolation act in

Nguyen Phuc Chu's stele.

Monk praying.

Panels illustrating the life of Buddha.

protest against the late President Ngo Dinh Diem's policy toward Buddhists. The back of Thien Mu is the residential area for the monks. As a working pagoda, many Buddhist prayer sessions are conducted throughout the day in the main temple. These are very good times for visitors to sit down, relax and to enjoy the soothing chanting of the monks. Whatever your faith, the rhythmic chanting and the exquisite panoramic view of the river behind is guaranteed to chase away the stressful pressures of modern life, if only for a fleeting moment.

The best time to visit Thien Mu is early morning, when layers of mist still linger over the surface of the river, on which heavily-laden small boats hurry past on their way downstream to Dong Ba market to unload their merchandise. The many hues of grey and blue tinged with the faint yellow streaks of a new dawn form a shimmering picture of indescribable beauty. Compared to the dreamy quality of dawn on the river, the sunset at this spot is breathtakingly dramatic. It is when the distant mountains suddenly loom clear and dark against the last rays of a flaming sun, a stunning spectacle comparable to a light show that constantly changes its colours, from red to brown to purple and then blackness as the tropical sunset rapidly reaches its conclusion.

Bonsai.

Van Mieu – The Temple of Literature

Travelling west for one kilometre from Thien Mu, we come to a brick façade, heavily damaged but still standing imposingly at the top of a set of steps and facing over the river. This is the remains of the Nguyen's Temple of Literature, a complex similar to its counterpart in Hanoi, but created exclusively to honour scholars who passed exams under the Nguyen. It is called Van Mieu or Van Thanh, a temple dedicated to Confucius' teachings.

It was built in 1808, under Gia Long, to worship not only Confucius but also his four disciples and the 12 wise men. It was a large complex of several structures but now only the façade and 32 stelea remain, arranged in two rows and sheltered under long roofs. They are engraved with the names of the 293 doctors of literature who passed their exams under the Nguyen, the first ones during the third year of Minh Mang (1822) and the last during the fourth year of Khai Dinh (1919) when the Nguyen proclaimed that they would no longer use Chinese characters but Romanised Vietnamese as the official written language of Vietnam.

As with the rest of Hue, the Temple of Literature has been heavily damaged by wars and bad weather. Most buildings on this site have been destroyed, with those remaining having been recently renovated. It is not much of a beauty spot but an important relic of the Nguyen dynasty, a haunting presence to remind us of an orderly past when Confucian teaching was the raison d'être for many Vietnamese scholars, and, certainly, for the early Nguyen Emperors in their opposition to the invasion of French culture.

Stelae.

The front entrance of Van Mieu.

Elephant gate into Ho Quyen.

Ho Quyen – The Tiger Arena

The contests between elephants and tigers during the Nguyen dynasty are one of the more shocking aspects of their rule. However, from their point of view, such contests expressed their admiration for the elephant as the noblest of beasts and for the tiger as an untamed and ferocious force of nature.

A Frenchman, Pierre Poivre, wrote of his experience as a guest of the Nguyen Lord Vo Vuong Nguyen Phuc Khoat (1714-1765) in the journal *Revue de l'Extrême-Orient*, volume III:

> '...They transported the tigers in cages to an islet in the middle of the Perfume River... Forty huge elephants were made to cross the river to line up in two rows at one end of the islet. The tigers were placed at the opposite end. The soldiers stood at attention in a line that stretched over the entire length of one side of the islet, their lances at the ready. That left only one side of the islet open for spectators to view the spectacle from their boats on the river...'

Under the Nguyen Lords (1558-1775), tiger and elephant fights took place on one of the islets on the Perfume River, the Da Vien. The Lords and their guests watched from the safety of their boats, the royal boat marked by a red parasol. The Lord gave the signal to begin the battle by beating on a piece of bamboo, whereupon the soldiers let the tigers out of their cages tethered with stout ropes around their necks. The elephants approached, the fight began and lasted until all the tigers were killed.

Later, under the early Nguyen Emperors, the fights were held on the river bank outside the Imperial Citadel. The royal party watched from their boats, until an incident occurred in 1829, under Emperor Minh Mang, when one of the hard-pressed tigers broke his restraining rope, jumped into the river and swam toward the royal boat, perhaps attracted by the red parasol. The animal was killed but its escape brought home the danger of having uncontrollable beasts in an unstable environment. Emperor Minh Mang thus ordered that an arena be built on the south bank of river, in an area adjacent to an old Cham Fortress called Thanh Loi.

The spot chosen for the arena was in Nguyet Bieu village, on the south bank of the Perfume River, about 5 kms from the Imperial Citadel. Ho Quyen was an open-air circular structure of bricks, with a circumference of 145 metres and a diameter of 44 metres. The outer circular wall was 5.90 metres high and was linked with a lower inner circular wall of 4.75 metres by the seating area. Like all arenas, the seating area was tiered, in a

series of narrow terraces. Under these, between the outer and the inner walls, were cells to house the tigers, with five tiger holding areas in all. All the tiger cells faced north where the Emperor and his entourage sat on the top tier, in an elevated position and under massive yellow umbrellas. Next to the arena were the elephant stables. From here, they were led in a dignified manner, through an iron gate, to their foe.

To capture tigers for the fights, a regiment of soldiers was set up and operated in the province of Quang Tri, north of Hue. As for the elephants, it is recorded that Emperor Gia Long organised his elephants into an army corps of several hundreds serving under a special mandarin, with each animal tended by a squad of four soldiers. Under Minh Mang, 800 elephants served in his army, with 130 kept inside the Capital City of Hue.

The elephant was also immortalised at the Nguyen Tombs, as part of an honourable court of stone. It is not documented whether any of the imperial elephants was used for the fights at Ho Quyen but it seems likely. Elephants represented the power of the royals, and a fight between the elephant and the tiger symbolised a triumph of royal power over a fearsome savage force. Many tigers were slaughtered during each of these contests that lasted hours. Several accidents occurred over the years, when soldiers and elephant-keepers were injured or killed by desperate tigers or enraged elephants.

Original drain sculpture on Ho Quyen wall.

Ho Quyen – The Tiger Arena.

Below: Inside Ho Quyen.

Gate to the elephant temple, Mieu Voi Re.

The contest was a big event with preparations starting from the early morning. People poured into the area to get a good place to view the royal party going past and, of course, the fights. Along the route, local people set up altars to welcome the Emperor. At noon, the auspicious hour, under a large escort of imperial guards, the emperor and his party would cross the Perfume River by Dragon boats, accompanied by a royal orchestra. On the South Bank, the royal party travelled along a route lined with more imperial guards, while the orchestra played, to reach the royal gate of the arena where courtiers knelt in wait on colourful straw mats.

After the fight was banned in 1904, the arena was used as a place to keep elephants until the last Nguyen Emperor Bao Dai left in 1945. Since then, the whole area has been abandoned to nature. Most of the original walls and seating tiers have been damaged, while the nearby lotus pond, once serving as a watering hole for the elephants, became a fish pond and was heavily polluted by a factory on the far side. In 1993, Ho Quyen and the nearby site of Voi Re temple were placed on the UNESCO's list of heritage sites of Hue. As a result, several archaeological activities have taken place inside the arena and uncovered some interesting facts about the quality of the bricks, the construction techniques, and the drainage system.

Although it appears an empty circular structure, it repays a short visit, if only to reflect on its history. The location is difficult to find without a guide, as the entrance is obscured by a market, and it is better to park outside and enter on foot. The site is quite spacious and, walking about and peering through the openings, one can

imagine the bewildered tigers being pushed through their cell gates to face a fearsome adversary. Today, on the contrary, the only animals to greet you might be a mother hen and her chicks.

Mieu Voi Re – Temple of Elephants

Once there, it would be remiss not to walk 200 metres further into the village to visit this rather shabby, but atmospheric temple complex dedicated to the brave elephants and even braver generals of the Nguyen Court. The temple was erected on the order of Emperor Gia Long soon after he ascended the throne to commemorate his four favourite elephants killed in battles against the Trinh and the Tay Son. All four were awarded the rank of admiral, a fact engraved on their funerary tablets placed within the two shrines at the site. Mieu Voi Re was named after a brave elephant that came to this spot to cry over the loss of its master, a Nguyen general who was killed in battle with the Trinh. Broken hearted the elephant died of grief and was buried by local villagers on this spot, with *re* meaning 'cry' or 'shriek'.

The complex occupies an area some 2,000m² on a raised piece of land facing a large pond and contains several buildings. The pond served as a waterhole for the elephants before their fights in the nearby arena. The main temple, Mieu Long Chau, was dedicated to the Nguyen Generals and the two small shrines flanking it were for the elephants, each housing a statue of a stone elephant. While the Nguyen were in power, they gave an annual sum for the locals to organise two ceremonies, in the spring and in the autumn, to glorify the elephants and the genies protecting the land.

Voi Re temple with the two elephant shrines on either side.

Inside Voi Re temple.

General view of Hon Chen temple.

Painting of the Goddess.

Altar for Cham and Vietnamese goddesses.

Hon Chen temple – a fusion of Cham and Viet beliefs

Next to Thien Mu Pagoda, another venue that has an intimate connection with Hue and the Nguyen dynasty is Hon Chen –Teacup Island, located 10 kms from the centre of Hue on the left bank of the Perfume River as the river flows up to Hue from the Valley of the Tombs. This is a small island in the shape of an upturned cup, which is probably why it acquired its name. However, many other reasons have been put forward to explain the name, from being a teacup from Heaven, a jade teacup that a fish/turtle returned to Emperor Minh Mang when he dropped it in the river during an outing, to the shape of the top of the mound that constitutes the entire island. The official name for the island is Ngoc Tran Mountain but Hon Chen is the popular name that is more widely used. It is a unique temple where the Cham Goddess Po Nagar and her Vietnamese version are worshipped on an equal footing.

According to local legends, the island was where the Goddess Po Nagar descended to earth to teach the Cham people how to plant rice and to cultivate the land. For them she was also the Goddess of Eaglewood, the precious scented tree core for which the Cham were famous in international trade. The temple was built to show their gratitude to her. When the Cham territory of the Ly became the Vietnamese land of Hoa Chau, the temple acquired a Vietnamese Goddess. Whether she was the Vietnamese version of Po Nagar, as at the Po Nagar Temple of Nha Trang further south, or another Vietnamese Goddess who had been assigned the same duty from Heaven, has never been ascertained. She was called Van Huong Goddess and enjoyed the same degree of reverence as Po Nagar.

It is not known when the original temple – said to be Cham – was built, but Hon Chen Temple was enlarged and renovated under Emperor Minh Mang in 1832. It acquired its royal status in an edict naming it Ngoc Tran Son Tu – the Temple of Teacup Mountain, issued by Emperor Dong Khanh, in 1886. Throughout the Nguyen era, the temple was well maintained and became a place of worship for both royalty and local people, with Cham and Vietnamese traditions fused into one. Hon Chen was most popular under Emperor Dong Khanh, who in 1886 ordered a more ornate temple in his favourite style and the holding of bi-annual celebrations supervised by court officials. These took place on the third and the seventh moons, equivalent to April-May and August-September of our Common Era calendar.

To reach the island temple, go by road to the right bank of the Perfume River opposite the site and take a little rowing boat across. Hon Chen is a small island that resembles a rocky mound rather than a mountain, the temple complex with its 10 structures perched on the slope of this mound. Apart from the main temple, most of the buildings are very small, being shrines dedicated to different deities of the site, or small caves such as that honouring Mr. Tiger, located on the right as we face the main temple, Minh Kinh Dai.

Minh Kinh Dai is a long building built in the same style as the pagodas and temples seen elsewhere in Hue, but it has an abundance of the royal phoenix motif, crafted from fine pieces of china and glass mosaic in typical Dong Khanh style. The interior is divided into three levels: the lower one has an altar and ceremonial equipment such as drums and bells; the middle has a tall nine-tier altar dedicated to Dong Khanh and various deities, while the top level is reserved for the two Cham and Vietnamese Goddesses and, again, Emperor Dong Khanh. This top level can be reached via a rickety stairway with no banister and should only be attempted by agile visitors.

Today, this temple is the main venue for colourful bi-annual ceremonies, when the Goddess Po Nagar and her Vietnamese counterpart are invited to come down to earth to join a grand celebration, which includes a boat procession on the Perfume River and a closing ceremony of floating candle-lit lanterns on the water at night. This spectacular part of the ceremony is re-enacted during Hue festivals.

Tiger shrine.

A woman prays at the shrine.

River view.

Temple interior.

Step-altar of Dong Khanh.

Dong Khanh's travelling chaise.

Bia Quoc Hoc – The Old War Memorial Stele

This large concrete screen in the form of a scroll stands on the south bank of the Perfume River. Unlike its name in Vietnamese, it has nothing to do with education and just happens to be called Quoc Hoc Stele because it stands on the riverbank across the road from the elite Quoc Hoc High School. Its correct description should be 'Monument to honour the dead of the First World War' because when it was erected in 1920, it was meant to be a memorial for those who died for France in 1914-1918, both French and Vietnamese; the French from the Hue area and the Vietnamese from all over Central Vietnam. The men were conscripted in Hue in 1914 and sent to France in batches, in 1915 and 1916, to fight on the French side in the First World War. It is not known how many of them died unrecorded in Europe, but 31 French and 78 Vietnamese names were once engraved on the surface. Sadly most of them have been crudely chiselled off, leaving only a few still faintly visible today.

Close-up of Bia Quoc Hoc.

Bia Quoc Hoc was planned in 1919 and a competition was organised to find the best design. A Vietnamese teacher, Ton That Sa, won and the monument was built in 1920 according to his design. It had the shape of a Sino-Vietnamese scroll displaying the motifs of 'long-life', dragons and flowers of the four seasons, similar to designs often found at royal locations in Hue. It also included French and Vietnamese motifs with the French 'Croix de Guerre' medal hanging under a Vietnamese *khanh* – an auspicious musical instrument. The monument stood at the top of a set of steps, flanked by two obelisks. On the flat surfaces of both sides of the screen, the 31 names of Frenchmen who lived in Hue in 1914 and the 78 names of Vietnamese from provinces in Central Vietnam, such as Thua Thien, Khanh Hoa, Thanh Hoa and Quang Binh, were engraved.

The monument was completed in 1920 and inaugurated on 23rd September 1920 by Emperor Khai Dinh and the French former

Bia Quoc Hoc from the front.

Inauguration of Bia Quoc Hoc, 1920.

Stele viewed from river.

A corner of Hue in 1911.

Minister of War, Paul Painlevé, who was visiting at the time. Although the names engraved on the stele have been chiselled off, perhaps to express displeasure at the French involvement in Vietnam and the contribution of Vietnamese soldiers to a distant 'French war', the stele remains on the river bank as a notable monument of Hue.

For many years under the early Nguyen Emperors, from Gia Long to Tu Duc, the south bank of the Perfume River remained under developed. It was here that the first French permanent delegation was allocated a piece of land on which to build their residences and offices. This corner of Hue, by the south end of the Trang Tien Bridge, later became a large compound housing the French Governor's imposing office and many associated buildings. Across the road from this compound was the symbol of French civilisation, the Morin Grand Hotel and Emporium, where European merchandise of all descriptions were available to French residents in Hue. Later on, after the French established their full authority in Vietnam, the South Bank of the Perfume River became the French Quarter, where French-style buildings, railway station, French schools and other institutions were established. Among these, stands a French-style palace, towards the southwest and by the banks of the An Cuu River: Cung An Dinh, a palace belonging not to a Frenchman but to the Vietnamese Emperor Khai Dinh.

Cung An Dinh – Palace of Emperor Khai Dinh

This was the residence of Prince Nguyen Phuc Buu Dao from when he came of age in 1902 to when he became Emperor Khai Dinh in 1916. Khai Dinh was the first son of Emperor Dong Khanh but did not inherit the throne straight away, having had to wait until Emperor Duy Tan was exiled before being called to occupy the Nguyen throne.

An Dinh was originally a modest wooden structure, where Khai Dinh lived with his favourite second wife, Hoang Thi Cuc, a commoner and mother to his only son, Prince Nguyen Phuc Vinh Thuy – Emperor Bao Dai, born three years before Khai Dinh became Emperor. After the French assumed total power in Hue, it was no longer certain that succession to the Nguyen throne would automatically go to the first son of the previous emperor, and Khai Dinh did not know if either himself or his son would ever inherit, a fact that he carefully engraved on an inscription in this palace. In this text, found inside a balcony on the third floor, Khai Dinh explained that he had built this Palace to commemorate the beauty of the place and named it Khai Tuong. Rather unusually for a prince who later became king, he stated that all the furnishings came from his own money, and, as such, it would be a private inheritance for his eldest son, whom he said was still a young boy while he was getting old. A cryptic line refers to his worry that, although he could not predict the future, his son might have an even worse time than he had had, implying he might never become Emperor, and hence the gift of the palace which he began as soon as he ascended the throne. First, Khai Dinh bought more land and then he proceeded to build a French-style palace in concrete to replace the old wooden structures.

An Dinh Palace was begun in 1917 and continued to be enlarged in different stages until 1922 with 10 peripheral buildings and a private theatre added to the original site. The extensive grounds have a private jetty, shrine, lake and animal quarters. As an Emperor who favoured

Today's gate.

Old gate to the canal.

Inscription inside An Dinh Palace.

Close-up of the top of An Dinh façade, showing the Nguyen Medal in the middle.

Above right: Quilin motif.

Right: Gate top.

European art, Khai Dinh created his palace in the manner of a sumptuous French villa, both inside and out. The main house, Khai Tuong, was built like a European palace with three stories and 22 rooms. The facade displays reliefs of Western-style vases, bunches of grapes, garlands and cherubs, giving the impression that it is a European villa in Western setting, not one built by a Vietnamese Emperor in the middle of a traditional Vietnamese City

Inside, each floor was carefully decorated in contemporary European style with sweeping staircases, ornate ceilings, crystal chandeliers, and walls covered in beautiful materials. The walls of the lower two floors were painted with exquisite murals. Six of those on the ground floor illustrated the six tombs of his predecessors, with each mural surrounded by a gilded frame. Over the years once the building ceased to be a royal domain, the paintings were severely damaged and the whole palace had an air of neglect. By 2009, however, the murals had been restored to their former state, while those on the first floor await their turn.

An Dinh interior.

French and Vietnamese guests watching
a play in the theatre, An Dinh Palace.

The double staircase.

A corner of An Dinh.

A room in An Dinh.

Outside, the front of the property opens onto steps leading down to a boat jetty, through an ornate gate, richly decorated with mosaic dragons, phoenix, quilins, flowers and couplets in Chinese characters. Between the main house and the gate stands an octagonal pavilion called Trung Lap, which housed a life-size bronze statue of Khai Dinh in European clothing with a row of French medals on his chest. This statue was moved in 1960 and is now displayed at his tomb. As with other structures in Hue, An Dinh Palace was damaged during the several wars and, although the main house is still intact, most of the other buildings have collapsed beyond repair.

Today, at the back of the property, two long houses stand opposite each other across a spacious courtyard. These were formerly homes for the staff serving at the palace and now are exhibition halls for artefacts taken from the Museum of Royal Antiquities, while the museum is closed for refurbishment.

An Dinh Palace has a unique place in the history of the Nguyen for many reasons. It is the only royal palace built outside the Capital City, on the South Bank of the Perfume River, and it was used as a permanent, rather than a summer or temporary, royal residence. Khai Dinh's premonition regarding his son and recorded in the palace's inscription became a reality in 1945, when Bao Dai lost all state privileges upon abdication and his family moved from the Imperial Citadel to here. When Bao Dai was reinstated by the French as Head of State in 1950, his wife, Queen Nam Phuong, and his children went to live in France. His mother, Lady Tu Cung, returned to live in Dien Tho Palace in the Imperial Citadel. However, after Bao Dai began his second exile in France in 1955, Lady Tu Cung returned and lived here until 1957 when she handed the property to the then government of the Republic of Vietnam and moved to another villa nearby, where she lived until she died in 1980.

In 1957, An Dinh palace became a dormitory for lecturers teaching at Hue University, and, later, in 1975, it became a refuge for displaced people. Only after transfer to the Hue Monuments Conservation Center in 2002 did the much-needed restoration of the palace begin. It is still on-going but the palace has featured a number of times in Hue festivals as part of cultural activities relating to the Nguyen dynasty.

Canons in front of the museum.

The Museum of Royal Antiquities

A visit to this museum is a must for visitors to Hue. Here thousands of priceless Nguyen artefacts are permanently displayed in the exquisite halls of a palace that once served as a resting house for Emperor Thieu Tri. The contents and the building are both works of art in their own right.

The building housing the museum was called Long An Palace and was originally located at a different site, north of the Imperial Canal, Ngu Ha, inside the royal quarter of houses and temples called Cung Bao Dinh. This quarter was built by Emperor Thieu Tri in 1845 as a resting place during the royal planting ceremony of Tich Dien, held every year at the beginning of the spring cultivation season. When he died, his funerary tablet was put on an altar here and Long An palace became his temple. However, after the French storming of the Imperial Citadel in July 1885, 'savage looting' took place in this area and his funerary tablet was moved to Phung Tien temple in the Imperial Citadel. The palace became the residence for the French General Prudhomme, commander of the occupation force. The general was asked by the Hue court to move to Thuong Bac pavilion in November 1885 and the area was left abandoned.

On the 4th day of the 2nd year of Duy Tan's reign (1908), the Emperor issued an edict ordering the court to relocate Long An Palace to a site next to Quoc Tu Giam – the Royal Academy. The palace was disassembled and its components, from wooden pillars to roof tiles, from brick to decorative motifs were moved and reconstructed at its present location. It was to become the National Library – Tan Tho Vien, serving the adjacent Royal Academy. All the materials of Long An palace were reused for the new library,

Khai Dinh's globe.

Duy Tan's decree.

The museum in 1925.

Screen from the original Imperial Palace (Musee Khai Dinh BAVH, apr-jun 1929-1).

exactly as per the original model, with some additional elements added. For examples, at its new site, all the wooden pillars of the palace were coated with European varnish and the wooden doors had iron locks made in European style. The cost of buying these new materials was listed as 4,719 piastres and 80 cents, according to a report from the Ministry of Public Works to the Emperor. The reconstruction was completed in November 1909. Four years later, in 1913, a part of the building was allocated to a French group of scholars and enthusiasts called the Association of Friends of Old Hue (Association des Amis du Vieux Hue) to use as their meeting place, and to house the artefacts that they acquired, some from the Imperial Palaces themselves.

In 1923, under Emperor Khai Dinh, the building became the Khai Dinh Museum to display all the artefacts, which by then were very numerous and needed more space. After the French left Vietnam, the building continued as a museum under different names and exhibited mainly Nguyen art. The Museum of Royal Antiquities is the latest name in use.

The main part of the museum – the former Long An Palace – is in fact two connected buildings and occupies an area of 38m x 25m. It was built by Vietnamese craftsmen in Nguyen royal style but without the colourful decoration seen in other palaces in the Imperial Citadel. Although the décor is more subdued, it is finely executed, creating a simple but elegant palace befitting its role as a museum. Constructed from brick and wood, the ornate roof supported by 128 ironwood pillars has wooden eaves densely carved with the royal motif of two dragons paying homage to the moon, and other mythical beasts such as the phoenix, turtles and quilins. The wood surface was unpainted but highly varnished. The interior of the building is clad with wooden panels illustrating scenes of the four seasons, flowers and objects of scholarly pursuit. The most remarkable feature of the interior is the panels displaying carved or embossed poems in Chinese characters, said to have been composed by Emperor Thieu Tri himself. The characters of the verses were elaborately inlaid with mother-of-pearl, ivory or other precious materials. Two of these panels are particularly interesting for Sinologists, as they display a group of Chinese characters arranged as a wheel of words, accompanied by a key to decode the poems contained in the wheel. Both sets of poems were composed by Emperor Thieu Tri. One wheel has the theme of a rainy moment on a mountain, the other is about a night of writing poems in Phuoc

212

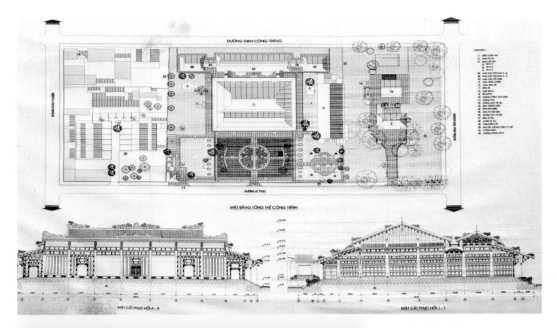

Plan of Long An Palace.

Emperor Thieu Tri's poetry wheel.

Vien garden. According to the Director of the Museum, this type of poem is the highest form of poetry writing and only the most talented scholars can master its intricate rules, with Emperor Thieu Tri being one of them. Each of the poems can be read in many ways, depending with which character we begin, what classical poetry rules we use to arrange the rhyming words, and in which direction we want to proceed around the wheel. The purpose of this literary game is to set an enigma that only scholars of superior intellect, at least equal to that of the composer, can decipher. It is also a challenge to see how many different poems can be read from each wheel. From the wheel of 56 characters describing a rainy moment on a mountain, so far a Vietnamese Sinologist has managed to read 64 different poems in different styles.

Bronze book.

Box of three precious metals.

Faience candlestick.

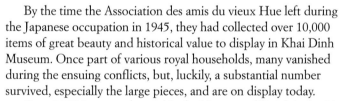
Silver wine set.

Vase.

By the time the Association des amis du vieux Hue left during the Japanese occupation in 1945, they had collected over 10,000 items of great beauty and historical value to display in Khai Dinh Museum. Once part of various royal households, many vanished during the ensuing conflicts, but, luckily, a substantial number survived, especially the large pieces, and are on display today.

Over 8,000 items are housed in the Museum of Royal Antiquities, including royal thrones, beds and travelling chaises, precious Blue and White dinner services and tea sets, Phap Lam vases and other objects, decorative trees with golden leaves and gem fruits, silver table screens and glass paintings, royal robes, embroidered shoes and hats and ceremonial attire such as Emperor Minh Mang's Nam Giao robe. They are grouped into collections and classified by their materials. Some are displayed in glass cases, while others hang on wooden pillars such as the priceless glass paintings which were commissioned under Emperor Thieu Tri.

The museum was closed for redecoration in 2008 and reopened in 2012. The key pieces are now on display here but some artefacts are still exhibited in different places such as the Ta Vu building in the Imperial Citadel, and at An Dinh Palace. Among the current exhibits at the Museum of Antiquities, some are singled out for particular mention as they are very unusual and, often, are the only such pieces so far known to exist.

The marble plate of Emperor Minh Mang

This magnificent decorative screen carved on a piece of composite marble illustrates a scene of peace and tranquillity representing a Taoist ideal of Paradise. Measuring 53 centimetres in diameter, it includes a poem composed by Emperor Minh Mang in 1829. The date on the back, probably added by the mandarins cataloguing the royal household effects, shows it was made in the Minh Mang year of the Rooster (1825).

The composite marble is both green and red, a very unusual quality according to the poem by Emperor Minh Mang, engraved on its surface. The colours occur as a result of the oxidising process and the presence of manganese. The process is continuing to this day and is why the plate is darker than in the past. Nevertheless we can still admire how the artist has managed to use the veins of colour to represent the scenery and create a dramatic tableau. The scene shows tall pavilions reaching the clouds and sail boats floating on the calm water of a lake surrounded by trees that will be forever green. Fluttering above the landscape are a pair of cranes, symbols of a graceful long life. It is a picture bearing the message of eternity, stability and durability that Emperor Minh Mang was very eager to impart. It is truly a work of art not to be missed.

Phap Lam objects

Over 100 Phap Lam artefacts are housed in the collection of the Museum of Royal Antiquities. They come in all shapes and sizes, from bowls and betel sets to serving plates and vases. Most of them were objects for everyday use that once belonged to three Emperors Minh Mang, Thieu Tri and Tu Duc. Unlike the Phap Lam panels used as architectural decoration in the Imperial Citadel and at the Nguyen Tombs, these pieces have finer patterns and more vivid colours.

Phap Lam urn.

The Blue and White ceramic and porcelain pieces

These exhibits show a high degree of craftsmanship and mostly consist of items made to order for the Nguyen Emperors at the imperial kilns in Jingdezhen, Jiangxi, China. Once described as 'Les Bleus de Hue' by French scholars, their unique feature lies in the combination of Vietnamese designs on the finest quality Chinese porcelain. Some are traditional, while others have unusually modern, almost Art Deco, themes. The shapes of some of the pieces are also interesting such as the covered steam cup that once belonged to Emperor Thieu Tri, or the Dau Ho vase of Emperor Tu Duc. Almost two centuries have gone by since they were created but the blue is still vivid, while the white has deepened into an ivory shade, giving the pieces a patina that is found only with the best antiques.

Also worth lingering over in An Dinh Palace are the coin collections, the prints displayed under glass, the Xam Huong game that belonged to Emperor Tu Duc, the bronze books bound with bronze rings, the paper edicts signed by Emperor Duy Tan, the lacquered boxes, the large European-made vases that were gifts to Emperor Khai Dinh and the set of royal seals.

At the Ta Vu building, it is worth paying close attention to the group of Dau Ho vases displayed in a glass case, as each is an art work in its own right and reflects the varying different artistic tastes of different Emperors.

Phap Lam bowl.

The textile collection

The textile collection on show in the Museum of Royal Antiquities represents a rich and intimate facet of Nguyen royal life. The museum has over 240 pieces of clothing and textiles, from royal robes and shoes to royal silk books and mandarins' court attires. In their last audit in 1994-1995, out of the 254 textiles, 112 were items of royal clothing. Unfortunately, since then some of the items have perished, or been torn or damaged beyond repair.

Rules governing the use of fabrics, their colours, the motifs embroidered and the styles of clothing for each class of person were strictly enforced under the Nguyen. Commoners were not allowed to use the same fabrics, styles and colours as the royals. The rules

Butterfly design on china.

governing royal clothing were even more complicated, with different styles of dress for every occasion, such as grand assemblies, daily meetings, state occasions and ceremonies etc. For everyday wear, they also needed particular garments with prescriptions as to colour, fabric, motifs, length and width of sleeves.

Royal robes were usually made of fine silk and brocade produced in China and at designated local factories. Factories throughout the country also offered their finest products as tribute to the Court and as part payment of their tax quota. The Nguyen encouraged and strictly controlled the silk industry in Vietnam in every reign. Edicts by different emperors, from Gia Long onward, showed that they wanted people throughout the country to cultivate mulberry leaves as part of their farming activities, and to raise silkworms. Even royal concubines were encouraged to raise silkworms in their spare time. The silk fabric was collected and stored by Phu Noi Vu. During the Nguyen, the Vietnamese produced silk was not just for royal clothing, but formed an important part of foreign trade.

Chinese silk and brocade were more favoured by the royals and could only be imported by the court. They were used for clothing, bedding, purses and other personal items for both male and female royals. Yellow and orange were reserved solely for the highest royals, with bright orange or gold for the Crown Prince and red for princesses. On the highest royals' robes, such as the emperor, the Queen, the Queen Mother, and the Crown Prince, the dragon motif was finely embroidered throughout, from the collars to the sleeves, in the shapes of a curled-up dragon or full-faced one to form the character Long-Life, or in profile. The five-claw dragon motif was reserved strictly for the Emperor. Other robes could only have the motif of a dragon with four claws, in whatever position. The phoenix, symbol of stability and/or femininity, was used liberally on all robes for the highest female royals along with flowers and other beautiful motifs. Since the reign of Emperor Khai Dinh, the Phoenix motif began to be included on the Emperor's robes, and this practice continued throughout Bao Dai's reign. Both motifs were mixed with flowers or strands of leaves and were embroidered in the most intricate detail. The beads used were extremely fine and made by hand. Each bead was so delicate and time consuming that the technique of production is almost extinct today. Museum research shows that the beads were of the same type as those used at courts in China and Korea and could only be imported from a small village north of Mumbai in India. To restore and reproduce some of these robes, the restorer, a Vietnamese artist from the United States, had to commission the villagers to remake the beads. It takes 18 months for the villagers to make half a kilogram of fine beads. The buttons on royal robes are made of precious materials such as gold, silver, or gems such as ruby.

Mandarin in grand court robe.

Queen mother's court robe.

Original Emperor's robe, daily court.

Original Long Tran, HCM Museum.

Military mandarin's robe,
grand court assembly.

Original Long Con,
HCM city Museum.

According to the Nguyen Book of Protocol, there were three types of robes for the Emperor to wear on state occasions:

Long Con – Great Dragon Robe for ceremonies displaying motifs of five-claw dragons and other auspicious motifs of clouds, bats and the characters for long life.

Long Bao or Hoang Bao – Great Dragon Robe for grand assemblies and other state occasions at Thai Hoa Palace. The golden yellow robe displayed a large full-face dragon at the front and other five-clawed dragons together with motifs of clouds, bats and the characters for long-life.

Long Tran – Great Dragon Robe – for outdoor ceremonies such as the Tich Dien – royal planting ceremony.

Apart from these Great Dragon Robes, the everyday clothing for the Emperor was also regulated by the Book of Protocol. Those for his daily assemblies are simpler but also display dragon motifs. However, the rules were broken under Khai Dinh's reign, when he decided to add more feminine motifs to his clothing. One of his court robes kept at the Museum shows the extra motifs of 18 roses and two large chrysanthemums embroidered in fine beads and satin threads on both the front and the back.

On state occasions or grand court assemblies, the Queen would wear her great robes but in different colours from the Emperor's and with the motifs of nine phoenix instead of dragons. Similarly, the Crown Prince would also wear Great Dragon Robes but with only four-clawed dragons.

Royal under robe.

The Great Robe of the Crown Prince

The double-sided robe in brilliant orange is made of fine silk and fastened on the right. It is 95 cms long with a flare of 90 cms in width at the hem. On the robe are motifs of dragons curled up in the shape of the character for long-life, a design favoured throughout Thieu Tri's reign. The collar has a motif of double dragons fighting for a pearl. The hems of the Nguyen Royal Great Robes are usually highly decorated with various motifs embroidered in silk and/or gold threads. On this robe, there is a mountain landscape with waves and Koi carp, symbols of good luck and achievement, created by fine embroidery stitches and extra-fine beads.

Crown prince's robe.

Also on display at the Museum is another robe, thought to have belonged to Emperor Bao Dai when he was still a child, after he was made Crown Prince. This golden robe has motifs of phoenix on its sleeves, apart from the required motif of dragons on the body of the robe. Its hem is also decorated with the same scene of mountains, waves and Koi carps.

Emperor Minh Mang's Ceremonial Nam Giao Robe

This black, or very dark blue, unlined robe was made in fine silk, and belonged to the category of Long Con – Great Robe. As a Great Ceremonial Robe, it followed the strict rules of the Protocol book, from the proportion of the sleeves to the motifs used. It is 100 cms long, with a flare of 98cms at the hem and wide sleeves of 68cms. It fastens on the right. The motifs embroidered on both the body of the robe and its sleeves show a solemnity befitting the occasion. On the front of the robe, is only one motif of a small dragon in profile showing five claws, but on the sleeves, this motif is magnified into two magnificent great dragons facing the openings. The back of the sleeves is equally impressive but instead of the dragon motif, we see a phoenix on each sleeve, a male bird on one and a female on the other to show the harmony between Yin and Yang. The back of the robe is much more of a work of art. Although

Nam Giao robe.

it looks simpler and less grand than the front and the sleeve, it is here that the meaning of the Nam Giao ceremony is made clear. Next to motifs of mountains, waves and clouds, a picture of the universe was carefully embroidered, showing the sky at night but with the sun embroidered on the left shoulder and the moon on the right. This is similar to the image of the universe on the ceiling of the theatre in the Tu Duc tomb. Although it is meant to show the sky at night, there is always an image of the sun hovering in one corner. This image of the universe was also present on the flag used at the Nam Giao ceremony.

Khai Dinh's Queen with bonnet.

The Royal bonnets

To crown it all, the Nguyen Emperor wore a variety of headdresses, depending on the occasion. For the highest state occasions, he wore a bonnet decorated with 31 gold dragons, 30 flowers encrusted with 140 beads of gems, diamonds and pearls. The Queen wore a similar bonnet decorated with nine dragons, nine phoenix and four silver pins encrusted with 198 pearls and 231 glass beads.

For Grand Assemblies, the Emperor wore a bonnet of nine gold dragons facing upward. The dragons were so finely made that they seemed to quiver at the slightest movement. Apart from these grandest bonnets used instead of crowns, there were other headdresses depending on the occasion. The simplest headdress would be a black or dark blue circular crown made of silk or cloth to accompany a dark blue or black Ao Dai. A similar style circular headdress of yellow silk was worn to accompany the Emperor's casual yellow robe; Bao Dai wore this style of headdress at his abdication ceremony.

Khai Dinh in Grand Court robe and hat with mandarins.

Khai Dinh's boots.

The Emperor's shoes

Under the Nguyen, silk and brocade were used extensively, not just on robes and everyday personal effects, but also for shoes and boots, sometimes as a cover over leather as with Bao Dai's slippers. Again, the material for the shoes, the motifs embroidered and their colours were strictly laid down in the Nguyen Book of Protocol

For Grand Assemblies, to accompany Long Bao or Hoang Bao, the Emperor wore black shoes lined with red silk and embroidered with dragons, clouds and flowers in tinsel or real gold. For State ceremonies, the black shoes had a dark blue silk lining. For the Nam Giao Ceremony, the Emperor wore black shoes or boots lined with red silk and embroidered with dragons and clouds, strands of leaves and flame motifs. Interspersed with these motifs were tiny diamonds, coral beads, pearls and gold beads.

On display are a pair of black velvet boots worn by Emperor Khai Dinh. They are lined with white leather and embroidered with dragons, clouds, mountains and waves in gold and silver threads.

Other royal footwear

Among the 21 pairs of shoes and boots on show at the museum, those for female royals give a fascinating insight into royal life and fashion within the Forbidden Purple City. These shoes once belonged to the Queen, the Queen Mother and the Emperors' favourite concubines. The Queen's shoes were in fine red silk, embroidered with phoenix motifs and decorated with jade, pearl and coral beads. A pair of clogs belonging to one of Emperor Thieu Tri's lesser queens shows an early attempt at high heels, and suggests the coquettishness of their owner, creating a moving but amusing image of a petite painted lady tottering on her elevated footwear along the Long Corridor to the Emperor's Palace to perform her duties of entertaining the Emperor.

The elevation of the clogs is 6 cms and they are somewhat reminiscent of Japanese Geisha shoes. The soles were painted in red lacquer and gilded with flowers and leaves, the outer parts are embroidered with dragons and the inside lined with red and purple velvet. More than a century after their owner departed this life, the pair of clogs never fails to invite a knowing smile among female visitors. Although they show clearly that their wearer valued comfort hence the soft lining, in the end, her vanity – represented by the precariously high elevation – won the day.

The Queen's shoes.

Concubine's clogs.

Exploring Hue and its environs

Most visitors to Hue do not linger long enough to fully appreciate the beauty and the long history of this city. For them, Hue is simply an old capital with fine buildings and a colourful imperial past. In fact, Hue was a thriving commercial centre before and under the Nguyen, although most of the trading activities took place outside the walls of the Capital City, in the adjacent peninsula of Gia Hoi.

Gia Hoi – the Old Quarter

To find traces of these long-gone days, we need to walk around the old quarter Gia Hoi, to the east of the Capital City, an area which is almost an island bordered by the Perfume River and Dong Ba canal. Gia Hoi was the main commercial quarter of Hue before the establishment of the Nguyen, being first used as a garrison for troops under the Nguyen Lords. The existence of a large number of people attracted Chinese traders from other locations in Thuan-Hoa and they join local merchants to transform the area into a thriving market. They opened emporiums to sell their goods, established club houses for members of the same Chinese clans such as the Hainan or the Guangdong clans, and built temples to worship their various deities, some of these being still well maintained, such as the Fujian temple. Later, under the Nguyen, the area became a spill-over residential quarter for princes, princesses, mandarins, generals and high-ranking court officials, a kind of suburb for Hue – the Capital City. On such residences, the favourite

Typical views in the Old Quarter.

Temple and detail of porch.

Roof details.

Night at Phan Thuan An's house.

dragon and phoenix motifs are clearly visible. Most of the old buildings, both Chinese and Vietnamese, are still standing along the main street running northeast-southwest of Gia Hoi, today's Chi Lang street, or in the areas immediately behind this street. Among these historical Nguyen houses, one is occasionally open to choice visitors who can visit the grounds and/or dine with the hosts.

The House of Princess Ngoc Son

This is a spacious house located in a large landscaped garden complete with miniature mountains and a lake. It was once the residence of Princess Ngoc Son, granddaughter of Emperor Dong Khanh and is today known also as her temple. The current owners are the granddaughter of the Princess and her husband, the well-known writer on Hue and former university professor Phan Thuan An, who open their doors to a few visitors, on application. Both the house and the garden have been well preserved in their original state. Most of the space on the ground floor is dedicated to altars worshipping the princess and other illustrious family members.

Altar in Professor Phan Thuan An's house.   A glimpse of the interior of the house.   Dau Ho vase and darts.

Many historically valuable artefacts, photographs, books and documents are also kept in the house and only a few fortunate visitors can glimpse a more intimate side of the Nguyen family through such items. Some artefacts are illustrated here with the hosts' permission. Also kept in the house are some precious blue and white ceramics and a wooden Dau Ho vase and its darts. Having spent months researching Royal Hue and many days recording the many historical sites of the city, the visit to the house was a crowning moment of our sojourn in Hue. We felt extremely privileged to be able to inspect at close quarter some of the intimate historical objects that once served the Nguyen royals. We were also saddened to learn that this historic house, as well as the whole of Gia Hoi, was prone to flooding, which regularly wreaked its cruel havoc on the house and the area.

The first iron bridge of Hue, leading into Gia Hoi quarter.

Gia Hoi lost its supreme market position to Dong Ba when that market was established at the beginning of the 20th century. Today, Gia Hoi is the sister commercial quarter of Dong Ba market, across a bridge over the Dong Ba canal. The original wooden bridge was replaced by an iron one in 1892, under Emperor Thanh Thai, seven years before the Trang Tien Bridge across the Perfume River. Accordingly it was known as the first iron bridge of Hue.

Thuan An Beach

One of the little-known gems of Hue is the beach at Thuan An, only 13 kms away to the east. The stretch of fine white sand was almost deserted the last time I visited it in 2009. Thuan An beach is by Thuan An mouth, where the Perfume River flows out to sea via a lagoon called Pha Tam Giang. The name Thuan An means 'peaceful and accommodating' and the beach certainly lives up to its name. Although the whole area of Hue, and Thua Thien province are often subject to bad weather during the monsoon, for half of the year, at least, the moderate surf of this beach can rival any of those further south, such as Non Nuoc (China Beach) in Danang and Cua Dai beach in Hoi An. The scenic beauty and the crucial defensive position of Thuan An made it one of the sites where the Nguyen Emperors chose to establish a fortress and a royal beach residence. They even composed poems eulogising its beauty, and immortalised its landscape on their Blue and White china, or on the Nine Bronze Urns.

Before the arrival of the Nguyen, this area was chosen by the Cham to build some of their spectacular temple-towers, now in ruins. One of these dating to the 7th-8th century can still be seen at nearby My Khanh village. In the 13th century, this area was where the Mongols under general Sodu came through to establish a garrison by Pha Tam Giang lagoon in 1284-1285, after they were defeated in the Kingdoms of Champa further south, and before they moved northward to try conquering Vietnam under the Tran. It was this historical event that led to this part of Cham territory being annexed by Vietnam in 1307 and assuming its new name of Thuan-Hoa. This land, in turn, became a refuge for the Nguyen Lords in the 16th century. From here, Royal Hue, home of the Nguyen, was eventually born.

A view from the Perfume River at dawn.

Life at Court

A tree with golden stem and flowers from gems.

Life at Court

Previous: The Nam Giao platform.

For most of their 143 years in power, the Nguyen Court in Hue ruled over a nation at odds with modernity and often restless with discontent, while the emperors themselves were often under pressure from France and other European countries. And yet, the Nguyen managed to accumulate enormous wealth and created a highly refined lifestyle that few of their contemporaries could rival.

To create an aura of mystique and grandeur, the Nguyen formulated many dynastic rituals that Emperor after Emperor followed religiously, each adding more details to make them even more awe-inspiring as time went by. Such ritualistic ceremonies continued to be performed even after the French installed themselves as masters at the Nguyen court, from 1885 onward, albeit with another layer – the French role in the performance.

Phoenix motif at An Dinh Palace.

The most significant ceremony was the coronation of a new Emperor. Logically, the next most important ritual should have been the investiture of a Crown Prince, but this ceremony only took place twice in the history of the Nguyen. Thus the second time was also the last when Bao Dai was named Crown Prince in 1922, at the age of 9.

As with the Chinese and most other dynastic traditions, the Nguyen followed the principle of primogeniture in which the first son would inherit the Mandate of Heaven from his father, the Emperor, and thereby gain the legitimate right to govern his land, his country and his people. This principle was strictly enforced, barring death and calamities, to ensure that the chosen Prince was seen as above reproach. It was also necessary in order to keep peace within an often large royal family, in which the Emperor sired many children with his queens and concubines. Emperor Minh Mang was a fourth son but the crown went to him after Gia Long's first born, Prince Canh, died in 1801, the year before Gia Long became the first Nguyen Emperor, and his next two children died young. Emperor Thieu Tri was Minh Mang's first son in an extended family of 78 children of both sexes. By invoking the primogeniture rule, Thieu Tri ascended to the throne without opposition from his brothers and half brothers.

However, the principle was seriously compromised when Emperor Thieu Tri died and left an instruction to bypass his first son, Hong Bao, in favour of his second. Indeed, trouble flared up as soon as the second son became Emperor Tu Duc. Hong Bao staged a coup against Tu Duc with alleged

An Dinh Palace.

help from European missionaries. The coup failed and Hong Bao committed suicide in jail. Furious at the missionaries' alleged involvement, Emperor Tu Duc initiated severe reprisals against them, which, in turn, became an excuse for France to further intervene in Vietnam.

From 1883 onward, the fact that Tu Duc had no blood children and the French now had a say in court matters made choosing a new Emperor a haphazard and hazardous affair. Three princes, related but not all blood brothers, were selected in less than a year, but all three died soon after being named. The next four emperors were plucked from Nguyen royal ranks out of necessity, in order to maintain legitimacy for both the Hue court and the French protectorate authority. Only under Emperor Khai Dinh was the succession order restored with his appointment of Bao Dai as Crown Prince. Later, Emperor Bao Dai also appointed his first born as Crown Prince Bao Long, but this prince did not reign, as Bao Dai abdicated in 1945 and the Nguyen no longer held power.

Despite the importance of having a clear successor, the Investiture of a Crown Prince, was held only twice during the Nguyen dynasty. The first time was in 1816, when Gia Long appointed his fourth son as the Crown Prince who later became Emperor Minh Mang. The second and last one was in 1922 when Prince Nguyen Phuc Vinh Thuy became the Crown Prince.

The Investiture of Crown Prince Vinh Thuy, later Emperor Bao Dai

The investiture of Crown Prince Vinh Thuy took place on 28th April 1922 with a decree from Emperor Khai Dinh, announcing to all that his first son has been chosen as his successor. The decree was followed by a grand ceremony in Thai Hoa Palace that Bao Dai described vividly in his Memoir of 1980:

> 'On the appointed day, the Mandarins arrived early in full court attire to prepare the Letter of Mandate, written on gold, and a Golden Seal to be given to the Crown Prince at the ceremony....The Emperor, sitting on a chaise carried by porters, arrived at 8 a.m. The chaise itself had a long history, it was a gift from King Louis XVI to Emperor Gia Long, to commemorate the signing of the Treaty of Versailles in 1787 and brought back to Vietnam by Mgr. Pigneau de Behaine. It was the chaise that all Emperors used to travel around the Imperial Citadel.... My father wore his Grand Court Robe in yellow, a jade belt around his waist, his head covered by a bonnet decorated with nine golden dragons, and he held in his hand the jade sceptre. His arrival was announced by the sound of seven canons, the beating of drums and the sound of the bell tolling from Ngo Mon.'

Following the arrival of the Emperor, the French Governor General came to Ngo Mon, to be met by a mandarin from the Ministry of Rites and the Royal Cavalier Escort. From there, the party walked to Thai Hoa Palace and was received by Bao Dai himself before being presented to the Emperor in the Throne Room. Both the French Governor General and the Emperor made speeches. On this occasion, the speeches also included an announcement that Bao Dai would be sent to France for his education. Then the Investiture Ceremony began:

'…. I kow-towed five times in front of the Emperor, then stayed down on my knees, a little to the left of the throne because no one should face the Emperor squarely. Two high-ranking Mandarins came to read aloud the Letter of Mandate and then presented it and the Golden Seal to me as my own symbols of authority. I handed them to two members of the royal family for safe-keeping and then retired to the waiting room, having kow-towed five more times in front of the Emperor…'

Crown Prince's Grand Court Robe.

The Emperor then authorised a decree to be displayed at Phu Van Lau – the Pavilion of Edicts announcing that a Crown Prince had been named and the ceremony had been completed. The next day, the newly-appointed Crown Prince went to offer his prayers at the Ancestral and Dynastic temples. Three days later, another Grand Ceremony was held at Thai Hoa Palace for the Court to offer their congratulatory letter to the Emperor, kept in a lacquer box covered with a red cloth. The day after that, the Mandarins went to congratulate the Crown Prince at his own residence, called the Palace of the East, and gave him a congratulatory letter kept in a similar lacquer box. These two letters of congratulations were, in fact, a pledge of allegiance to the Emperor and the new Crown Prince.

Emperor's Robe.

Apart from the Investiture of the Crown Prince, there were many other royal ceremonies, such as the grantiing of new titles to the Queen Mother or the Queen, or the awarding of official titles and posts to the many princes. Each occasion took place in front of a grand court assembly and lasted a varying length of time, but all took many days to prepare. The Coronation of a new Nguyen Emperor was the grandest event of all.

Emperor Dong Khanh's Queen.

The Coronation of a Nguyen Emperor

A coronation ceremony had many stages lasting several days. The first stage was when Mandarins of the Ministry of Rites performed an announcement ceremony at the Nam Giao Platform, a place where it was believed the Son of Heaven could communicate with the power from above, and at the dynastic and ancestral temples of Thai Mieu and Trieu Mieu. This was to inform everybody, high and low, of the Coronation so that all should be prepared to set up altars where different parts of the ceremony would take place. After that, each stage of the ceremony was meticulously conducted by the Ministry of Rites according to the Nguyen rulebook.

The day before the Grand Ceremony, two yellow altars were placed facing the Throne in Thai Hoa Palace, with two more in the back room on the left, and on the right. Two musical groups of Small Ensembles were positioned on either side of the Throne, and two Grand Ensembles waited outside, on the steps of Thai Hoa Palace. At dawn on the Grand Day, ceremonial objects such as the Golden Book, the Royal Seal and the Phoenix scroll box were fetched from Can Chanh Palace and brought to Thai Hoa Palace to be put on the yellow altars. The Royal red inkpad to accompany the Royal Seal was placed on an altar at the back. Boxes containing congratulatory letters and other ceremonial objects were arranged on the remaining altar. Ceremonial Officials stood waiting on the east side. Princes of all ranks and court Mandarins waited at their appointed places, both inside Thai Hoa Palace and outside in the Courtyard. Outside the Imperial Citadel, dignitaries, villagers and town elders waited on either side of Phu Van Lau – the Pavilion of Royal Edicts.

At the appointed auspicious hour, a drum roll was sounded on Ngo Mon, a ceremonial flag was raised on Ky Dai and the Emperor-to-be was transported to Can Chanh Palace, behind Thai Hoa. After sitting on the throne there, he was carried on a chaise to the north steps of Thai Hoa Palace, from where he walked into the Hall of Audience, accompanied by the sounds of drum and bell from Ngo Mon and music from the ensembles, in an atmosphere of thick incense smoke. Upon reaching the throne, all sound ceased to be replaced by nine cannon after which the new Emperor sat on his throne to begin the coronation ceremony. Everybody waiting prostrated themselves five times and stayed kneeling on the floor to await the next stages of the ceremony: the reading of the Golden Book and the congratulatory letters,

The coronation of Emperor Bao Dai.

The Coronation of Emperor Duy Tan.

The coronation of Bao Dai – next to him is the regent who looked after state affairs while he was studying in France.

The Court Grand Ensemble waiting to perform.

Bao Dai in a French carriage on the way to Nam Giao 1936.

followed by the first use of the Royal Seal on the Royal Scroll announcing that a new Emperor had been successfully crowned.

The Coronation of Emperor Khai Dinh followed the established tradition of his predecessors, but with the added participation of the French Governor General, who, by then, had the right to approve any new Emperor. It began on the fifteenth day of the fourth moon – 16th May 1916. First, a delegation was sent from the Imperial Citadel to An Dinh Palace where Khai Dinh – still only a prince – lived. The mandarins solemnly announced that the prince was to become Emperor and to move into the Forbidden Purple City. Khai Dinh was then carried on a chaise to the Imperial Citadel, stopping at the French Governor General's Office to thank the Governor for his approval the day before. Moving on to cross the river on Trang Tien Bridge, the procession entered the Imperial Citadel by the Hien Nhon gate and proceeded to the Forbidden Purple City. Here, the entire court waited to welcome him in the courtyard of Can Chanh Palace – the place where Nguyen emperors conducted their daily affairs within the Forbidden Purple City. The Prince, dressed in a green robe, walked slowly through Can Chanh Palace to arrive at his temporary residence, Quang Minh Palace. There, a Receiving Ceremony was conducted with prescribed speeches and formalities to welcome the new Emperor-to-be.

The next day, the second stage of the Coronation Ceremony began at 8 a.m in Can Chanh Palace, where a yellow altar had been set up for the ceremonial objects. Khai Dinh, dressed in a green robe and a black circular headdress, arrived to inspect the yellow altar in the presence of the High-Mandarins, and then retired to wait for the next stage. Meanwhile, lower-ranking court mandarins began to assemble in the Courtyard of Salutation.

At the appointed auspicious hour, Khai Dinh, now wearing layers of yellow robes, and a yellow circular headdress, arrived and stood at his designated place in Can Chanh Palace, facing west. From there, he slowly approached the yellow altar, stopped and kow-towed five times. In the courtyard, following an order by the ceremonial official, the assembled mandarins did the same. Khai Dinh then went down on his knees and waited. Two High-Mandarins, one civil and one military, brought him the Royal Seal and the Imperial Robes, which were formally accepted and then placed back

Emperor Khai Dinh.

Can Chanh Palace – now in ruins.

on the yellow altar. Another Mandarin then kneeled down and handed him the Golden Book, which he opened and read out at the page marked with his name. The book was placed open on the table. Khai Dinh returned to his original position and the mandarins knelt in front of him and read out the name of the Emperor-to-be once more, which was then written down on a piece of red paper. The Golden Book was returned to the box and was carefully locked. All the mandarins returned to their appointed positions. To conclude this stage of the ceremony, Khai Dinh went to the yellow altar, saluted three times and then retired to his private quarters. The ceremonial symbols of Royal Authority were put under lock and key and this part of the Coronation Ceremony was over.

The following day, 18th May 1916, the Grand Ceremony of Coronation began at Thai Hoa Palace, where Nguyen Emperors conducted their bi-monthly court assemblies. Two yellow tables stood in the middle of the hall, with two red tables to their left. On one of the red tables, the High-Mandarins put the Royal Seal and the First Royal Edict, rolled up in a tube painted with a yellow phoenix on the outside. On the second red table, was placed a box containing a red inkpad. One of the yellow tables, would later receive the Golden Book and the Letter of Congratulations. Outside, in the courtyard, all the princes and mandarins waited in place to participate in the Coronation Ceremony.

At the appointed time, a mandarin of the Ministry of Rites and a Military mandarin announced that all was in order and invited the new Emperor to leave his temporary residence for Can Chanh Palace. From here, he mounted a chaise carried by 16 bearers to travel a few steps to Thai Hoa Palace. A band playing court music accompanied the procession, while bells and drums were sounded to announce his arrival.

Emperor Khai Dinh.

Mandarins kow-tow in front of Thai Hoa.

Tu Duc's silver coin.

Khai Dinh's coin.

One of Khai Dinh's seals.

At this point, the French Governor General and French guests arrived and entered the Imperial Palace by the Royal Gate – Ngo Mon, to be greeted by high-ranking Mandarins of Rites and taken into Thai Hoa Palace. There, the French Governor saluted the Emperor who was standing to receive him and the Emperor inclined his head in return. The French Governor then read out a congratulatory speech and the Emperor replied. When all speeches had been read, the Emperor sat on his throne. All mandarins then took turn to come to kow-tow in front of him, with the name of each mandarin and the number of required kow-tows announced by the Master of Ceremony.

After this, a High-Mandarin brought in the box containing the Golden Book and placed it on the yellow altar in the middle of the room. Another High-Mandarin came to kneel down and read what was engraved on a new page of the Golden Book. In effect, the Golden Book attested to the new Emperor's legitimacy and announced that Emperor Khai Dinh was beginning his reign now that his father had passed away. When the reading was over, more kow-tows from the mandarins followed. Then came the ceremony of congratulation when the Letter of Congratulations was taken from the red table and read to the assembled court and guests. The Master of Ceremony then asked the Emperor to use his Royal Seal on the red inkpad to stamp his First Royal Edict, announcing the beginning of his reign and listing the grace and favours to be distributed to the people in the capital and throughout the country. The now stamped Edict was put on the first yellow altar. The mandarins withdrew and the Master of Ceremony proclaimed that the ceremony was completed. A nine-gun salute announced the end of the ceremony and a Minister of Rites came to kneel in front of the Emperor to inform him of the ceremony's completion. The Emperor left to return to his quarters and the mandarins and guests dispersed. The reign of Khai Dinh had now begun. Next, the First Edict of the new Emperor was taken out to Phu Van Lau, to be read aloud to the assembled dignitaries and elders, and then pasted on the display board for all to read in the days to come.

Nguyen Rituals

The Nguyen's refined lifestyle, with its indulgence and excesses, has been admired and vilified in equal measure. Nevertheless, the emperors and their courts have left behind a legacy of cultural artefacts and precious objects that have become part of Vietnam's national heritage. In addition to material items, they also left an extensive legacy of rites and rituals.

During their time, the Nguyen calendar was full of dates for various ceremonies that the Emperor – in his capacity of 'Son of Heaven' – was required to perform. Under the early reigns of Gia Long, Minh Mang, Thieu Tri and Tu Duc, the ritualistic ceremonies were a necessity to uphold their Mandate from Heaven. Later,

Bronze Bells used for the Nam Giao ceremony.

however, after the French Protectorate Authority took over the administration of the country in 1884, these were the only duties left for the Emperors and their courts to perform

The Nguyen year began with the Lunar New Year – Tet celebration – and then progressed to other ceremonies, some annually, others periodically. The most important ceremony of all was the Nam Giao, the oldest and most traditional of the Nguyen rituals, created by Emperor Gia Long in 1803, with the last one being performed by Emperor Bao Dai in March 1945. It was an occasion designed to allow the Son of Heaven to communicate directly with the power from above, in a moment when Heaven and Earth converged on the Nam Giao Platform.

One final Nam Giao ceremony was performed by Bao Dai at a different location in 1953, in his capacity as Head of State. This took place in Ban Me Thuot, his private domain in the Central Highlands.

The Nam Giao Ceremony

This is the grandest of all Nguyen's ceremonies and was held annually until 1907 when it was changed to every three years under Emperor Thanh Thai. Nam Giao can be described loosely as a ceremony for the Emperor to talk to his superior beings – his celestial parent(s) – and ask them to grace the country with peace, good weather, good crops, and to thank them for past blessings.

A lamp post at the Nam Giao Platform.

Bao Dai arriving for the Nam Giao ceremony, 1939.

Nam Giao ceremony with French guests, 1924.

It was the most solemn and most significant occasion in the Nguyen calendar of rites. It was also a sacrificial ceremony where animals such as buffaloes, pigs and goats were killed and offered to Heaven. French officials who witnessed such ceremonies wrote many articles about them from 1914 onward and called them 'Le Sacrifice du Nam Giao', as they focussed on the sacrificial aspect, rather than its spiritual significance to the Nguyen Emperor – as a re-affirmation of his Mandate from Heaven.

The tradition started in 1803, before the building of Hue, at a location nearby, called An Ninh village. Then it was simply an occasion for Emperor Gia Long to express his thanks to Heaven for his victory, his newly-formed dynasty and to pray for the well being of his people. In 1806, with his capital now complete, Emperor Gia Long decided to turn the Nam Giao ceremony into a dynastic ritual and moved the location to an auspicious venue on the south bank of the Perfume River. Here, he built a large platform called Dan Nam Giao – Dan meaning a platform or an esplanade, a name that is still in use today.

The Nam Giao Platform is an elaborate 4.65 metre high earthen structure of three tiers. It was built using soil collected by an Imperial edict from villages throughout the country. The result was a large platform with two square tiers as the base and a circular tier at the top. The three tiers symbolise the three elements that need to be in harmony with each other: Heaven, Human and Earth.

Preparing the sacrificial animals for the ceremony, 1927.

The whole structure resembled an enormous cake, each tier connected to the next or to the ground by elaborate stone steps. An iron parapet surrounds each tier with openings on all four sides, each gap shielded by a screen to keep the bad air out. The parapets were originally painted in different colours: red for the largest, bottom tier, yellow for the next and blue for the top, representing the blue sky of Heaven. The floor of the top tier was paved with large slabs of blue stone, each drilled with holes for inserting tent poles. During most of the year, the Nam Giao Platform was left empty but during ceremonial times, several large blue tents were erected on the top to shelter the altars dedicated to Heaven and the spirits of the sky, the stars. On the next tier, were tents of yellow cloth to shelter more altars.

The most remarkable feature of the Nam Giao Platform is its acoustics. Despite being an open-air platform, any sound uttered on the top tier of the platform will be heard by all around and below. In this regard it is similar to the construction of the most sophisticated ancient Greek and Roman open-air theatres. During the ceremony, the chanting, the sound of drums and music were magnified many-fold and reverberated through the surrounding pine trees, making the event a grand performance that could be heard from afar.

The area around the platform was planted with pine trees, a Nguyen favourite, which add a foliage element

Goats ready for the Nam Giao ceremony, 1924.

Pine tree labels.

Khai Dinh's procession on way to Nam Giao, 1924.

to the harmony between Heaven and Earth. During the early Nguyen, under the order of Minh Mang, the Emperor and his mandarins planted the pine trees themselves, each tree marked by a copper plaque inscribed with the name of the planter, and they were subsequently nurtured by an army of servants. Later, the original pines died and have been replaced by a new species that we see today.

The Nam Giao Platform does not just refer to the platform alone. Around the structure were several buildings used for the emperor to rest and purify himself prior to the ceremony, for the kitchen to prepare the sacrificial animals and for many other functions necessary to the grand ceremony.

The preparation for the Nam Giao ceremony began months before the actual date, and the organisation fell on two ministries: the Ministry of Rites and the Ministry of Work. Firstly, the Emperor would issue several decrees calling on the people to get ready, and ordering fortune-tellers to choose auspicious dates. Then he awarded his mandarins with favours and ranks and gave an amnesty to prisoners for good luck.

The purpose of the ceremony was solely for the Son of Heaven to speak with his celestial parent(s) and the gods of different elements and had nothing to do with Buddhism, ancestor worship, or any other beliefs in Vietnam. The date was announced three months in advance, not to the populace, but to the divine power from above. Two weeks before the ceremony, the souls of the ancestors were informed and invited to participate in the ceremony. To prepare himself, the Emperor went into retreat for three days beforehand to purify himself, as he was required to be chaste and abstinent before he could present himself to the Celestial Power. The original period of three days was shortened to one under Emperor Bao Dai.

When the time came, the Emperor and his entourage departed for the ceremony the day before, at an auspicious time in the early

morning, with a canon being fired to announce the royal departure from Can Chanh Palace in the Forbidden City. The procession comprised two thousand people, divided into three groups, preceded by elephants garbed in colourful ceremonial gear. Behind the elephants came the parasol bearers, drums, gongs, ritual objects, musicians, and most important of all, the Emperor's Sword of Mandate. The next group was the bearers of flags symbolising the universe, the sun, the moon and the stars, then the royal cavaliers, the dancers, and the chaises carrying the Crown Prince and the Emperor. Behind them was the third group carrying bells, large and small, drums, musical instruments, and last of all, more elephants, caparisoned sumptuously.

Before the Trang Tien Bridge was built, the royal party took a long time to cross the Perfume River, before continuing on the road known as the Nam Giao route. Along the way, local people erected decorative gates and roadside altars to greet the Emperor. The procession of people and animals took several hours to cross the city at a slow and solemn pace arriving at the Platform just before noon. On arrival, the Emperor was taken directly into Trai Cung – his Palace of Purification, located in a separate area at a corner of the Nam Giao Platform, where he meditated until the ceremony began.

Bronze bells ready for the Nam Giao ceremony, 1924.

Elephant leading the procession to Nam Giao, 1924.

Bao Dai's procession at Thuong Tu gate en route to the Nam Giao ceremony, 1936.

Khai Dinh in Nam Giao robe.

The Nam Giao Ceremony began at 2 a.m, a time considered as the most auspicious for communication between the Son of Heaven and his Celestial Parent, and lasted three hours. It was also the quietest moment of the night when the prayers from below had the best chance to reach as far as Heaven, magnified manyfold by the special acoustics of the platform. In his Memoir of 1980, Bao Dai recalled his own Nam Giao:

'...I left the Palace of Purification to arrive at the platform by palanquin. The Great Flag was unfurled. I walked up to the top and stopped to wash my hands. Enormous torches lit up all corners of the platform while, at the southeast corner, an enormous fire was ready, the buffalo – animal of sacrifice – waited.... Men seemed to be mesmerised by the atmosphere of mystique and solemnity while the music played.... All my gestures at the ceremony were meticulously calculated according to regulations. Each step, each gesture was announced by the Master of Ceremony. On the yellow tier of*

The Emperor returned to the Citadel after the Nam Giao ceremony.

Child dancers.

A rare stone badge c. 1884: the Nguyen troubled period.

Trai Cung – the purification palace today.

the platform, the altar for offering was placed under an yellow tent. Eight other altars were also placed nearby, to make offers to the genies, the moon, the cloud, the wind, the earth, the stars...'

The nine stages of the ceremony took three hours, each stage accompanied by 128 singers and dancers. The most solemn stage involved the Emperor kneeling and reading aloud a prepared text, written on a tablet, listing the names and achievements of all his ancestors. He invited them to come down from Heaven to participate in the ceremony and then asked the Celestial Power to accept the offers of precious silk, wine and freshly killed meat. When the reading was over, the offerings and the prayer tablet were put in copper urns and set alight so that the flame would propel the essence of the offerings to heaven. With the offerings ascending to heaven, the ceremony was pronounced over. The Emperor descended to the ground, got back in his palanquin and returned to

Urn for the Nam Giao ceremony.

A gate to the Nam Giao Platform.

the Palace of Purification where he was congratulated by the princes and other members of his extended family. The royal party then took the same route in reverse back to the Capital City on the North Bank. When they reached the Imperial Citadel, a nine-gun salute signaled their return and the Nam Giao was over for another three years.

Today, the Nam Giao platform is bare, standing in the middle of a spacious gated park, its dense foliage mainly provided

Urn for the Nam Giao ceremony.

by pines. At first, the platform appears as a circular terrace and only on closer inspection does it become clear that it is a three-tier structure. The bottom tier measures 340m x 265m and appears as if it is part of the general landscape. The top tier has a diameter of 40.5m and is 3.8m high.

Whichever of the three entrances to the park is chosen, one must walk several hundred metres to the foot of the platform. One of the entrances has modern iron gates, while the north one is marked by a large screen, once highly decorated with royal symbols but now tarnished by time and neglect. At one corner of the park, several hundred metres from the platform, is the Trai Cung where the Emperors purified themselves prior to the ceremony. It is now used to house old ceremonial objects and newly created items for re-enactments of the Nam Giao Ceremony during the Hue Festival. On the walls hang many black and white photographs of past ceremonies, and plaques explaining the process of the ritual under the Nguyen. In this once solemn royal domain, old and the new ceremonial objects stand side by side in readiness for their next performance demonstrating aspects of a unique Nguyen practice that will never be held again for the purpose it was originally intended. Rather, it is now a colourful spectacle performed by artists and accompanied by live elephants and horses.

Tet and the Phat Thuc preparatory ceremony

Tet is the beginning of the Lunar New Year, which falls in either late January or early February, depending on the position of the moon. It is celebrated in China and Sinicised countries such as Vietnam. Under the Nguyen, it was a grand celebration for both the Court and common people. Like all Nguyen ceremonies, it took many days and much preparation. The most remarkable preparatory event was the cleaning of the Royal Treasure called the Phat Thuc ceremony in Vietnamese. This ceremony usually fell on the last few days prior to the end of the old year and was an occasion for the court to inventory their treasure in the presence of the Emperor and his princes.

The Inner Court first presented a date and a list of persons they thought would be suitable for the Phat Thuc ceremony to the Emperor, who then granted his approved and chose the necessary personnel. On the appointed day, six large cabinets were brought into Can Chanh Palace and opened in the presence of the Emperor, his princes and the chosen mandarins. One by one, the chests were unsealed to reveal the Nguyen treasure to be cleaned. The treasure was a huge collection of different precious objects: Royal seals in gold, silver, jade, bags of precious stones, royal swords, golden books, silk books, and many other valuables. The cleaning of the Nguyen treasure was a solemn occasion that was first held in the 17th year of Minh Mang's reign (1837 CE). To perform this ceremony, the mandarins dressed themselves in their formal court

An urn for the Nam Giao ceremony.

robes, in deep blue with large sleeves. As they washed the valuable objects in scented water and dried them with a soft cloth, another mandarin noted what came out and was put back into the chests so that when the task was finished, the list of treasure had been updated. The chests were sealed again and would not be opened again without an order from the Emperor. The Phat Thuc ceremony ended with a grand banquet for all those who took part.

When the first day of the new year arrived, it was an occasion for yet another great ceremony beginning with a seven-gun salute announcing the arrival of the New Year. It was followed by a day of feasting and mutual visits before culminating in a flamboyant Royal procession through residential areas of the city, accompanied by music, dancers, horses and elephants. The procession was called a Royal Rite of Spring – Du Xuan – and was meant to be a joyful occasion for all to display their finery. In reality, everyone stayed indoors when the royal party went past as nobody dared to show their faces for fear they might be whipped out of the way by the imperial guards.

As a joyful occasion, bad spirits had to be kept away by the noise of firecrackers, let off constantly all over the city. On one Tet celebration under Emperor Dong Khanh (r.1885-1889), the royal party was accompanied by General Prudhomme, riding at the side of the Emperor's chaise. The sound of firecrackers frightened the general's horse so much that he had to dismount and walk, like a humble foot soldier, to avoid being thrown into the canal. It was an amusing anecdote told with glee in *La Guerre illustrée* by a French journalist who also wrote for the French newspaper *Le Figaro*.

Gia Long's main seal.

A large ceremonial urn.

A Royal silk book.

Stone elephant at Thieu Tri tomb.

Opposite: The Tiger Arena.

Elephants kneeling to show respect to the Emperor.

The Nguyen at Leisure

Elephant-Tiger contests

Ever since the 16th century, when the first Nguyen Lord settled in the south, the Nguyen are known to have indulged in certain blood sports, with the favourite being a fight to the death between tigers and elephants. This was a typical royal pastime until 1904 in the reign of Emperor Thanh Thai, when the game was banned.

Tiger and elephant fights began as military training exercises, at a period when the Nguyen were trying to consolidate their power in the south while facing constant threats from the Trinh in the north. Accordingly, they had to keep their army in a state of readiness in case of war. Traditionally, elephants played an important role in Vietnamese and most Southeast Asian armies. By their sheer size, they acted like modern tanks and provided prestige to their commanders, who sitting atop the huge beasts could see how the battle was progressing below. The Nguyen valued their elephants highly and trained them to become used to the scent of blood by involving them in regular military exercises. Under Emperor Gia Long, such exercises were held three times a year. Under Minh Mang, these were increased to four times a year and then became even more frequent, once every moon. During the training exercises, the tactics that the elephants employed in their fights with dummies would be carefully analysed by generals and soldiers in order to apply them to their war plans. As a result, elephants' fighting tactics evolved into a blood sport to be staged periodically for the Nguyen Lords and their entourage to enjoy. On such occasions, the elephants fought real adversaries – the tigers – instead of dummies. Over time, the spectacle was conducted in a festival-like atmosphere and enjoyed by the populace from far and wide

As evidenced by inscriptions at the temple erected in memory of a brave elephant – Mieu Voi Re – the Nguyen clearly saw the elephant as the most powerful, the most loyal and warriorlike animal. At the same time, like most peoples who coexist closely with fearsome wild beasts, they feared and respected the tiger as an unpredictable

but noble beast. By pitting the two animals against each other, the Nguyen created one of the most savage spectacles that enthralled and revolted the spectators in equal measure. The elephant-tiger fights left a lasting impression on those who witnessed them, with French guests often writing of them with awe and revulsion, with allusions to similar Roman spectacles held in the Colosseum.

Dau Ho game

This is a dart game with a difference. With *Dau* meaning head or dart and *Ho* meaning jar or vase, the game involves throwing darts into a vase – something that is more difficult than it sounds calling for a good eye and a steady hand. It was a favourite game among the Nguyen and Emperor Tu Duc was said to have been very skilful, setting out the rules of play in the Royal Book of Rites. Dau Ho was mainly an indoor game played after a meal, but sometimes, it was played outside, on the veranda of the palaces or in the courtyard.

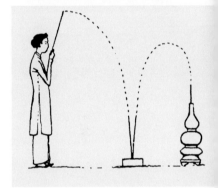

Dau Ho game.

A Dau Ho vase.

The game necessitated three items: a tall vase, bulbous at the bottom and with a narrow neck and 5 cm wide mouth, a square block of wood and a set of darts. The height of the vase is about 60-65 cms and usually stands on a block of wood about 40-45cms high to raise the mouth of the vase to the height of an average Vietnamese chest. As part of a royal game, the Dau Ho vase tended to be a work of art in its own right, made from precious wood, bronze, porcelain or fine ceramic and heavily ornate, often inlaid with precious gems. Inside, a small drum is placed at the bottom, or something that would sound when the dart managed to enter the narrow mouth and hit the bottom. The whole process was supervised by a master of games who kept scores and regulated complaints.

Each player had 12 darts, representing the 12 moons in a year and each dart was about 40 cms long or even longer, according to the regulation of each Emperor, with the longest almost 80 cms.

The longer the dart, the more difficult the game. Darts were made of soft wood to increase their flexibility and bounce.

The player stood away from the vase at a distance three times the length of the dart, with the block of wood placed on the floor equidistant between the player and the vase, to act as a bouncing point. The player threw his dart onto the wooden block and hoped that it would bounce and somersault into the narrow mouth of the vase. The prize was a small souvenir gift or a cup of wine that the loser would humbly offer to the winner. Needless to say, it was a very difficult game designed to test the player, both mentally and physically, and to train him in the practice of total concentration.

The Nguyen loved the game and cherished their vases, with several being created in each reign. They later became collectors' pieces and many have been taken out of Vietnam. As each Nguyen Emperor had his own specially created vases, they also offer an

Xam Huong set which once belonged to Emperor Tu Duc.

insight into his preferred style. Some vases were of blue and white porcelain, while others were polished wood, inlaid with gem stones.

Two vases created by Emperor Tu Duc show great decorative skill, one was porcelain encrusted with precious stones and mother-of pearl, the other was bronze and inlaid throughout with gems and jade. A third one, carved from a single piece of wood, without any decoration, is simple but exquisitely elegant in shape. Some Dau Ho vases still survive and are on show at the Museum of Royal Antiquities or at other locations during festival times, when the game is re-enacted and visitors are invited to participate, often with dismal but hilarious results.

Xam Huong game

Another typical game was the Xam Huong, a dice game much loved by the Nguyen. Like Dau Ho, this unique game is also re-enacted during festival times. The rules are fairly complicated and need lengthy demonstration before spectators can grasp the highly volatile process, which evolves with the combinations of sticks that each player accumulates.

First players throw their dice and pick a corresponding stick from the box. In all there are 63 sticks, usually made of flat ivory, with their values engraved on the upper parts. The values are not numbers or symbols like in a card game, but academic degrees, each colour-coded on the flat stick. The higher the degree the more valuable the stick, with doctorate obviously the most sought after. Each degree is divided into levels and engraved in different colours, so each stick has many different levels of value, adding another layer of complexity. The players count the sticks at the end of the game and decide the winner. Each Emperor owned his own box of Xam Huong, but today only one such box survives and is on display in the Museum of Royal Antiquities. It once belonged to Emperor Tu Duc and is still kept in pristine conditions, although only 56 out of its original 63 sticks remain. The sticks are kept in five compartments of the wooden box, the outside of which is richly decorated with precious materials such as ivory and mother-of-pearl, with a small drawer in the box for the dice.

A collection of Dau Ho vases.

Models for burning at funeral ceremonies.

Incense sticks drying in the sun.

Life after death

Like all Vietnamese, and other Asians, the Nguyen took death seriously, not as the end of life but as a passage from one form of being to another. According to this philosophy, a person's time on earth is just an interlude in a long chain of being, in many diverse forms, until the soul achieves enlightenment. Until such time, the soul of the dead lives among the living, where it may occupy a newly-born mortal body to begin another life, although the essence of the soul continues to be around in an ethereal form. As such, the dead are believed to continue to exist in an afterlife and need all their favourite things. To make this afterlife comfortable, it is the duty of their relatives to burn models of their possessions, such as cars, motorbikes, money, or houses at the altar during their funerals, in the hope that the essence of these will follow the dead into his/her afterlife. In 1926, a model of Kien Trung Palace, Emperor Khai Dinh's home that he loved so much was burned at his funeral, along with many other possessions that the royal family deemed he might need in his afterlife.

At Nam Giao ceremonies, one of the rituals that the Emperor was required to perform was issuing an invitation to his ancestors, asking them to come to the ceremony. At the end of which, the offerings were burned so that their essence could travel upward to the sky for the Emperor's celestial parent(s) to enjoy, or permeate in the air to reach the souls of the ancestors in their afterlives.

Burning of model offerings.

Under the Nguyen, an Emperor's funeral was a grand affair that took days to complete, sometimes, after months of waiting for an auspicious burial day. According to the late Emperor Bao Dai, after leaving his father's body to rest in Can Chanh Palace until the auspicious day, more than a month later, 50 mandarins took turns to carry his coffin in a long cortège from the Imperial Citadel to his tomb in the Valley of the Tombs, on the South Bank of the Perfume River. Here, Emperor Khai Dinh's body was buried but his soul lived on in his new imperial palace that the tomb represents.

Khai Dinh's funeral.

Royal arts

Phap Lam panels at Thieu Tri Tomb.

As scholars and gentlemen of leisure, the Nguyen emperors were very fond of poetry and art, with the happy result that a treasure house of Nguyen calligraphy and arts still exists in Hue today. Despite many valuable pieces being destroyed or stolen during periods of conflict, what remains is still substantial in quality and diversity of style.

Characteristically, each Nguyen Emperor was keen to imprint his signature style on buildings and structures built or renovated under his reign. The style of each was so different that it is often possible to assign items to a specific reign, just by studying the materials and the techniques. For example, the Phap Lam panels on Ngo Mon and the Terrace of Five Phoenix are clearly from Minh Mang's reign, as he was a well-known champion of this painted enamel technique. Similarly, both Emperors Dong Khanh and Khai Dinh are well known for their fondness for ceramic and glass inlay. That said, such visual hunches need to be properly verified by documents.

Apart from their distinctive architectural decorations, the Nguyen also assembled a wealth of art objects, porcelains and curios. These came to the court in all shapes and sizes from all over the world. Many were diplomatic gifts from Chinese and neighbouring courts, or inducements from European ship captains who sought to trade with the Nguyen.

Many of the latter can be recognised by their alien subject matter or scenes. One such example is an oval serving platter depicting a large turkey, a bird unknown in Vietnam at the time. It was a gift from a Portuguese delegation to Emperor Gia Long, according to the stamp underneath. Later, European-made gifts tended to display a more oriental design, perhaps in the hope that they would be more pleasing to the Nguyen. The British willow

pattern – still in manufacture today – was the most popular. The pattern, showing a scene of castle, bridge, people and a willow tree from a Chinese story, was so appreciated that Emperor Dong Khanh used it extensively to decorate his birth father's tomb in the Valley of the Tombs, on the South Bank of the Perfume River. The majority of the foreign-made objects, however, were purchased by agents on behalf of the Nguyen emperors.

Roof corner of Thai Hoa Palace with Phap Lam panels.

Although it is not widely known, the early emperors engaged in commercial activities through the ports of Danang, Hoi An and Saigon, sending ships and commercial junks to trade with China, Thailand, Singapore or even India. It is documented that between 1835-1839 Emperor Minh Mang sent ships every year to Singapore and Cambodia, selling rice, raw silk, animal skins, oil, salt, salted fish, bird nests, shark's fins, buffalo horns and elephant tusks among other valuable products. In return foreign products were bought such as opium, wool, tea, silk, spices, paper, porcelain, copper, arms and ammunition. On their return, the Vietnamese ship captains or officials in charge bought objects that they thought the Emperor might appreciate, such as jewellery, clocks, glass beads and mechanical toys, sometimes at exorbitant prices. If the items did not find favour, the captains and officials could be jailed for having wasted money.

Under the Nguyen, Vietnam continued to have a thriving pottery industry with kilns working throughout the country catering both for all types of domestic consumer and for export. High quality Vietnamese-made tiles and paving stones from Bat Trang kiln, near Hanoi, were used on royal palaces and to pave the paths of the Imperial Citadel, but for everyday use at court, foreign-made china and porcelain objects were more popular. Porcelain vases, urns, tea sets, and dinner services, together with boxes gilded in gold and silver and painted in different colours, or inlaid with precious and semi-precious stones, were cherished by the Emperors and aspired to by courtiers.

The majority of the porcelain used in the palace came from China, a place seen as the height of refinement by most Asian courts. Many pieces had designs in cobalt blue on white and more

Screen at Kien Thai Vuong's tomb.

Detail of Minh Mang Phap lam.

A mosaic bowl of fruit.

Fayence lime pot commissioned from Copeland & Garrett by Emperor Minh Mang. c. 1840.

Teaset marked 'for inner palace'.

than 3,000 such pieces, having survived war and escaped theft, are currently on display at the Museum of Royal Antiquities in Hue. Large pieces have survived better than the smaller ones, which were easy to pilfer in troubled times.

The Royal Collection of Blue and White china

The unique feature of this large group of ceramic and porcelain pieces is that most were made to order for the Nguyen Court – who supplied their own designs – at the Imperial kilns of Jingdezhen in Jiangxi, China. Some were also made in fine kilns in Guangzhou and Fujian. From the dates and marks stamped on these pieces, it is known that four Vietnamese Emperors, Minh Mang, Thieu Tri, Tu Duc and Khai Dinh, commissioned them from Qing China. The first Nguyen Emperor Gia Long tended to favour locally-made china as some pieces bearing his stamp were clearly made in Vietnam. His Chinese objects usually came to Hue as gifts.

The period when no ceramic wares are known to have been ordered during the reigns of Tu Duc and Khai Dinh reflects a turbulent era in Vietnamese history, when France took over the administration and five Nguyen emperors succeeded each other within short periods of time. None of them had the opportunity to enjoy a peaceful reign, let alone indulge in the refined lifestyle that their predecessors had enjoyed.

The one exception was Emperor Thanh Thai, who had a long enough reign to imprint his style within the Imperial Citadel. However, he favoured European designs over Chinese and commissioned many pieces from France and England. His penchant for European ceramics led to unique items where European pieces were made for uniquely Vietnamese functions, such as lime pots or spittoons, receptacles vital for betel-chewers but non-existent in European culture. His son, Emperor Duy Tan did not order any personal chinaware but still left a small number of fine ceramic objects bearing his stamps – gifts from China on his birthdays.

Each of the four Emperors who did order from China had their own sets and designs, with the stamp dates, and, sometimes, the signature calligraphy of that particular emperor. Many pieces depict paintings and accompanying poems composed by the emperors themselves. The process of commissioning chinaware from Jingdezhen was lengthy and carefully controlled. On the order of the Emperor, the artists produced their designs on paper, and then submitted them for consideration. Once approved, a delegation was despatched to China with the designs and orders were placed at the imperial kilns. According to Vietnamese historical records, there were 26 missions – called embassies – to China under the Nguyen. These embassies were mainly diplomatic missions but they also handled the Emperors' orders for bespoke china. When the cargo of china arrived in Hue, the royal household officers would stamp them with the mark 'for Emperor's use' on the bottom of each piece, or the characters 'sun' and 'long-life'.

By any definition, the Nguyen's collection of Royal Blue and White china is refined in production technique and rich in design, especially those pieces from Jingdezhen. The Jingdezhen imperial kilns in Jiangxi have been renowned for their fine china since the Song dynasty (960-1279) and attained their highest reputation under the Yuan (1271-1368), when Mongol rulers imported the cobalt blue dye from the Middle East. This dye revolutionised the production techniques at Jingdezhen as the artisans could create clearer, more durable and more vivid blue designs on white than with the previously-used organic blue dye. The kilns maintained their high reputation throughout the Ming (1368-1644) and the Qing (1644-1911) dynasties. The fine porcelain wares are greatly admired for their translucence, achieved by using the local high quality clay and skilful firing techniques. The quality control at these kilns was extremely high and only the best pieces would pass the inspection of the kiln superintendents. Any imperfect pieces were broken at once to keep the designs exclusive to the clients.

Blue and White ceramic made in Jingdezhen.

The high quality of the Jingdezhen kilns, combined with the more fluid Vietnamese designs, make the Nguyen collection of Blue and White china unique. Designed by Vietnamese artists, they were diverse in size and shape, with subjects that could only have come from Vietnam. Many designs derived from the region surrounding the capital, and often incorporated royal calligraphy or brush strokes. Not only is the collection valuable in material and artistic terms, but it provides an historical record of the political and social climate under the Nguyen. By deciphering a simple couplet on a royal porcelain plate we may see how the Emperor was feeling at a particular time. Similarly, the painting of a local landscape can become an historic document. For example, the severe typhoon of 1904 changed the shape of Thuan An port, 13 kms northeast of Hue and moved the entrance. Without the painting, the original site of the entrance and a piece of geographical history would be lost.

A steambowl in blue and white ceramic.

Although the Nguyen brought the design of imported porcelain to new heights, the practice of ordering from Jingdezhen was not invented by, or exclusive to, the Nguyen emperors and other Asian courts, such as the Thai, were also customers. In Vietnam, the custom started in the 16th century under the Le, and became more established in the early 18th century with both the Le emperors and the Trinh Lords placed orders in China. When the first Nguyen Lord established himself in the south, he started the Nguyen's own collection of Blue and White ceramics from China. At the same time, courtiers and wealthy merchants also ordered fine china from Chinese kilns, although not necessarily from the imperial ones, and not always from Jingdezhen.

The identity of some former owners can be gleaned from the stamps on the underneath, or by the way the character was formed. On some of the Nguyen imperial pieces, by checking the shape of the character 'sun', we can link it to the reigns of Minh Mang,

A plate in blue and white ceramic.

Vase, a gift from France.

Phap Lam tray.

A large Phap Lam vase.

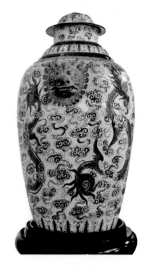

Thieu Tri or Tu Duc: Minh Mang's 'sun' is calligraphically refined and slightly open at one corner, Thieu Tri's is closed and square and Tu Duc's is top heavy.

Apart from the Chinese collection, the Nguyen owned a smaller number of ceramics either received as gifts, or ordered from Japan and Europe. These pieces bear Japanese calligraphy or the stamps of Spode and Royal Staffordshire in England, or Sèvres in France. An even smaller group of European ceramics are said to have been painted with Vietnamese subjects and landscapes after manufacture in Europe and transport to Hue. A few survive and allegedly bear the stamps of Minh Mang's reign. However, whether they were painted for the Emperor or someone else during his reign, is still unclear.

The Nguyen Phap Lam technique

The Phap Lam technique is today considered typical of the Nguyen, but it was originally imported into Vietnam by Emperor Minh Mang and became a favourite form of decoration under his successors Thieu Tri and Tu Duc, before gradually dying out during the French occupation. It is still visible today on the two ceremonial gates straddling the path leading from the Ngo Mon (Royal Gate) to Thai Hoa Palace, on buildings within the Imperial Citadel and at the Nguyen tombs. Phap Lam has also been used to decorate smaller royal objects such as bowls, plates, boxes and vases.

The origin of the name Phap Lam is rather complex and there is debate in Vietnam as to whether it is a direct translation of two Chinese characters meaning French/European and the colour cobalt blue, or whether it simply represents one word Phap-lan(g) meaning France. In the latter case this could be a reference to its possible origin, before it was imported into China and then to Vietnam. The technique was once called Canton enamel after the location where it was produced en-masse in the 18th and 19th centuries. Exactly how the technique came to Canton (Guangzhou) is still uncertain. It has also been suggested that the character Lam was originally Lan and was later changed to Lam to avoid being a Nguyen taboo word.

In any event, Phap Lam is a technique of freehand painting on ceramic glazed on copper sheets or artefacts. It differs from the better-known Byzantine art of cloisonné, which also uses enamel and copper, so beloved by French and Russian courts in the 18th and 19th centuries. With cloisonné, liquid enamel or precious stones was used to infill tiny compartments created by copper wire, or indents, on a copper base. With Phap Lam, the enamel was used first as a glaze on a copper base, then over painted with flowers and other motifs, before the pieces were fired once more to fix the colour and the shine.

There are three variants of Phap Lam: the first is that described above; the second fixes fine copper wire onto the enamel glaze before freehand painting on top; while the third adds a transparent glaze over the top of the first and second methods before firing once more. The end result in all three methods looks like a colourful miniature bas-relief.

As with their Jingdezhen chinaware, the Nguyen preferred to order ornamental pieces from China, and some of the earlier Phap Lam objects came to Hue from Guangzhou. Under Minh Mang, however, Phap Lam artisans were brought to Hue from China to help decorate new structures in the Imperial Citadel. Once the Vietnamese learned the techniques, Emperor Minh Mang set up his own royal factory in Hue known as Phap Lam Tuong Cuc in 1827. From here, many pieces were produced and used throughout the Imperial Citadel and at the Nguyen tombs. Unfortunately, the production techniques have since been forgotten. Nevertheless, nearly one hundred pieces of old Phap Lam are housed in the Museum of Royal Fine Arts, as well as the architectural pieces on buildings and gates mentioned above. Indeed, almost all Nguyen royal buildings have panels of Phap Lam under their roofs, on their walls, decorative gates and doorways. The subjects depicted are often flowers from the four seasons, symbolic objects associated with gentlemen's pursuits, scholarly scenes or poems. The colours are vivid and the designs are finely executed.

Today, three main factories are operating in Hue to produce Phap Lam panels and objects. Although they cannot yet rival the originals, new Phap Lam pieces are used to renovate temples and other royal buildings throughout Hue. Recently, demonstrations of the technique have been included in the biennial craft festivals. Visitors can also purchase small Phap Lam objects as souvenirs such as decorative table-screens, plates, panels, boxes and jewellery.

Stage 1.

Stage 2.

Stage 3.

Stage 4.

The four stages of Phap Lam production.

Pineapple wine bottle for royal food display.

Royal Food – *Cung Dinh* Cuisine

If eating is an art, as is often said in the East, then royal food under the Nguyen was a fine art indeed. It was an unique cuisine in the sense that it was not a range of fancy dishes cooked to perfection and presented in the most elaborate way possible, as seen on most royal tables throughout the world. Rather the Nguyen's *Cung Dinh* cuisine was a mixture of pedestrian dishes found in the kitchen of the poorest Vietnamese family and the set royal dishes in Qing Chinese style. This peculiar mixture reflects the humble early life of Emperor Gia Long who once had to hide among the poorest farmers and fishermen in the southern province of Ha Tien, and, on Phu Quoc island. Another reason for this fusion of taste was that some dishes were introduced to the court by women brought to Hue to serve the Emperors. Like all Emperors, the Nguyen admitted a number of commoners into their harems, some whom later became their favourites, and even queens or queen mothers such as Lady Tu Du, Emperor Tu Duc's mother who came from Go Cong in the deep south, or Lady Tu Cung, Bao Dai's mother who was a street vendor on the outskirts of Hue. These women brought with them humble dishes such as fermented fish or shrimps, *mam* in Vietnamese, a spoonful of which can go a long way to making plain rice palatable. This was food made from ingredients that could be scavenged from ditches, wet-rice fields or little rivers, made tasty by the fermentation process. Whether such dishes reached the Emperor's table is not documented. Later on, *mam* became a staple Hue condiment that is found in many Hue dishes today, from noodle soup to fried shrimps. Let us not forget also that Hue was originally a Cham territory, and as such, some Cham dishes or ingredients entered the royal cuisine. Perhaps the most influential source for Royal cuisine, however, were regional products regularly sent to Hue as tributes. Local An Cuu rice and Perfume River cockles were two of the staple ingredients for the royal table, but barbecue dishes from the Truong Son mountain tribes were also included via the game that the highlanders sent to Court. Similarly Anh Vu fish from the Bach Hac river in the north found its way into royal cuisine through the tribute system.

When Gia Long died, Emperor Minh Mang regulated royal cuisine in a book of rules that set out the number of dishes to be served at each meal, along with meal times and how they were to be served. In so doing, he also outlined the punishments that would be meted out to those who violated these rules.

According to the Nguyen rule book, the Emperor ate alone, three times a day. Each meal had a set of 50 dishes prepared by 50 chefs, one for each dish. The chefs were strictly forbidden to engage in impure activities, whatever these were. They were strictly

About to start carving a vegetable food display.

supervised by the Ministry of Interior and had to abstain from many things. Each chef was solely responsible for his dish, with his well-being, or even his life, depending on it. Before the dish was ready, it went through many preparatory stages. Then when ready, the dishes were put in ornate boxes with the name pasted on the lids and carried by Eunuchs to the dining room. They were then handed to five royal maids responsible for feeding the emperor. A royal meal usually had meat, fish, vegetables, fruit, cakes and sweets presented one by one to the Emperor on special Blue and White china or Phap Lam dishes. He then picked at the food with a special pair of chopsticks, made of fine young bamboo that were destroyed after each meal. Emperor Dong Khanh, however, preferred a different type of chopsticks, made of a special wood that changed colour if the food contained poison.

Nguyen royal cuisine began in the fields and gardens where special plants, fruits and herbs were grown especially for the delicate royal palate. The royal banana – *chuoi ngu* – is a good example of this fine culinary tradition, as they were developed to grow only to a tiny size to fit the dainty royal hands, and had a special aroma different from other types of bananas to entice the refined royal taste buds. It is not known where this banana originated but, as with other Nguyen royal foods, *chuoi ngu* is now a common sight in everday markets in Asia, and is even imported into Europe, despite being once reserved exclusively for the court of Hue. The rice the Emperor ate was examined grain by grain and cooked in a tiny clay pot. Even the water for cooking had to be checked for impurity each time it was used. All the dishes, humble or not, would be presented exquisitely as befitted a royal table. The presentation followed the popular royal designs of

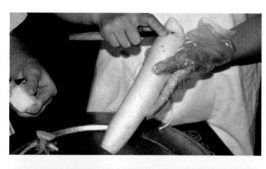

dragons, phoenix, flowers and animals, although the quantities of each dish were tiny.

Throughout the Nguyen dynasty, the production and preparation of royal food were under the supervision of a special department related to the Medical Institute of the Interior Ministry and responsible for the entire meal, from the selection of ingredients to the provision of after-meal toothpicks. Created in 1802, the year that Emperor Gia Long came to power, the Royal Food Department operated under different names over the years but retained the same function; providing the most suitable food for the royal

A set of food decorations waiting to be used for a mock royal banquet.

family. They worked hand in hand with the tea department, which as the name suggests provided tea and other drinks to the royals. Both were supervised by the Medical Institute to ensure that all the dishes were health giving and the balance between Yin and Yang was strictly observed. A chef who gave the Emperor an incorrect type of food would be caned 100 times. If the food was not clean enough, the chef would be caned 80 times. If a wrong ingredient was used, the chef would be caned 60 times. If the chef did not taste the dish first to check it was not poisoned, he would be caned 50 times, and so on.

Emperor Gia Long was said to be a simple eater and not a drinker, his plain tastes perhaps reflecting his earlier hard life as a Lord in exile battling enemies on all sides. His favourite dish was said to be steamed rice and stewed fish. Emperor Dong Khanh was the most elaborate eater who expected his 50 dishes three times a day, while Duy Tan was the first emperor to eat with his wife, a tradition Bao Dai later heartily endorsed. While he was living with his wife, Queen Nam Phuong, in Kien Trung Palace, Bao Dai ate his meals with her and their children en-famille. His father, Emperor Khai Dinh ate a little less than his own father, Emperor Dong Khanh, with only 35 dishes, served sometimes on an European dinner service.

What were the dishes that the Nguyen Emperors ate? Such a question might require volumes to answer, for apart from every day food, the Emperors had to preside over many banquets both in honour of numerous guests, and as rewards for faithful subjects, from high-ranking generals and mandarins to newly qualified scholars. The banquet was known as Ban Yen – giving bird's nest – a peculiar term indicating the highest cuisine available in Vietnam. As bird's nest is a very expensive and most precious food, it was indeed the highest honour that the Emperor could bestow on his guests.

In general, according to a cookbook left by Lady Truong Thi Bich called *Thuc Pho Bach Thien* – 100 royal dishes, the Nguyen royal family ate more river fish, shellfish and seafood than meat, followed by vegetables, with meat occupying third place. Fermented fish and pickled vegetables were also favourites. Surprisingly, the more precious food such as game, shark's fin, abalone and bird's

Food presented in royal style.

Dragon boat made of carrot.

Inside the red fruit *Gac*.

Strings of *nem* on sale at the local market.

nest were used only sparingly. All were presented with intricately carved vegetable dragons, phoenix or flower shapes. The dessert dishes were often shaped into little birds or tiny flowers. The fruits were seasonal and came from all over the country. Some of these dishes are found today not just in restaurants specialising in *Cung Dinh* cuisine, but also on the street and in local eating houses. *Com Hen*, for example, is a special Hue dish of rice and tiny cockles, served with vegetables, nuts and other condiments such as fiery bird-chillies. This dish uses local rice and cockles from the Perfume River, once a favourite ingredient for royal food. The names of royal dishes have also been woven into traditional Hue songs such as the Nam Ai, where the names of dishes were sung, such as: peacock rolls, rabbit casserole, beef, eels, crab, pigeon, duck's feet tendon, abalone soup etc...

Occupying its own position in the league of Nguyen royal food is royal vegetarian cuisine. All the Emperors were devout Buddhists so, like all Buddhists, they preferred to eat vegetarian food once or twice a month to purify their systems. The Emperor also had to abstain from meat and impure ingredients before performing solemn ceremonies such as the Nam Giao. Such requirements elevated vegetarian cuisine to a separate Nguyen art with Hue as the capital of vegans. For the royal table, each vegetarian dish was cooked to perfection and presented just as well as meat and fish dishes in order to give an impression that being abstemious was not such a hardship after all. On special family occasions, the Nguyen would offer their guests a vegetarian banquet with dishes that looked and tasted like their meat and fish counterparts. Such banquets were usually served on the anniversaries of the death of their ancestors, a grand tradition in the Vietnamese calendar of rites and a good occasion for a family reunion. Beancurd or tofu in many forms was used regularly to give texture and body to the food. Quite often, it is impossible to differentiate between a vegetarian and a meat dish because the tofu was shaped and seasoned to taste like meat, fish or poultry, a concept that is sometimes difficult for true vegans.

At the other end of the spectrum was the high royal cuisine: the Great Banquet in the Chinese tradition. Under the Nguyen, the royal Great Banquet offered 60 dishes, eight of which belonged to the set royal banquet dishes called *Bat Tran*, a must-have. The rest were dishes that Nguyen royal members ate daily, and could be quite ordinary but presented in a special way with extraordinary names that belied their humble origins. A documented royal Great Banquet for a Qing Ambassador had the following *Bat Tran*, which reads like a list of the most endangered species:

Nem Cong – Fermented Peacock meat: uncooked fermented meat is a Hue speciality and usually comes under the term *nem,* although today *nem* generally means minced meat, cooked or uncooked, shaped like a small cigar or little pillow. Peacock *nem* was special because the peacock is a precious bird symbolising beauty and pride.

Peacock meat was believed to be an antidote for poison and was always included in the eight precious dishes as a safety measure.

Cha Phuong – Phoenix roll: Like *nem*, *cha* is a term used for anything minced and shaped into tiny morsels. *Cha* is minced meat usually mixed with other ingredients and then steamed, fried or grilled. Pheasant is used in this dish to emphasize its rarity.

Khai Dinh's dinner service, Tomb of Khai Dinh.

Da Tay Nguu – Rhino skin: This is a small square of soft skin under the leg of the rhinoceros. It was stewed with other ingredients to create a rare dish symbolising strength.

Tay Gau – Bear's Paw: as a wild animal, the bear represents untamed power and its powerful paws were particularly valued.

Gan Nai – Venison tendon: the deer is one of the fastest animals in the wild and it was believed that by eating its leg tendon, the eater would absorb this quality.

Moi Duoi Uoi – Orangutang's lips: it is not known what the significance of this dish was but it was clearly very rare and worthy of a royal table.

Chan voi – Elephant's foot: as we've seen the elephant was highly valued by the Nguyen. Stewed elephant foot was believed to impart

Emperor Khai Dinh presiding over a banquet in Can Chanh Palace.

strength to the eaters. By serving this dish, the Nguyen Emperor was demonstrating the esteem in which he held his guests. However, when Emperor Tu Duc sent one to the French Legation, they were baffled. An observer who worked at the Legation at the time, Dr. Auvray, noted that they were perplexed as to why the Emperor kept sending them such inedible things in an article published in France in 1883.

Yen Sao – Bird's nest: The rarity of these nests and the peril involved in harvesting them make this dish a precious must-have for the royal Great Banquet, even though the taste and the texture of the nests are unremarkable. However, it is believed that it will bring long life and good health to the eaters.

The above list of eight most precious dishes for a royal Great Banquet changed over time and, apart from bird's nest, all the other exotic dishes offered by Cung Dinh banquets today have been substituted by ones created from less endangered species.

Hue Factsheet

Hue is located 645 km (400 miles) south of Hanoi and 930 km (575 miles) north of Ho Chi Minh City.

For many years, Hue was an optional destination or a quick stop-over on many tour routes but the situation has changed recently with Hue being recognised as one of the most important destinations for learning about Vietnamese culture. It is now easy to get to Hue by plane, train, bus or private car.

By plane
From Ho Chi Minh City and Hanoi, there are daily flights to Hue which take 1 hour 20 minutes and 1 hour 10 minutes respectively. From Hue-Phu Bai airport, you can travel to the city centre, 15 kms away, by taxi for approximately US$10-15 per car, although if it is rush hour or bad weather, it can be slightly more. It is also possible to travel to the city centre by airport bus.

From Danang airport, 100 kms (60 miles) away, you can hire a private car and driver, or a taxi, for around US$40-50 per car/per trip. The journey takes about 2-3 hours. This is a good option for those who can fly directly from China, Cambodia and Singapore to Danang. It's best to arrange with a tour company by phone or online to hire a car in advance to avoid waiting around and being subjected to a lot of hassle. There are trains and local buses from Danang to Hue but the journey can be long and uncomfortable.

By train
Hue is one of the major stops on the national North-South railway. Train travel in Vietnam is relatively slow but it does provide an interesting experience and great coastal views. From Ho Chi Minh City, it takes 14-15 hours and 12-15 hours from Hanoi. Hue Railway Station is located in the city centre at 2 Bui Thi Xuan Street.

By road
Public buses from Hanoi to Ho Chi Minh city stop in Hue and other major towns and cities along the National Highway 1. The journey can be slow as traffic is heavy on this route. Alternatively, you can negotiate with a tour company to tag along on their tour bus and only pay the fare for the journey.

Travelling by car from Hanoi or Ho Chi Minh city is possible and more comfortable but it is slow and can take up to 12-14 hours.

It is now possible to take a bus or car from Vientiane-Savannakhet in Laos to Hue via the international crossing at Lao Bao. The sleeper bus with toilets is a popular route with backpackers but can be crowded. The journey can take up to 15 hours.

Best times to visit
Weatherwise, there is no best or worst time to visit Hue for the climate of central Vietnam is unpredictable. The dry season is from April/May-September/October and the wet season is any time from September onward. Sometimes, Hue can experience torrential rain if there is a typhoon. However, Hue weather can be very pleasant. As there is no hard and fast rule, a rain jacket or umbrella is advisable.

The Hue festival and craft demonstrations in June can be dry and hot but sunny with clear blue skies. It is a lot of fun but some may find it crowded and noisy. Humidity is high all year around but toward the end of the year it can be cool enough for a light jacket or sweater. During November-February, days may start misty but turn into drizzle or bright sunshine.

Christmas is not a big holiday in Vietnam but many sites may be closed during the Lunar New Year (Tet) which falls between January and early February, depending on the lunar cycles. It is better to check in advance.

Opening times
Since May 2014, the opening times for all heritage sites are:
Daily: 07:00 to 18:00
Last ticket sales are at 17:30

Ticket prices vary from site to site, for foreign visitors:
Imperial City + Museum of Royal Antiquities: Adult: VND105,000. Children VND 20,000
Minh Mang / Tu Duc / Khai Dinh Tombs: Adult VND 80,000. Children VND 20,000, per tomb
Museum of Royal Antiquities / An Dinh Palace / Thieu Tri Tomb: Adult VND 40,000. Children free, per site.

Rulers contemporary with the early Nguyen

Electric Shuttle Services:
Bus Station Nguyen Hoang – Ngo Mon Gate:
VND30,000-50,000 depending on the size of the cart
Imperial City – Museum of Royal Antiquities:
VND30,000-70,000
Museum of Royal Antiquities – Bus Station Nguyen
Hoang: VND70,000 - 80,000
Imperial City – Bus Station Nguyen Hoang:
VND70,000 -150,000
Citadel District (surroundings of Imperial City):
VND90,000-180,000
-Within the Imperial Citadel: 30 minutes:
VND100,000-180,000; 1 hour: VND150,000-280,000

Elephant services:
15-20 minute ride on an elephant, with imperial
costumes: VND150,000
Sit in imperial costumes on an elephant for a
photograph: VND50,000
Stand with an elephant for a photograph: VND30,000

Tickets for art performances:
Royal Court Music / Ceremonial Music at the Royal
Theatre: VND100,000 per person.
        Two performances daily: 10:00-10:30 and
        14:30-15:00

Free performances are held daily:
Changing of the Guards: 09:00-09:30
Concert at The Mieu Temple: 10:00-10:30 and 16:00-
16:30
Concert at Thai Hoa Palace: 08:00-08:30 and 14:00-
14:30

**Sightseeing regulations issued by the Hue
Monument Conservation Center:**
Do not carry explosives, inflammables, poisonous
substances or weapons.
Wear appropriate clothing and be quiet in palaces
and solemn places. Camera and video recorder are
not allowed inside the Imperial palaces.
No smoking in palaces, pine tree areas and other fire-
susceptible places.
Do not pick flowers or twigs, no graffiti.
Do not lie, sit on or touch artefacts.

China:
Qianlong Emperor (r. 1736-1796)
Jiaqing Emperor (r. 1796-1820)

Thailand:
King Taksin (r. 1767-1782)
King Rama I (r. 1782-1809)
King Rama II(r. 1809-1824)

Cambodia:
King Ang Eng (r. 1779-1796)
King Ang Chan II (r.1806-1835)

Laos:
King Chao-In (r. 1792-1805)

Japan:
Emperor Kokaku (r.1780-1817)

Korea:
King Jeongjo (r. 1752-1800)

France:
King Louis XVI (r. 1774-1789-92)
French Revolution (1789-1799)
First Consul Napoleon Bonaparte(1799-1804)
Emperor Napoleon Bonaparte (r. 1804-1814-1815)

England:
King George III (r. 1760-1820)
King George IV (r. 1820-1830)

Portugal:
Queen Maria I Francisca (r. 1777-1816)

Spain:
King Charles IV (r. 1788-1808)

The United States:
President George Washington (1789-1797)
President John Adams (1797-1801)
President Thomas Jefferson (1801-1809)

Glossary of names in Vietnamese

In order of appearance

Bao Dai	Bảo Đại	Thai Hoa	Thái Hòa
Nguyen Phuc Vinh Thuy	Nguyễn Phúc Vĩnh Thụy	Thai Binh Lau	Thái Bình Lâu
Hue	Huế	Duyet Thi Duong	Duyệt Thị Đường
Phu Xuan	Phú Xuân	Phu Noi Vu	Phủ Nội Vụ
Tran (dynasty)	Trần	Thai Mieu	Thái Miếu
Dai Viet	Đại Việt	Trieu Mieu	Triệu Miếu
O (territory)	Ô	Hien Lam Cac	Hiển Lâm Các
Ly (territory)	Lý	Cuu Dinh	Cửu Đỉnh
Thuan Chau	Thuận Châu	The Mieu	Thế Miếu
Hoa Chau	Hóa Châu	Hung Mieu	Hưng Miếu
Huyen Tran	Huyền Trân	Phung Tien	Phụng Tiên
Quang Tri	Quảng Trị	Dien Tho	Diên Thọ
Binh Thuan	Bình Thuận	Truong Sanh	Trường Sanh
Thang Long	Thăng Long	Cuu Vi Than Cong	Cửu Vị Thần Công
Le (Dynasty)	Lê	Vac	Vạc
Le Loi	Lê Lợi	Tang Tho Lau	Tàng Thơ Lâu
Mac (Dynasty)	Mạc	Tinh Tam	Tịnh Tâm
Trinh	Trịnh	Ky Dai	Kỳ Đài
Nguyen	Nguyễn	Phu Van Lau	Phú Vân Lâu
Nguyen Hoang	Nguyễn Hoàng	Nghenh Luong Dinh	Nghênh Lương Đình
NguyenPhuc Nguyen	Nguyễn Phúc Nguyên	Thuong Bac	Thương Bạc
Nguyen Phuc Chu	Nguyễn Phúc Chu	Vinh Thuy	Vĩnh Thụy
Dang Trong	Đàng Trong	Nam Giao	Nam Giao
Dang Ngoai	Đàng ngoài	Tet	Tết
Nam Tien	Nam Tiến	Phap Lam	Pháp Lam
Phu Quoc	Phú Quốc	Ho Quyen	Hổ Quyền
Con Lon	Côn Lôn	Dau Ho	Đầu Hổ
(Prince) Canh	Cảnh	Xam Huong	Xâm Hường
Thien Mu	Thiên Mụ	Cung Dinh	Cung Đình
Hoi An	Hội An	Tuc Mac Hau	Tức Mặc Hầu
Gia Long	Gia Long	Thien Tho Lang	Thiên Thọ Lăng
Minh Mang	Minh Mạng	Hieu Lang	Hiếu Lăng
Thieu Tri	Thiệu Trị	Xuong Lang	Xương Lăng
Tu Duc	Tự Đức	Khiem Lang	Khiêm Lăng
Duc Duc	Dục Đức	An Lang	An Lăng
Hiep Hoa	Hiệp Hòa	Tu Lang	Tư Lăng
Kien Phuc	Kiến Phúc	Ung Lang	Ứng Lăng
Ham Nghi	Hàm Nghi	Long An Palace	Long An
Dong Khanh	Đồng Khánh	Long An Temple	Long Ân
Thanh Thai	Thành Thái	Van Mieu	Văn Miếu
Duy Tan	Duy Tân	Hon Chen	Hòn Chén
Khai Dinh	Khải Định	Bia Quoc Hoc	Bia Quốc Học
Truong Tien or Trang Tien	Trường Tiền/Tràng Tiền	Cung An Dinh	Cung An Định
Ngo Mon	Ngọ Môn	Gia Hoi	Gia Hội
Dai Noi	Đại Nội	Ngoc Son	Ngọc Sơn

Auvray, M.A, 'Dix-huit mois a Hue: Impressions et Souvenirs' in *Bulletin des Amis du Vieux Hue (BAVH)*, No.3 Jul-Sep. 1933; reprinted from *Bulletin de la Société de Géographie de Paris*, 1883

Bao Dai, *Le Dragon D'Annam*, Paris: Plon, 1980

Bao Dai and Philippe Lafont, *Hue La Cite interdite*, Paris: Edition Mengres, 1995

Bao Tang My Thuat Cung Dinh Hue, Vol. IV Chuyen De Phap Lam, Hue Monuments Conservation Center, Hue 2005

Bao Tang Lich Su, Hanoi, Vietnam.

Bao Tang Vien Thanh Pho Ho Chi Minh.

Bonhomme, A, 'La Pagode de Thien Mau: Historique' in *BAVH*, No.2, 1915

British Museum, The, London, United Kingdom.

Cadiere, L, 'Tombeaux annamites dans les environs de Hue', in *BAVH*, 1928

Cadiere, L, 'Les Urnes dynastiques du Palais de Hué: Notice historique' in *BAVH*, No.1, January-March 1914

Chapuis, O, *The Last Emperors of Vietnam: from Tu Duc to Bao Dai*, Contributions in Asian Studies, No. 7, Greenwood Press, Westpoint, Conn., 2000.

Chovet, P, 'Les Urnes dynastiques du Palais de Hué : Technique de la fabrication' in *BAVH*, No.1, January-March 1914

'Chuyện thoái vị của vua Bảo Đại qua lời kể của Huy Cận' in *Viet Bao*, 31 August 2003

Chronological table of the monuments of Hué, www.UNESCO.org

Complex of the Temple for the worship of the Nguyen Emperors (The Mieu), www.UNESCO.org

Đại Nam Nhất Thống Chí, Phạm Trọng Điềm, trans., Đào Duy Anh, ed., Hanoi: Khoa Học Xã Hội. 1969.

Đại Việt Sử Ký Toàn Thư, Hanoi: Khoa học Xã hội, 1967

Đại Nam Thực Lục, Chính Biên, all volumes, Hanoi, Viện Sử Học, 1962-1873.

Đào Duy Anh, 'Cuộc Kháng Chiến Của Nhà Trần Đã Ngăn Chặn Đà Bành Trướng Của Mông Cổ Xuống Đông Nam Á', in *Nghiên Cứu Lịch Sử*, No. 42, 1962

Đào Duy Anh, *Lịch Sử Việt Nam, từ nguồn gốc đến thế kỷ XIX*, Hanoi: Văn Hóa Thông Tin, 2002

Delvaux, A, 'La Legation de France a Hue et ses premiers titulaires (1875-1893)', *BAVH*, No. 1, Jan-Mar 1916

Dumoutier, L, 'Sur Quelques porcelaines europeenes decorees sous Minh Mang', in *BAVH*, No.1, January-March 1914

Fall, Bernard, 'Indochina', in *Revolution Warfare, Vol. V: French counterrevolutionary struggles: Indochina and Algeria*, U.S. Military Academy, Westpoint, New York: Department of Military art and engineering, 1968.

Gaide & Peysonneaux, H, 'Les tombeaux de Hue, Prince Kien Thai Vuong' in *BAVH*, 1925

Gia Pha Nguyen Phuoc Toc, Ban Lien Lac Nguyen Phuoc Toc tai Thanh Pho Ho Chi Minh, 1992.

Hai Trung, *Choi Chu Han Nom, Nhung Bai Tho Doc Dao*, Hue: Thuan Hoa, 2002

Hue Monuments Conservation Center publications: *The Imperial City and the Forbidden Purple City, Minh Mang Tomb, Tu Duc Tomb* and *Khai Dinh Tomb*, and other information on www.hueworldheritage.org.vn.

Kham Dinh Viet Su Thong Giam Cuong Muc, Quoc Su Quan Trieu Nguyen, trans., Vien Su Hoc, Hanoi: Giao Duc, 1998

Langrand, G, 'Le Tombeau de Thieu-Tri', in *BAVH*, 1939.

Le Bris, E, 'Le Monument Aux Morts de Hue' in *BAVH*, No.4, 1937

Lê Thành Khôi, *Histoire du Vietnam des origines à 1858*, Paris: Sudestasie, 1981.

Lichtenfelder, Ch, 'Notice sur le Tombeau de Minh Mang', in *BAVH*, 1937 Museum of Royal Antiquities: *Chuyen De Do Det*, Internal Documents, 2009.

National Archives of France.

Pham Khac Hoe, *Tu Trieu Dinh Hue den Chien Khu Viet Bac*, Hanoi: Nha Xuat Ban Ha Noi, 1983

Pham Van Son, *Viet Su Toan Thu, Tu Thuong Co Den Hien Dai*, Electronic Edition, acc. July-August 2009.

Phan Thuan An, *Kien Truc Co Do Hue*, Hue: Nha Xuat Ban Da Nang, 2009.

Proclamation 1993: "Nha Nhac, Vietnamese Court Music", www.UNESCO.org

Quoc Trieu Chanh Bien Toat Yeu, ed. Cao Xuan Duc, trans. Quoc Su Quan Trieu Nguyen, Hanoi: Nhom Nghien Cuu Su Dia Vietnam, 1972

Réalités Vietnamiennes, Saigon: Ministère des Affaires Étrangères du Vietnam, 1966

Sogny, L.L, 'Les Urnes dynastiques du Palais de Hué: Notice descriptive' in *BAVH*, No.1, January-March 1914

Taylor, Keith, 'Nguyen Hoang and the beginning of Vietnam's southward expansion', in *Southeast Asia in the Early Modern Era: Trade, Power and Belief*, Anthony Reid, ed., Cornell University Press, Southeast Asia, 1993

Than Kinh Nhi Thap Canh, Tho Vua Thieu Tri, Phan Thuan An, Pham Duc Thanh Dung, Phan Thanh Hai & Nguyen Phuoc Hai Trung, Hue: Thuan Hoa, 1997

Tran Dinh Son, *Thuong Ngoan Do Su Ky Kieu Thoi Nguyen 1802-1945*, HCM City: Nha Xuat Ban Van Nghe, 2008

-'-, *Nhung Net Dan Thanh*, HMC City: Nha Xuat Ban Van Nghe, 2007

Tran Duc Anh Son & Le Hoa Chi, *Phong Vi Xu Hue*, Hue: Nha Xuat Ban Thuan-Hoa, 2003.

Trần Trọng Kim, *Việt Nam Sử Lược*, Hanoi: Văn Hóa Thông Tin, 2002

Vietnam, Conservation and Restoration of the Select Monuments in Hue City, UNESCO Report, 1992

Warder, Vũ Hồng Liên, 'Mongol invasions in Southeast Asia and their impact on relations between Đại Việt and Champa (1226-1326 C.E.)', PhD thesis, SOAS,

Index

TL 4

TL 8

Bồ

Đặng Huy Tá

Bùi Điền

ga Văn Xá 🚉

TL 8

Lý Nhân Tông

Lê Thuyết

TL 8B

HƯƠNG TOÀN

HƯƠNG VĨNH

PHÚ MẬU

TL 4

QL 49B

HƯƠNG CHŨ

HƯƠNG SƠ

Vạn đò
Phú Bình

PHÚ HẬU

PHÚ THƯỢNG

QL 49B

TL 10

Lư Chữ

Tăng Bạt Hổ

PHÚ BÌNH

PHÚ HIỆP

VỸ DẠ

AH 1

Lý Thần Tông

HƯƠNG LONG

TÂY LỘC

THUẬN LỘC

Imperial Citadel &
Forbidden City
PHÚ CÁT

AH 1

Lưu Bảo

KIM LONG

Lê Duẩn

THUẬN THÀNH

PHÚ HỘI

XUÂN PHÚ

AN ĐỒNG

HƯƠNG AN

Thien Mu
Pagoda

PHÚ THUẬN

THUẬN HÒA

Lê Lợi

VĨNH NINH

PHÚ NHUẬN

Tomb of
Duc Duc

Tố Hữu

Hoàng

Temple of
Literature ■

PHƯỜNG ĐỨC

Phan Chu Trinh

PHƯỚC VĨNH

An Dinh
Palace

Tư Đức

🚉 Ga An Cựu

tp. Huế

THỦY BIỀU

THỦY XUÂN

TRƯỜNG A

AN CỰU

Nam Giao
■ Platform

Tiger Arena

Tomb of
Tu Duc

Võ Văn Kiệt

THỦY DƯƠN

Kim Long

■ Tomb of
Dong Khanh

AH 1

QL 49

AN TÂY

Chằm

AH 1

Hon Chen
■ Temple

Bến Than

Võ Văn Kiệt

N

■ Tomb of Thieu Tri

QL 49

Tomb of
■ Khai Dinh

Minh Mạng

Kim Phụng

Tomb of Minh Mang

AH 1

Copyright © River Books 2015

Tomb of Gua Long

THỦY BẰNG

HƯƠNG THỌ

Đò Gia Long

tx. Hương Trà